A PLUME BOOK

FOREVER YOUNG

WILLIAM SYLVESTER NOONAN is a graduate of Boston College. He lives outside of Boston with his wife and four children.

ROBERT HUBER is a senior editor at Philadelphia magazine. He lives in Philadelphia, Pennsylvania, with his wife and two sons.

William Sylvester Noonan

WITH ROBERT HUBER

FOREVER YOUNG

MY FRIENDSHIP WITH
JOHN F. KENNEDY, JR.

A PLUME BOOK

PLUME
Published by Penguin Group
Penguin Group (USA) Inc., 375 Hudson Street, New York, New York 10014, U.S.A.
Penguin Group (Canada), 90 Eglinton Avenue East, Suite 700, Toronto,
Ontario, Canada M4P 2Y3 (a division of Pearson Penguin Canada Inc.)
Penguin Books Ltd., 80 Strand, London WC2R 0RL, England
Penguin Ireland, 25 St. Stephen's Green, Dublin 2, Ireland (a division of Penguin Books Ltd.)
Penguin Group (Australia), 250 Camberwell Road, Camberwell,
Victoria 3124, Australia (a division of Pearson Australia Group Pty. Ltd.)
Penguin Books India Pvt. Ltd., 11 Community Centre, Panchsheel Park,
New Delhi – 110 017, India
Penguin Group (NZ), 67 Apollo Drive, Rosedale, North Shore 0632,
New Zealand (a division of Pearson New Zealand Ltd.)
Penguin Books (South Africa) (Pty.) Ltd., 24 Sturdee Avenue, Rosebank,
Johannesburg 2196, South Africa

Penguin Books Ltd., Registered Offices:
80 Strand, London WC2R 0RL, England

Published by Plume,
a member of Penguin Group (USA) Inc.
Previously published in a Viking edition.

First Plume Printing, November 2007
1   3   5   7   9   10   8   6   4   2

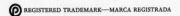

REGISTERED TRADEMARK—MARCA REGISTRADA

CIP data is available.
ISBN 0-670-03810-5 (hc.)
ISBN 978-0-452-28892-8 (pbk.)

Printed in the United States of America
Original hardcover design by Katy Riegel

To my children, TJ, Kiely, Bridget, and Lilly, and especially to their mother, my wife, the gingerlady, Kathleen.

Acknowledgments

THERE ARE DIFFERENT areas of my life in which certain people have played an important part. None have made a more substantive contribution than my parents. In my father's case, I did not have enough time with him, yet he taught me to always do the right thing, never talk down to anyone, and be willing to go the extra mile, especially in sales, to find excellence. My mother's devotion to her faith and her God is an invaluable gift that has sustained me in different periods. The extraordinary person who restored my faith and healed my heart is my wife, Kathleen, whose steely strength and perseverance have made all the difference in my recovery. Her parents, Bob and Lorraine Maguire, stood behind me and supported my efforts to write this telling story; to them I am eternally grateful not just for their support, but also for the daughter they sculpted, and for Dennis Maguire. Finally, there are my children, for whom I have oceans of love and who will understand how much I adore them only when they have children of their own.

Thanks to the team at Penguin—Clare Ferraro, Carolyn Carlson, Katherine Carlson, Ann Day, and their staff; to literary agent Gary Morris; the indispensable super agent Steve Mountain and his team at Cornerstone Management in Bryn Mawr, Pennsylvania; and to Dr. Bob Arnot,

Kevin Cullen, Aidan Browne, Richard Kearney, and Billie Fitzpatrick, who were there when this all started.

I have been blessed with many friends, some have come and some have gone: My oldest friends, my Irish mother, Mary Ruane, and husband Michael. My friend Marty Galligan, who insisted I write this book, and his wife, Nancy. Michael Grace and his associate Lauren Puglia at Adler Pollock & Sheehan's Boston office. Brian and Miriam O'Neill, and Peter Katsikaris and family, who run the Fells Market in Wellesley, Massachusetts. My sister, Patty Cronin, who filled in the details. Mr. and Mrs. Sargent Shriver and their son Timothy, who has always been there with good counsel and friendship in triumph and tragedy.

Contents

CONTENTS

FOREVER YOUNG

Introduction

ONE CANNOT have grown up Irish Catholic in mid-twentieth-century Boston without, at some point, crossing paths with America's most famous family. There were many Irish families I grew up with that were wealthier, wilder, or more religious than the Kennedys, but none more famous or powerful, and none that left a wider wake.

Long before I was born, my uncle played football with Robert Kennedy at Harvard. My father, Tom, was recruited by him to campaign in 1952 for his older brother, John F. Kennedy, then a young congressman who wanted to become a senator from Massachusetts. My father forged a personal relationship with both John and Robert; the connection evolved from Brookline neighborhoods all the way to the White House.

Tom Noonan served in the Kennedy administration and played golf with the President when I was just a young boy scrambling along the dunes in Hyannisport, so it was natural, probably inevitable, that John F. Kennedy, Jr., and I would become friends. Our friendship was rooted in the fact that our fathers were contemporaries, political allies, and friends. And the bond grew, as we did, in the shadows of these absent men. (My father died when I was thirteen.)

Our friendship extended back to the days of Secret Service protection, teenage dances, and trying to score beer. It continued into our adult life of careers and marriages. I was his oldest and most trusted friend—something John told me many times.

My role in his larger-than-life family has become clearer to me as I think about him now—as I think, especially, about my need to write about him. I was as close to John as his closest and most trusted cousins, Timmy Shriver and Anthony Radziwill; I shared a friendship with all three. I was an usher in all their weddings, and all three were involved in mine. We were like a foursome in golf.

Since John's death seven years ago, I have said little about him publicly, partly because comments I did make were edited down to irrelevant trivia and partly to honor John's privacy. Recently, however, I realized that it was time for me to reveal the guy I knew—that, in fact, I *had* to; many of the books and articles about him do not capture John at all. For a man who spent his whole life being photographed and written about, who was largely accessible to the media and then became *part* of the media, John—the real John—remained elusive. The myths are abundant, of course, and began from the moment he was a little boy saluting his father's casket. They continued to his death at age thirty-eight, and now beyond.

Sitting down to write this book, however, was difficult. It is rooted in my culture and background to follow a certain edict: If you are going to say anything, don't say anything at all. This is age-old Irish advice, and it's a good idea to follow it. There is, however, another cultural tradition: The Irish are great storytellers. So I felt caught between two ingrained parts of of my personality. But something else is pushing me to speak. I believe that the stories—the *true* stories—of the people we love create the meaning of their lives.

I shared, as John's friend, his struggle to establish his own persona. He had enormous pressure on him. He had become so many things to others, while still trying to become himself. For the most part, he accepted his strange status; more than that, he took on our ideas of who he was supposed to be. He remained loyal to his family and respected their history. He was intensely close to his mother, sister, and a few cousins. Yet he struggled with what it meant to be his father's son; it was a relationship he never developed and hardly remembered. As an adult he embraced his father's legacy and character in order to define himself. Yet he was determined to live his life on his own terms, as he pleased.

That's the John I knew but the world does not. He thought hard about being more responsible than many of his cousins—yet he was the guy named "The Sexiest Man Alive" by *People* magazine. He started his political magazine, *George*, to tweak his family and their idea of what he was supposed to be but also to get into the world of ideas, to join the national discourse on politics, and to honor his father. Especially as he got older, John read his father's speeches and favorite books, studied the careers of other national and historical leaders, and reveled in his Irish roots. He helped keep his father's legacy alive at his Presidential Library and Museum and the Kennedy School of Government at Harvard. He also maintained the President's only home, in the Kennedy compound on Cape Cod. We talked all the time, about politics, about money—I was his stockbroker—about women, about our lives. And about what he saw in his political future.

At the same time, friendship with John involved theater and fun. John was lively and assuredly real. He could not sit still. He smoked grass. He loved the blues, he could eat more than anyone I've ever known, he had a cavalier attitude toward danger, and he had a thing for hardheaded—and beautiful—women. He respected his uncle Teddy, although some of the Senator's shenanigans drove him nuts; John always responded to his uncle's requests to participate in campaigns or fund-raising events for his family. He also was an incredibly thoughtful and caring friend: John drove up to Boston from Brown University the night before my cancer operation because he couldn't bear the thought of me lying in a hospital, alone, contemplating the worst.

I owe John these stories—ours—told accurately. He believed in the idea of Camelot and the sense of responsibility it created; he hated

people using the myth to try to make him into a prince. He preferred the
metaphor of life being like a banquet, where he could choose what he
liked and leave the rest.

And what a banquet it was! John and I spent many weekends as adults
at his house in Hyannisport; it was our habitual retreat, up until his death.
Sometimes, still, I dream about John (and Anthony, whom we've also lost)
in rooms white and full of light, with music playing , as it always did, and
I get a feeling, as I always did with John, that something is about to happen: some fun, some bit of intrigue, an adventure—John was always *going*
somewhere—and, of course, I get the overriding sense of where he might
eventually have landed. His death ended something important for me. It's
a little like the memory of watching a football game, a long time ago,
with my father. "Don't ever bet against Notre Dame," he'd tell me. "It's
bad luck—never mind the odds." Nobody ever tells me things like that
anymore. And when I leave the dream to start a new day, I think about the
rich friendships that I've lost.

I was John's confidant. I believe it helped that I wasn't part of the family; I could give him perspective on the huge pressures and conflicting ties
all Kennedys feel. Contrary to published accounts, it was me John was
visiting—or was going to visit—the night he died. Never has that day
been truthfully presented. Which is also true of his life; the bits and
pieces that have emerged are recognizable to me only as fragments of
John. Here, then, is my best friend, from the four-year-old pedaling furiously around the Hyannisport compound on a tricycle to the guy who
didn't show up to help me celebrate my fifth wedding anniversary.

1

A Midsummer's Nightmare

JOHN KENNEDY was meant to meet me for dinner the night he died. The plan was for a group of eight of us—including John and Carolyn—to celebrate my fifth wedding anniversary at a favorite restaurant on Nantucket. This third weekend in July had become, like so many other milestones in our lives, a time for John and me to get together and enjoy our friendship and accomplishments.

The past few years, my wife and I had visited John and Carolyn at his mother's estate on Martha's Vineyard. Since Mrs. Onassis's death, John had been using Red Gate Farm for the month of July; his sister, Caroline, stayed there in August. Carolyn and John assembled different groups of friends for their four or five weekends there.

These weekends—especially the previous summer, when relationships were tense, and now with John's cousin Anthony Radziwill fighting cancer—tended to be pitched higher than we thought would be desirable for our anniversary celebration. It would be Kathleen's and my first night away from our children, aged two and one. We wanted to celebrate with the ease and comfort of an evening we had arranged.

The plan was to meet on the Hyannisport pier early that Friday evening and take a leisurely sunset ride to Nantucket aboard the *Bryemere,* a fifty-three-foot Ocean Yacht that belonged to Brian and Miriam O'Neill; Brian was a close childhood friend of both John's and mine. The captain was a seasoned local, aware of the tides; he decided we should depart at five-thirty. We planned to return to Hyannisport later that evening. It was no big deal to us—just dinner on a neighboring island, something we did easily, as experienced Cape Codders, in our own backyard of fun and low-level glamour.

Kathleen and I had taken the day off from work and headed down from Boston to her parents' house on Cape Cod the night before to prepare for our night out. It had been a clear, beautiful midsummer day. About two-thirty that afternoon, John called to explain that he was entangled in some late-afternoon business in New York—he'd been editor of *George* magazine for four years by then—and might not be able to meet our group in Hyannisport. Though he assured me he was not out of the picture quite yet. This was typical John—he was always late for everything, especially when he had to escape New York or when Carolyn was involved.

John also explained that he was having a mutual friend of ours, Dan Samson, fly into Boston and then to the Cape instead of meeting him in New York and flying to the Vineyard. Samson was not yet at John's Hyannisport house; John asked me if I would collect him later so that we could all meet on Nantucket. Sure, whatever—I had learned long ago that John was too unpredictable for scheduled events such as these.

Later that afternoon John called me at my in-laws' to say he was really late now, and because he was coming to Hyannisport to meet us, he felt obligated to attend his cousin Rory Kennedy's wedding there the next day. Since Carolyn's summer dresses were at Red Gate, he had to stop there to pick up a dress for the wedding. Plus, since he was stopping on the Vineyard, Carolyn's sister wondered if she could hitch a ride, but because of her job she could not leave until well after five. This was the usual confusion that always seemed to swirl around John. He promised he would still try to make it to the restaurant on Nantucket.

"Listen, Billy," he told me, "if all of this doesn't work out, when you guys get back to the Cape, come up to the house for a glass of champagne."

"Fine." We'd see him when we'd see him. It turns out that another couple had bailed, too, because they couldn't get out of Boston and to the Cape in time for a five-thirty boat, but I was still heading out for a sweet night with my wife and our good friends the O'Neills.

At five that afternoon Kathleen and I headed over to John's house to pick up Dan, who was just getting up from a nap after taking the red-eye from Seattle, but Dan said he was more comfortable waiting for John than coming to a couples dinner on Nantucket. We left our car there and walked down to the pier to meet the O'Neills, then headed off to the island sipping champagne.

About halfway there we stopped and floated for a while, since we were way ahead of schedule; the tides were right and the sea calm, and with Nantucket only twenty-five miles away the *Bryemere* could make the crossing in only forty-five minutes under such ideal conditions. We caught up with each other and listened to music, then meandered the rest of the way to Nantucket.

John and Carolyn did not make dinner. Though I was sure that John would—as always—show up eventually.

When we arrived back at the *Bryemere* later that evening, the captain, Francis O'Neill, another Hyannisport native (no relation to Brian), told us that the weather had gotten bad, that there was a strange mist that could eliminate visibility and cause radar abnormalities. This is par for the course when boating on Nantucket.

Miriam O'Neill is a cautious boater at best and uncomfortable with any nighttime travel no matter how big the boat and knowledgeable the captain. Kathleen was nervous as well, but for different reasons—she was edgy about spending an entire night away from the children, and she did not like sleeping on boats. But she called her parents, who told her that everything was fine, and we decided to spend the night on the *Bryemere*.

Francis and his mate, Scotty, headed out for some island fun, looking to break a few debutantes' hearts. Given the looseness of John's plans, there was no need to call him. We had a nightcap and went to sleep.

The next morning we got up early, as most yachters do, and walked over to the Downyflake for coffee and doughnuts. When we got back to the boat, Francis, who knew that John and I were close and that John had planned to be with us the night before, pulled me aside. "Listen, I just got off the phone with the mainland, checking weather conditions, and was told that John's plane is missing."

I blanched but then made a half-humorous remark about how John was probably on Long Island eating his way through an IHOP breakfast buffet. Deep down, though, I immediately knew that this was bad. It was not like his other miscalculations.

Kathleen hadn't heard the conversation but saw the look on my face and—feeling guilty about being away from TJ and Kiely—screamed at me to find out what was wrong. *Is it the kids?* I stood on the Nantucket wharf trying to get my thoughts together. She was panicked, but I wasn't helping. My head was spinning—what had John said? What was the last thing he said? Was he staying at the Vineyard? Why wasn't he in Hyannisport? Where could he be? Did he stay in New York? No, he would not have done that—

"Billy, for God's sake, what is it?" Kathleen wondered desperately. "The kids . . . ?"

"No, Kathleen, it's not them. There's a problem with John."

She stared.

I didn't want to say it, because just saying it might make it true. "John's plane is missing."

I jumped off the wharf into the boat and went below. Brian asked me what was up. I told him. Immediately we started back. When we were out of the harbor, Francis came down and reported that he had verified the information. "I'm sorry, Billy," he said. I've known Francis since we were kids. "I'm sorry for you."

Clearing the harbor, we turned on the TV, and I grabbed the phone. I called John's house—busy. Kathleen called her mother. The kids were awake and all was fine, her mother reported, but Timmy Shriver had called three times, which she found unusual, since it wasn't yet eight o'clock. I dialed Timmy's house repeatedly—busy. I knew he would tell me that everything was all right, if I could only get through. I called John's house again—busy. What the hell was the number on the Vineyard? I had dialed it thousands of times, but I couldn't remember it now, and I couldn't exactly call directory assistance to ask for the Onassis estate number. I needed my Rolodex, but it was Saturday and my assistant was away for the weekend. Where the hell was John?

Finally I got through to Timmy.

"Billy, is John with you?"

"No, he never showed up last night, and I can't get through to his house. What the hell is going on?"

"Dan called me this morning—apparently he never showed up on the Vineyard, and we were hoping he went directly to Nantucket and spent the night because of the weather conditions and the rule about bottle and throttle. [It's against FAA regulations to fly within twenty-four hours of drinking.] Now I can't get back in touch with Dan, and I don't know what's happening."

"Listen, I'll be in Hyannisport in a few minutes. I'll call you from there."

As we approached the Hyannisport break wall, it was still early; the remnants of the mist, the stillness of the air, and the encroaching heat made the morning light surreal and eerie. Hyannisport neighbors were waiting for us with what they'd heard—John's plane, missing—hoping for different news. I saw the flag flying proudly at full staff at the main house in the Kennedy compound and took this as a positive sign, yet the faces of the neighbors were filled with dread. I knew then that I might be headed for the worst news of my adult life; one expects to lose his parents, but not friends, and especially not the one with nine lives.

Kathleen and I thanked the O'Neills and dashed up Irving Avenue to the President's house; still dressed in dinner attire, we threw unneeded articles into the car and headed for the back door leading into the kitchen. I was praying to see John there reading a newspaper, eating his breakfast, shaking his head at our fear: "I can't believe you guys. After all these years, you have no faith in me? What's the big fuss about?"

Now as I approached the door, our history—John's and mine—washed over me. This was the house we reenergized after it sat empty for a few years when his mother moved to the Vineyard and before he bought out Caroline. This was the house we held together, kept upbeat and interesting with friends, constant dinners and conversation, *ideas*. This was a house that, in some respects, I grew up in, too, and that we now returned to for vacations with our wives and my own children. This was the house where the candidate awaited the presidential election results, where the First Family came to recover after the assassination; this is where Caroline had come to get married, John had come to heal after his mother died. If he was gone, so were all those happy memories, and so much more, irretrievable. It would be just another sad Kennedy house.

There would be, obviously, no grieving mother or wife waiting for John. There would be only Providencia Paredes, a family staff member from the Dominican Republic who had been with the First Family since John's parents were newlyweds. She was in the White House, she was in Dallas, she was bequeathed money from Mrs. Onassis to buy herself a condominium, and now, in her retirement, John had her come up every summer to look after things. She adored John.

When I crossed the threshold, she was sitting at the small kitchen table. "Where's Yahn?" she asked me desperately, in her Dominican accent. "Is he with you, Billy Noonan?"

Her head sank onto the table when I told her that he was not. I was her last hope for his survival.

2

Hyannisport, 1963

EVERY FRIDAY afternoon in the summer of 1963, my Irish nanny, Mary Ruane, would wait for the sound of the helicopter. It was Marine One, and its passenger was the President of the United States, John Fitzgerald Kennedy. The helicopter was heading along the southern coast of Cape Cod from Otis Air Force Base, toward the front lawn of his father's home in Hyannisport. Mary would drop everything she was doing in the kitchen, grabbing me, her charge, to head through the privet to get a glimpse of her hero, the first Irish-American president, who was just back from Ireland. To her, John Kennedy was as important as the pope.

For a five-year-old, too, it was an amazing sight. With great fanfare the drab green helicopter would land softly on the football-field-size front lawn of Ambassador Kennedy's summer home, the main house in the Kennedy compound, as the press had come to refer to the clubby cluster of three houses and a number of outbuildings. I remember it even now by the vibrant colors: the lush emerald green lawn; the softer green sea grass just beyond, waving in the wind; the deep blue waters of Nantucket Sound meeting, in a perfect line, the light blue sky. Everything was so *crisp*, so alive. The whirling of the blades would slow to a stop. Out he would come, "The President"—as if there could be no other.

He always disembarked first, out of protocol, so tan, wearing a navy blue suit and a paler blue shirt, smiling broadly. After saying hello to his father and children, he would climb into the backseat of a white four-door Lincoln Continental convertible and then be driven slowly up the hundred-yard lane leading out of the compound. He would wave and sometimes touch our hands—that's how close we could get. Mary would be beside herself. Then the Lincoln would turn left, down to the causeway and over to the peninsula known as Squaw Island, where he stayed for security reasons. This was my first brush with the Kennedy family.

My own family had been coming to Hyannisport since the 1940s, when my grandmother Bessie, recently widowed with young children, talked my father, the oldest of ten and in his mid-thirties, into renting a house; like most of the Irish, she found the heat and humidity of Boston summers unbearable. Also like many first-generation Irish, my father's family had come a long way from humble beginnings. Bessie's father had emigrated to America during the mid-1800s to escape starvation in Ireland and to search for gold in California. He ended up serving in the Civil War and was able to return to County Mayo drawing a pension from the Union Army, which made him a wealthy man by Irish standards. He married his best friend's daughter and started his own family. Ireland was a poor country and still under the boot of Britain, but he was able to bring his family to the western coast of Ireland in the summer, where they had a small shop and took in tourists.

"America is a country where you could be born poor and die rich," my great-grandfather was fond of saying. So—as many Irishmen did in those days—he sent his children over to Boston to start a new life. When it was Bessie's turn, she was met by her older sisters, who promptly threw her luggage into Boston Harbor. "There are presents in there for you!" Bessie protested. "There is nothing from Ireland that you will need here in America," they informed her. Bessie found work as a domestic.

Soon after she met James Noonan, a day laborer from County Roscommon, at an Irish social, they married, and a son, my father, was born, the first of ten children over the next twenty-six years. The young couple settled in Brookline, a Brahmin outpost for the wealthiest of Boston's captains of industry. Bessie worked in their homes while James got a job for the town's Department of Public Works. The maintenance facility building was located in "Whiskey Point," where the Irish laborers settled down. The Brahmins attempted to rationalize the slanderous moniker by explaining that the area was shaped like a whiskey bottle, but the Irish were proud of their turf and its young lads who were making their way in the prestigious Brookline public-school system and on the town's playing fields.

One of these grand lads was my father, Thomas Joseph Noonan. He was an industrious youth who worked three jobs while still in school and became a standout athlete to boot. Tom was recruited by Brown University in Providence; the first telephone call he received there came after his first freshman football game. It was not, however, a congratulatory call: His father had suffered a near-fatal heart attack. Tom was on the next train home. From this point on, it was up to him to support the family.

On the other side of town, a young banker named Joseph P. Kennedy was raising his own brood. Disgusted by the poor treatment of the Irish by the Brahmins, Kennedy moved his family to New York, where he would learn how to manipulate the stock market and make his millions. The Noonans and the Kennedys might have crossed paths with one another on a playing field or maybe in a department store in Brookline, but they didn't socialize until Jimmy Noonan, Tom's younger brother, showed up at Harvard University after the war to play football.

Jimmy went to Harvard as the past captain of the Brookline High School squad, after two years in the navy; he wasn't very big, however, and some of his teammates, who had served as many as five years in the war and had started families of their own, were older. But Jimmy was a tough, feisty halfback, and his size pleased at least one teammate: "Finally," young Bobby Kennedy said, "there is someone smaller than me on the team."

In Capraesque fashion, Tom Noonan vicariously enjoyed an Ivy League athletic career through his kid brother. He attended most practices and was quoted each week by a sports reporter who mistook him for a Harvard official. But his interest wasn't just in the game. Each member of the varsity team received two tickets, with seniors getting four, and since money was tight, the players sold their tickets to my father; he gave them to the best clients of the T. J. Noonan Company, the medical-supply business he had started. In those days a Harvard ticket was a coveted item, as many games were sold out. By the time Jimmy graduated, Tom Noonan had become New England's largest medical-supply dealer.

It was after Jimmy's freshman year at Harvard that Bessie convinced my father to rent a bed-and-breakfast in Hyannisport so that she and the younger kids could beat the heat of the city; she would run the B&B, and it would pay for itself. Jimmy's friend Bobby Kennedy sometimes hosted the footballers at his father's house down by the pier. One time, when a ragged Bobby Kennedy came by to recruit Jimmy for a touch football game, Bessie commented that maybe Jimmy should lend him some money to buy new clothes. Jimmy pointed out where Bobby lived and noted that the Kennedys probably could do without their help.

After graduating from Harvard, Jimmy married Jane Connors, a Manhattanville College socialite from Brookline. Some of the Harvard squad served as ushers, including team captain Ken O'Donnell and Bobby Kennedy. Jimmy and Bobby stayed in touch. In 1952, Ken O'Donnell and Bobby Kennedy found themselves running a disjointed Senate campaign for Kennedy's brother Jack, a congressman from the eleventh district (now the eighth) who was waging a gargantuan battle for the seat of Henry Cabot Lodge, Jr., a well-heeled Boston Brahmin. Lodge had been a senator before the war, served his country well in the war, and returned to get reelected; it was the same seat his father had had before him and that his ancestors had held going back to the founding of the republic.

So the odds against the Kennedys were high; Democratic infighting and having the campaign financed by an overbearing father who wanted to call the shots didn't help. Kennedy and O'Donnell approached Jimmy about getting involved; he was not interested but agreed to speak to Tom,

who was an elected official on the school committee in Brookline and creating quite a political name for himself.

The young Kennedy Turks did have a plan: starting a grassroots
movement throughout Massachusetts by hiring local politicians and
anointing them "secretaries"—this was not a term easily associated with
postwar machismo, but better than the outdated "ward boss." Tom Noonan heard them out. They explained that if they could win Brookline,
which is surrounded by Boston on three sides, they could gain momen-
tum and win Newton and then Dedham and so on. Lodge was running
the national campaign of General Dwight Eisenhower's presidential bid
and never took any Democrat seriously, especially young Kennedy; however much money Jack's father had, it was a pittance compared to the
wealth of a Cabot or a Lodge. Tom Noonan loved the challenge and signed
up as the Kennedy secretary for Brookline, one of the wealthiest towns
in the country.

Tom Noonan started his assault on the Republican powerhouse
through his contacts in the medical community. He asked them to open
their homes along Commonwealth Avenue and invite their friends for
small gatherings to meet Jack Kennedy, congressman, war hero, and candidate for the U.S. Senate. Down they would go—my father and Jack
Kennedy—along Commonwealth Avenue, stopping at shops and homes
on the way, down to Fenway Park. Tom would call upon his friend Neil
Mahoney, part of the Red Sox organization, and they'd stay for a couple
of innings to work the crowd. Up the avenue to Brookline's "Pill Hill,"
where Boston's prominent doctors lived. Down the hill into Whiskey
Point, into the fire stations and police precincts, the tenements, to finish
up in Hancock Village, a residential community on the West Roxbury
line. Then Tom would pass Kennedy off to the next secretary and head
home.

A friendship of mutual admiration had begun. Jack Kennedy told
Kenny O'Donnell, "This Noonan guy knows every doctor, fireman, cop,
and baseball player in town, and he introduced me around as 'Brookline's

native son'—we took in a small fortune." The Kennedy machine proved to be effective. Although there was a national Republican landslide in 1952, the year Dwight Eisenhower was elected to his first term as president, Jack Kennedy beat Lodge by more than 70,000 votes; he was only the third Democrat ever elected as a senator from Massachusetts.

My father remained part of the Kennedy machine—now known as the Irish mafia—as their Brookline secretary. In 1958, when he helped Jack Kennedy get reelected to the Senate, Tom Noonan himself was elected a selectman in Brookline. He used to say, "I knew Bobby better, but I had a better working relationship with Jack." My father would go on to serve as a delegate to the Democratic National Convention in Los Angeles in 1960, and, after selling his business and finishing a term as selectman, was appointed Northeast director of the U.S. Small Business Administration by President Kennedy. My father was happy to stay in Brookline and fund government loans to companies, including projects coming out of Harvard and MIT; NASA was then based in Cambridge.

During the summer of 1963, after President Kennedy returned from a European trip, he and my father played golf, and the President broached the possibility of my father's becoming ambassador to Ireland; the President was assassinated, of course, that November, before anything came of the idea.

In sixty years my family had come a long way, from the peat-heated cottages of Ireland to America, to attend college and make their fortune, and now we were helping fund the President's project of sending a man to the moon. We'd also become accustomed to summers on the Cape; sailing, boating, waterskiing, and fishing came naturally to my family. In the 1950s my parents had bought a cottage in Popponesset Beach. Much to her displeasure, my mother was forced to drive my older brothers to Hyannisport for sailing instruction from the famous Johnny Linehan. In the early sixties, when my brother John needed sailing instruction and I swimming lessons, my mother suggested we rent a house in Hyannisport rather than drive thirty miles every day; my father could play golf, and she could get a glimpse of Jackie, the paragon of style and taste for every woman, especially the administration wives.

So down to Hyannisport we went. It was an exciting time in an exciting place, the epicenter of national attention, something even a five-year-old could feel. We lived in a house directly across from the News Shop, within the six blocks cordoned off by the Secret Service, where sometimes you could see the President go for an ice cream cone holding the hand of his little boy, John.

3

Boys of Summer

ONE DAY in Hyannisport, during the late summer of 1974, I was hanging out with Timmy Shriver, and he said that before heading to the pier to go sailing we should stop to see his cousin John. I had gotten to know Timmy from being in Hyannisport; I was sixteen, a year older than he was, and was spending the summer with my mother in our house in Osterville, five miles away.

Since my father's death in 1971, my mother was struggling. His death had taken everyone by surprise, and my mother was overwhelmed. There were real estate businesses to dissolve, property to unload, clubs to resign from, and a lifestyle to maintain. Plus two of her five children were still teenagers who needed to be educated.

Slowly, she simplified her life and took on the role of a well-to-do widow. Her children coined the nickname "Annabelle" for her high-minded Victorian manner. "She's as tough as nails," my father used to marvel; it was a quality my mother, a real grande dame, never lost. As a high-spirited sixteen-year-old, however, I found living within a secluded golf community with a sixty-year-old widow far too staid.

Hyannisport, on the other hand, was like a kids' club, with warrens and hidden pathways, where it felt as if kids had the run of the place. I could always find somebody to sail or water-ski with. At night there were dances, games of truth or dare and spin the bottle; we drank beer. A lot of the kids were Kennedys.

Timmy told me that John had just returned from the second part of a scuba-diving vacation; Timmy had been with him in Hawaii earlier that summer, on the first part of his diving trip. Now Timmy wanted to hear about the rest of it, which had taken place off the Greek island of Skorpios—the private island of Aristotle Onassis.

We approached the stockade fence of the Kennedy compound that faced Irving Avenue, which was not something you would do on your own, as a Secret Service trailer was there, and every time the gate opened, an agent would stand up to check you out. Of course, the Secret Service knew Timmy—Eunice and Sarge's son—and nodded us in.

We entered the back kitchen door. This was not a kitchen that families hung out in; it was a workstation, with two stoves, pantries, and a sitting area for the staff that led to a back set of stairs up to three bedrooms, typical of the way Cape Cod houses were built when families regularly had staff, as this house still did. There was a lot going on, with Secret Service, neighbors, guests—and who was standing there chatting but Dicky Gallagher, twin brother to my swimming instructor and neighbor back in Brookline. Dicky, whose family ran an insurance business, was a buddy of Teddy Kennedy's, and he made sure that the staff—some of whom had been working for the Kennedys so long they were like extended family—knew I was okay. In fact, a couple of the staff remembered me from cookouts when my family summered in Hyannisport a decade earlier.

As we talked, Jackie Onassis came into the kitchen looking for iced tea. I had never met her, though I had seen her walking on the Hyannisport golf course. Jackie would go power walking before the term was invented—lengthy strides, her hair in a kerchief, those big sunglasses. The surprising thing, at first blush, was her size: Jackie was about five-ten. She was wearing a cabana jacket—like something you'd wear over a bathing suit—and slacks. She was not thin and petite; her shoulders were wide, she had a long, graceful neck. She was very tan. In her early forties, she

looked like a woman who rides horses and rides them well. Timmy introduced her to me. Jackie, in her soft, slow, careful way of speaking—"So
very nice to meet you"—would have you waiting for pearls to drop off
her lips. Nothing, even the ordinary, felt ordinary around her. "This is a
perfect day," she might say. "We have to celebrate it as a perfect Cape Cod
day." You'd think that was a terrific idea.

Timmy and I sat with John in the living room. I didn't know John
either—I remembered him as a little kid pedaling furiously around his
driveway on his tricycle. He would have been three or four. Now John
was thirteen, nearly fourteen, and was in an awkward—almost comically
awkward—stage between being a kid and an adolescent. He moved dis-
jointedly and had no build. He had a big nose, braces, and pimples.
He wore an untucked button-down shirt and cargo pants—he looked
like an unmade bed, which would always be standard John, until he got
into his public dress-for-success mode. I listened to Timmy and John
catch up.

John had had some New York friends join him on Skorpios for scuba
diving, and he regaled us with the beauty of the underwater Greek
world—exotic fish, coral, and so on. And he told Timmy how much he
missed him. Timmy and John had a rapport like brothers, always getting
on each other.

"You know how when we were on that reef and you weren't supposed to go down in that spot and you practically got stuck—then we
broke surface and just . . . whaled away," John was saying. He was being
careful with his language, since his mother was sitting within earshot, and
he didn't want to make it sound like life or death. What he'd *really* said to
Timmy, when they'd gotten back to the surface, was something like,
*What the HELL were you doing, playing down there in the coral like that, you
asshole?* To them, even scuba diving was a contact sport, because *everything* between them was a contact sport. Which was something his more
polite New York friends—maybe a little in awe of being taken to Skorpios
by JFK, Jr.—didn't share.

That same easy, busting-on-each-other rapport that Timmy and John

shared came immediately to John and me, too. Timmy and I started going out sailing with John in his little Sunfish; even at thirteen he was inde-
pendent from his other cousins, especially the RFKs. He liked using his
Sunfish rather than joining in on big, all-day trips with his uncle Ted—
Teddy had a big boat, there'd be a lot of people on it, and it could be a long
day. My uncle Jimmy Noonan once went sailing with Bobby Kennedy, got
smacked in the head with the boom, and Bobby had to fish him out of the
water. Ethel was the same way. She once loaded about thirty people on
her twenty-six-foot boat; the weight sank it. It was all too much for John.
Better to go off on his own. Already he was sailing against the Kennedy
wind.

This time of year—the end of summer—Hyannisport got trans-
formed from a quiet hamlet to a bustling party scene, especially in the compound: Jackie's friends, the Lawfords, the older RFK kids, the Smiths—they
all started showing up. But off we went—Timmy, John, and me—on his
Sunfish, all twelve or thirteen feet of it, and it could hold *maybe* four
people. But it was a perfect boat for a kid: light and easy to sail, and if you
capsized, you could easily right it. John kept his in front of Ambassador
Kennedy's house. Timmy and I would grab John, late morning, and we'd
slip across the compound, get on the beach, pull the boat down, put the
sails up, and off we went. We'd sail around the break wall and in would
come ferry tourist boats, which held about a hundred people, hoping to
get an eyeful of Kennedys. To John they were annoying, so we played
chicken with them, seeing how close we could get before we'd jump off,
capsize, and save ourselves from bouncing off the ferry's steel hull. Given
that the ferries were going only four or five miles an hour and the captains
kept an eye out, the danger was probably more imagined than real. John,
inevitably, would be the last off the boat. If the captain or the tourists ever
knew who it was that was fouling up their sightseeing, forcing them to
veer off course, it would have made their day. Sometimes, at night, John
liked to walk along the top of the break wall. Everything with him was an
adventure, with an edge of danger thrown in.

Half the point of sailing with John was getting dumped into the wa-

ter. Because of my size—at fifteen I was over six feet and about two hundred pounds—I'd be on the windward side, Timmy leeward, John at the
helm. When the boat heeled out, he would tighten up the main—which
threw Timmy into the water. We'd capsize, so I'd go flying, too. Then
we'd scramble to get the boat up, and they'd gang up on me; coming into
the wind, as I'd start to get back up on the boat, John would suddenly shift
the main and knock me off.

"Listen, this is getting a little juvenile!" I'd yell after about the fourth
time.

"What's the problem?"

My one knee back up on the boat, John would twist the tiller, and I
was back in for a swim. *"Listen,* CHOWDERHEAD . . ."

And so it went: I would hitchhike over late mornings, or take
my Boston Whaler; early afternoons the three of us would go out,
sometimes, on Shriver's Wianno Senior, a racing sloop sailboat made in
Osterville—it's the same type of boat you see JFK on in photographs.
We'd pack a lunch, head out to Egg Island, go for a swim and eat, take our
sweet time getting back.

Late afternoons, by three or four, the wind sits down and the water
flattens, so we'd go waterskiing, using Timmy's boat. Then we'd swim in,
walk up the beach, cut across the compound, sometimes take a dip in Ambassador Kennedy's pool, though Rose didn't like that. The pool was
roofed in, and whatever noise we made reverberated, disturbing her nap
(that didn't stop us from occasionally sneaking in for a swim at midnight).
Next—there was always a next, always *doing* something, with John—we'd
throw a Frisbee around or maybe get into a touch football game with the
RFKs. But John wasn't very good at the traditional ball sports—football,
baseball. The couple times we played tennis, the ball was over the fence
more than it stayed on the court. Plus, football on the compound was a little too Kennedyesque—not just for me but for John. Early evenings I'd go
home in my thirteen-foot Whaler, back to Osterville as the sun set, and often scrounge dinner alone; my mother went out to dinner every night.

Or sometimes I hung around into the evening. Those last few weeks of summer would go on for ages, or so it seemed at fifteen or sixteen years old. We thought we had the run of the place; still, without drivers' licenses, we were forced to find a beach or an unparented house to have our little parties. We smoked Old Golds, tried to score beer.

John didn't drink or smoke yet, though, and stayed away from girls—he wasn't ready for that. Besides, in our group of fifteen, eight would be Kennedys, so there wasn't a lot of romance; it was mostly girls hanging with girls, boys with boys. John was still small, younger than a lot of us, and not just younger but a little bit out of place beyond the confines of the compound. I would not say he was shy, but guarded—*literally* guarded.

John was making the transition, this summer, from being a kid to a teenager; Timmy and I were bringing him along. On the Cape, John didn't really know anybody outside of the compound; our friendship was the beginning of his stepping into a wider circle.

The world knew, or thought they knew, Caroline—the little girl from the White House, sixteen now, the subject of endless women's-magazine articles. John blended in and was anonymous, partly because he was unrecognizable as the heartthrob boy until he was about eighteen. He was fine with that—he would have worn a mask if he could have and dropped the Kennedy thing altogether. Yet he wasn't shy with family and a group he was comfortable with. John had already been all over the world and had a sort of cultured confidence. He told amazing jokes that were more like stories. Most thirteen-year-olds throw out one-liners based on bodily functions or what you call a nun. But John, for example, told the story of Angus MacPherson, a Scottish lad who wants to propose to his lassie and goes to a weaver to buy a kilt in which to do it. Well, says the weaver, a kilt requires nine yards, at this much a yard. John imitated the Scottish accent perfectly:

"Och, man, I'm not made o' money. Haven't you got something less dear?"

Being a Scotsman—and frugal—poor MacPherson is forced to buy eff0of

the weaver's own family tartan. The weaver blows the dust off a swath and says, "I'll throw in an extra three yards as a scarf for yer lassie." However, as MacPherson walks to see his girl along the moors in his new kilt, it catches on a thistle and, unbeknownst to him, proceeds to unravel completely underneath his long gray coat.

When he gets to her door, MacPherson opens his coat and says, "Lassie, now what do you think of this?"

She looks down and sees his manhood. "Oh, Angus," she says, "I like it just fine."

"That's great," he tells her, still blissfully ignorant of what's missing, "because I've got three yards at home to wrap around your neck."

John, who at thirteen could mimic anybody and loved to tell stories, had everyone laughing their asses off.

He used to tell me about New York and his apartment. In Boston, if you lived in an apartment, you were usually a college student or living in subsidized housing in tough areas; everyone I knew lived in suburban sprawl. "An apartment? Why do you live in an apartment?" I teased him.

"It's more like a house than the apartment you're thinking of."

"If you have an elevator, it's an apartment."

"So?"

"I thought your family was rich."

He couldn't understand why I didn't get it. "You'll see," he told me. "Come down sometime, and I'll show you around." A standing invite—that was the friendliness and informality of John. Two years later I would take him up on it.

After getting off to a smooth start, though, John and I hit a bump. He made some joke about my being involved in vandalism, and I wasn't too pleased.

A group of us were riding one night in the truck of a Hyannis guy, a local greaser a little older who would occasionally buy us beer. This guy got into ripping off hood ornaments from cars. It circulated back to Timmy and John that I was somehow involved, and I heard that John had made some sort of crack about me and another guy being involved.

The first chance I got, I took John aside, grabbed him by the shirt, and was not exactly subtle. "You don't know what the fuck you're talking about. I should smack you, because you've implicated me in this thing, and I had nothing to do with it."

"Well, I'm sorry," he said, surprised, backing away. I was much bigger than John.

And angry. "Well it's not funny, because I don't want to be thought of as some juvenile delinquent." I had already had a small problem at a local dance.

"I'm sorry," he repeated, his eyes wide. "I didn't know."

"So why didn't you shut up? If you didn't have Secret Service, I might give you a pop to let you know you shouldn't be talking about stuff like this."

"All right, all right. I'm sorry."

"If you want to act like a fucking girl, then be a girl. If you want to be a guy, then learn how to keep your mouth shut."

"All right, all right. I understand. I'm sorry."

And that was it—I was pissed, yes, but merely needed him to own up to the fact that he was having fun at my expense over something that wasn't true. Once he apologized, I let him off the hook. And I think we had inadvertently proved a point to each other. John didn't try to deny saying something about me (he later told Timmy that I scared the shit out of him, but he didn't try to weasel out of it), and I wasn't going to give him any bogus slack merely because of who he was. I wasn't going to be a Kennedy acolyte. If we were going to be friends, we had to trust each other, and that was the real start of it.

JOHN'S COUSIN from England, Anthony Radziwill, was the son of Jackie's sister, Lee, and Stanislas Radziwill, a deposed royal prince of Poland who had escaped Hitler and was living in the shadow of Buckingham Palace. The marriage had fallen apart, and Anthony and his sister, Tina, remained with their father in England. I never met the man, but

from pictures I saw, he had that regal, mustachioed look of European aris-
tocracy. Although Anthony grew to look like him, he had a different appearance entirely when he showed up at John's house that summer.

"Wait until you meet this guy," John told me one afternoon when we
were hanging around his bedroom. "Give him shit"—pronounced, in
faux British style, *shite*—"about his shoes."

"What are you talking about?"

"Just wait."

Soon enough he appeared, on another afternoon when John and I
were hanging upstairs in his house. John's room had been added onto the
house at some point, maybe as a nursery; I remember it had strangely an-
gled corners. It was painted light blue—with a baby blue floor—and fur-
nished with white-painted chairs and two twin beds. John had two
foot-tall candles of the same color, one a wax Nixon and the other a de
Gaulle (one of them had been burned down some, though I can't remember which). There was a small bathroom attached to the bedroom, where
there was a montage of John and his father. John and I would lie around
looking at magazines—he read a lot of aviation stuff; even then, at thirteen, he had the flying bug. Or *Sports Illustrated*. John was a big football
fan. Or we'd check out, from his window, the inevitable beehive of people coming and going at the RFKs'. Mostly, though, we'd be talking about
what was next, outside, what we were going to *do*. We really didn't spend
much time in his bedroom. John didn't like to sit still.

So in walked Anthony: skintight, open-necked polyester shirt with
horizontal stripes and no buttons, high-waisted, skintight, massively bell-
bottomed pants, finished off by large, thick-soled, high-heeled shoes. And
a wicked Cockney accent to boot, as John introduced us.

"Nice shoes," I said, shaking his hand. "Does your sister know you're
wearing her shoes?"

Anthony took one look at John and then attacked him. Laughing like
a hyena, John kept pushing him off, protesting, "I didn't say anything!"

"Yes you did, you bastard! Why would someone I just met say something like that unless you put him up to it?"

He had a point. Thus began my twenty-five-year friendship with Anthony—until his death, from cancer, in 1999, three weeks after John's—watching him battle John in a constant ball-busting scrimmage and trying to keep up with it.

My relationship with Anthony was built, from that first meeting, on the fact that I was different from the Kennedys in the compound, as Anthony, with his dry British wit and glam-rock dress, surely was as well. That summer I had spent two weeks in Europe, the second week in Ireland and England, with a friend and his parents. My friend and I hung out in Piccadilly Circus, especially the original Hard Rock Cafe. We were trying to touch the underbelly of mid-seventies European life, though we took in all the hot spots in our blue blazers and, I'm sorry to admit, sunglasses, to look cooler and more hip. I got turned on to *Ziggy Stardust*; a taste for David Bowie was something Anthony and I shared.

Anthony had been brought up in a very crisp, British way. He was far more sophisticated than most of John's cousins and much closer to actual royalty than John and the Camelot aura. But the two princes in the family both loved to play with language, to bust on each other over an ocean's gap in their English. And they were both interested in glam rock, drawn to gritty, bad-boy, West End trouble. They would sing together; I remember them teaching me a song about skinhead boot boys of London. Two boys exposed to such elitism were fascinated by—and needed—what felt real.

It was Anthony who eventually shared my family's connection to the President with both Jackie and John. The Kennedys owned a few acres of land in Osterville, up the street from my house there, a place the locals called Mike's Pond and the Kennedys referred to as "Grandpa's Lake." At one point Joe Kennedy kept horses and had built a riding ring. The common story was that, during Prohibition, John's grandfather hid liquor in the basement of Sloppy Joe's, a black-owned and -frequented speakeasy there. Once a summer we'd go for an overnight of a campfire, songs, and beer drinking. The Secret Service would be at the property's entrance, so we were protected from any interference. I had no intention of sleeping in a sleeping bag, though, and neither did my friend Dennis Maguire, who'd driven us there, and apparently neither did Anthony. We escaped into Hyannis—John, who enjoyed camping, stayed behind—for a late-night dinner, then drove around listening to Bowie. Anthony came back to my house, and we all crashed. In the morning my mother supplied some English muffins as I explained who Anthony was. Actually, she already knew, as she knew a lot about the Kennedys, and she was delighted to have him as a guest. She asked some questions about his family, so it was natural to share something of ours: She retrieved a framed letter written to my father from JFK encouraging him to run for the board of selectmen in Brookline, "my native town." Anthony grabbed it against my protest, saying that he had to show it to Jackie.

My mother was hoping it would solicit a luncheon invitation; I was mortified. It was exactly what I didn't want to happen, for my father's connection to Jack Kennedy to come out like this. Jackie, like John, didn't know anything about it.

I was well aware, of course, of the way people treated the Kennedys in and around Boston. Practically everyone there, including my mother, would say to the First Family, if given the chance, "God love ya, I knew ya fatha." Jack Kennedy may have become the most powerful man in the world, but every woman who went to a Kennedy tea was responsible for his start in politics and every man was there with him in the beginning. I didn't want to ride the coattails of that idea. I didn't want to expose myself as the son of one of those secretaries—the men who were part of Jack Kennedy's inner circle and so crucial to his political rise. I didn't want to be seen as part of the Irish mafia.

That day, it turned out, when we returned to the President's house in Hyannisport, Jackie was having lunch with Dave Powers, President Kennedy's closest adviser and a friend of my father's. Anthony showed Jackie the letter, and Dave immediately told her all about my father and the Brookline organization.

Jackie stared at me. "This is your father? I did not realize that, Billy Noonan."

I suppose this wasn't such a bad way for the connection to come out—of course I knew that it eventually would. I was already friends with John, and trusted by his mother for that, and I hadn't tried to leverage my way into the world of the Kennedys by using my father's connection. I think, at that moment, Jackie understood me perfectly. As for John, not only had we already established a bond, but I'd also made the point that I wasn't going to put up with any crap from him.

A few days later, Jackie shipped Anthony off on a bus to Newport to see her mother—his grandmother. A bus? Why the hell didn't we drive him, since it was only an hour away? It was not until I lived in Ireland for a few months a couple years later that I realized that the rest of the world does not work this way, and a kid from England was bloody well capable of taking a bus like the rest of us, no matter that he was a prince and leaving one famous estate for another. Anyway, Anthony and I stayed in touch. He came back the next year, and by then I had my license and a car. The following spring his father died; Jackie told me that someone had to pry his fingers off his father's casket and gently guide him away. That was a level of shock and grief I understood all too well. Anthony joined John and me, boys trying to preserve the memory of our absent fathers.

JACKIE'S MOTHERING OF JOHN was complex. She had an innate sense, I understood much later, of how to walk the line between protecting him and giving him the freedom to figure out his own way. If John read something in *National Geographic* and decided he wanted to learn how to scuba-dive, she would make the contacts so that it would happen— that's what triggered the Hawaii and Skorpios trips. Or she'd set up his visiting ruins in Guatemala or bicycling in France, or, in the coming years, trips to Africa.

At the same time, Jackie was all over John; she wanted him to be a regular guy but also wanted him to be polite and dignified. He told me once he'd overheard her reprimand someone for having a patronizing manner toward him, saying, "I don't want John to grow up to be some 'screw you, Charlie' guy." This was a boy who, quite naturally, had the staff fighting over who would make his breakfast in the morning. Jackie directed him away from the misadventures of the RFKs and steered him toward the more responsible Shrivers. At the same time, she never dictated whom he could or couldn't hang out with.

John, in turn, went along with her rules. Caroline was somewhat rebellious; not John. Caroline seemed older—even beyond their three-year age difference—because her closest friends were cousins who had older brothers. It seasoned her. Caroline was something of a hippie; Jackie wanted more of a debutante. They'd squabble over clothes and hair. John, on the other hand, was dutiful and never quarreled with her. I really don't know if that's because they were of the same mind or more out of respect. Certainly he respected, and was intrigued by, her vast knowledge. And I never remember him whining or complaining about his mother.

Not even when he had to spend his summer mornings getting tutored in math. It would emerge later that John had a learning disability, especially in math. At age thirteen, every morning he was instructed by a math tutor for an hour. He hated math, and he hated being tutored, especially as Timmy and I threw a Frisbee outside the open windows of his dining room waiting for his release. We tormented him, of course.

"Hey, Timmy, go out for a long one . . ."

John was trying to focus, and the more he wanted to get outside—and he was *always,* all his life, trying to get outside—the longer it took.

Years later I was contacted by a journalist to ask if I would comment about John's being gay; the journalist told me that John's math tutor had a revealing story about an encounter with him and was coming forward with it. I quickly learned a lesson about tabloid fishing expeditions when I called John and joked about what exactly *was* going on in that dining room.

"Hey, Billy, you asshole, that tutor was an FBI agent," he snapped. "Do you think my mother would arrange for me to be tutored by some queen?"

"Now that you mention it . . ."

"So don't get fooled again by that—don't even talk to them. They're just pulling your string."

John's absolute vigilance, when it came to not taking bait, was part of his grooming. I decided not to talk to journalists and never to suspect that Jackie would ever put him in a compromising situation.

But what I remember, mostly, from the time I first became friends with John, was his easy rapport with his mother, the sweetness between them. When we'd return from a day of sailing and waterskiing and swimming, we'd sometimes go back to John's house and take a quick outside shower to wash off the salt water. He would dress, and I would hang out for a while in a towel. Jackie, as ever, was out on her patio, working away editing some manuscript or talking on the phone. We'd join her.

She would grab her knee and pull it toward her chest, stretching, as she asked us about our day as if it were as important and interesting as hers; then, changing knees, she'd tell us a little story about some language conundrum she was dealing with and how she was searching for the correct handling of it. Jackie had an amazing grasp of language—both in a literary sense and as a speaker—and from that John had acquired a healthy vocabulary. He would say a word—and the word I remember, from one particular late afternoon, was "parameter"—and she would stop him and ask if he knew what the word meant and whether he was using it properly. He defined "parameter," and before he went on, she said, "There are fewer than five people in the whole United States who know what the true meaning of that word is and how to use it, and you are one of them."

That might be laughable in the literal sense, but her point wasn't: that language, and learning, and knowledge, are special. Then, before heading out on one of her walks around the golf course, she would ask, "Billy, will you come to dinner tonight? We're having lobster."

Ye-*es*.

"Good. I'll tell Marta on my way out. See you at seven?"

I would head home in my Whaler, tell my mother where I was having dinner; she would offer a ride.

"No thanks. I'll take the boat."

My mother would groan. She was missing out on a chance to get a glimpse of her social barometer.

At dinner Jackie would ring the bell for course changes. In my house we once had a good laugh about a maid my mother had who objected to the buzzer under the rug and asked her to use a small bell instead. My mother loved the idea, the men of the family found it a bit too patrician, and ultimately the maid was let go. Yet somehow, Jackie—as she could with so many things—made ringing that bell just the right touch.

The dining room in the President's house, a massive room loaded with antiques, glowed like candlelight even before the candles were lit. The table was antique tiger maple with dips and raises that made everything on it seem unsteady. Each place setting had its own salt and pepper shakers and very large goblets of water, with bowls of ice set out for them. The chairs were ancient and appeared breakable, they were so petite. Jackie's chair at the foot of the table, though, was big and strong, like a throne; I had hoped to be seated in it the first time I had dinner there, then prayed that I wouldn't shatter my tiny seat into antique kindling. In spite of my size, the little chairs never even creaked. Just as the table and chairs appeared too fragile to use, they were, like Jackie herself, delicate and refined, yet strong as steel.

The opposing chair at the head of the table was seldom used in my presence. It was obvious why: The presidential portrait was taken with Jack Kennedy sitting there; it was the one that graced the cover of *Time* (my father had a copy of the photo on his library desk, hand-inscribed with unusual penmanship; I still cannot determine exactly what is written, and even John could not decipher his father's scratch). Beyond the empty seat was a handsome sea captain's portrait.

It might have been the rich wood of the hand-hewn antiques, or the painting from Sunset Hill looking down over what is now the Hyannisport Golf Club, or maybe the burgundy drapes, but the room glowed with serenity. I watched my manners and listened intently to the visiting luminaries who were sometimes there as well, adding something only when I understood what the hell they were discussing. But John, even at thirteen, used this setting as a theater; he pondered aloud his interests and concerns, gesturing with his hands, cutting the air to make his point. He might be talking about saving the whales. Or scuba diving. In a year or two, it would be the politics of Africa. Eventually, when this room, and house, were his—ours—he would be sitting in his mother's seat, riding a discussion with different luminaries or friends, or both. It was a scene that would be replayed again and again not just in the President's house but in many different dining rooms, everywhere I had dinner and conversation with him over the next quarter century. But it was in this room where John developed, like an actor, his love of debate and engagement.

4

Native New Yorker

JOHN REVELED in the energy, pace, and variety of New York, a place where I'd never spent much time. There was a song in the seventies called "Native New Yorker"—he was that kid. I was intrigued to go see him there; I still wondered what it was like living in an apartment. I had a vision of a crowd of people standing in a fluorescent-lit hallway, waiting for an elevator, only to have it arrive full, with another coming soon. Something like a New York subway during rush hour.

During the bicentennial summer of 1976, a mutual friend of ours and I went into Boston to pick up my newly painted '73 Cougar convertible and then head down to Hartford to catch a Grateful Dead show. After the concert we decided to drive to New York; John had just returned from some summer vacation. Besides, we had very little money, and it was easier to slip down there than head to the Cape.

Small problem: By the time we got to 1040 Fifth Avenue, it was well after midnight, and we could not get a response from John's apartment. A couple of his Secret Service agents were still around, so it didn't look wise to push too hard. Total Deadheads, we slept in my car and waited for morning light. Then we went around the corner to get some coffee and hang out in Central Park until it wasn't too early to impose on our friend.

John was surprised to see us but, as always, enjoyed company and the possibility of adventure, especially on his home turf. The apartment was nothing like what I'd expected. The elevator had a bench in it and a closed-circuit camera, and it opened up directly into a faux marble–painted vestibule at the Onassis front door—not a fluorescent light in sight. John immediately called Anthony, who lived only a few blocks away, to come over. We were ripe for a day in the city. We had another small problem, though: Our mutual friend was a big pot smoker (I was more of a beer drinker), and he had gone through what he had at the concert. He was looking for some pot for the ride home.

John suggested we drive up into Spanish Harlem in my car. In little bodegas there, he had heard, there were NO POT TODAY signs in the windows—we simply needed to find one without the sign, he reasoned, sort of like a motel with a vacancy.

He assured me it was safe, so up we drove. When we got to a corner where a couple guys were hanging out, John urged our friend to "run over there—go ask that guy." So out he leaped, a preppy in his little Lacoste shirt, and within five seconds my Cougar—with the top down and with that brand-new hunter green paint job—was getting pelted with vegetables and fruit from windows above.

"*What the hell . . . ?*" I yelled. "Get back in the car!"

John, in the backseat, started laughing. Then a guy in a suit and dark glasses was at my door.

"Listen," he said. "We don't know what you guys are up to, but we better get out of here."

It was the Secret Service—there they were behind us, a couple of cars back, in their Crown Vic. And I could not have agreed more.

Food kept raining down; we were on a side street and stuck behind another car for a moment. But as soon as our friend got back in—needless to say, without the weed—we hightailed it out of there.

John laughed the whole way back to his apartment, with the Secret Service tailing us. I was spooked; as one of my first experiences in New York, it didn't exactly make me feel comfortable. No doubt the locals saw the Crown Vic, not to mention these preppy kids in a convertible, and thought it was some sort of sting operation.

Later we went across the street to the plaza in front of the Metropolitan Museum of Art and threw a Frisbee and ate Sabrett hot dogs—much tamer action. I looked around, suddenly curious about the Secret Service: One was standing by a mailbox, wearing a raincoat and shades, looking official. Two guys were parked nearby in the black Crown Vic; in Boston the Crown Vics were blue. On the Cape the Secret Service was less obvious.

That was my first taste of New York, John-style. After borrowing a few dollars from him (for a change), we headed to the Cape, where we'd rendezvous with him in a few days.

THAT FALL, John started at Phillips Academy in Andover, and I was a freshman at Boston College, so I saw him frequently. The Secret Service would drive him into Boston, and we'd go to a BC football game, and maybe to Charlie's Kitchen in Harvard Square. Behind the bar were photos of President Kennedy, and some of them included two-year-old John. But nobody knew who he was; John was still getting around under the radar.

Or I'd go down to see him in New York when he was home; the shuttle flight from Boston was only about thirty-five bucks round-trip. I remember one weekend flying down with him—and a Secret Service agent. We were met at La Guardia by three more agents in a station wagon that took us to 1040 (our shorthand for Jackie's apartment). By the time we got there, it was dark. Jackie was all dolled up, about to head out for dinner with Lord Harlech, who had been British ambassador to the United States during JFK's administration; Harlech quickly regaled John and me with stories about his daughter's boyfriend, Eric Clapton. Jackie told us that dinner would be served in the library on trays, that she had gotten some magazines for us—*Rolling Stone, Sports Illustrated*—and told John that some of his New York friends had called wondering when he was getting in. We watched cable TV as we ate. I'd never seen anything like it before; there were hundreds of channels, and we landed on a movie on HBO—what was HBO? I felt like the country mouse.

John's friends started coming over. They were Upper East Side kids, rich, longhaired, street-smart; they knew where to buy beer, they knew how to avoid the Eighty-fifth Street gang. They wanted to go up to John's roof to check out the Met's new wing, which was going to house the temple that the Kennedy administration had saved from being ruined by the Aswan Dam—a project (and I would learn of many more over the years) with Jackie's fingerprints all over it. Then we went out and prowled the streets. I was sure we were going to get mugged—I'd seen *Death Wish,* so I knew what happened in New York. We ended up at a friend's apartment. I was disappointed: We got off the elevator in a hall—after experiencing Jackie's elevator taking us right to her *apartment*—so I thought this was pretty low-rent. Though there were no fluorescent lights.

"Billy," John informed me, "we're on Park Avenue, one of the nicest addresses in the world."

The country mouse.

The next morning I got up early at 1040 and went back into the library to figure out that TV; I couldn't, so I checked out the books—my God, there were books everywhere. There was also a beautifully ornate mahogany desk with gold filigree around the drawers and corners—later I found out, when the desk was sold at auction, the Nuclear Test Ban Treaty had been signed on it. I sat down to fiddle with a knife set from the Scottish Highlander Black Watch Regiment; it included a fork and a dagger and was small enough to carry in a sock.

When I looked out over the terrace, down to the street below, I saw the Secret Service's light blue Crown Vic, parked right in front of 1040, the same one that had driven us to the airport in Boston: An agent had brought it down here. What an operation! I looked around to see if anyone else was up. Jackie was not about, John was still asleep. The apartment was like a museum, with Egyptian statues, Greek busts, John Singer Sargent paintings. Only two things in the communal rooms announced that the Kennedys lived here; both were in the dining room: a large photograph of Robert Kennedy, sleeves rolled up, with a microphone in his hand addressing a crowd; and a gold box, about the size of a cigar box, with the presidential seal and some inscription. I was reading it when out came . . . *Charlie!*

Well, I had never heard about Charlie. He was flamboyant, with a shock of white hair, seemingly right off the boat from Ireland and with about three inches of air under his feet.

"Good morning, Mr. Noonan—a fine Irish name that is—now, will you be having breakfast?"

"Yes I will, please."

"A full breakfast?"

I must have looked somewhat puzzled, but he checked me out and decided, "Yes, a full breakfast. I'll bring you some coffee and the newspapers. Please sit down."

Off he went behind a screen, to a kitchen door.

Bang! A door swinging wide open. "Here we go." He set the table with monogrammed silver, poured some coffee, and handed me the three New York daily newspapers. The coffee was strong and wonderful; it had a hearty aroma like the kind in European markets. I sat there overlooking the park, reading, quite content.

Bang! Out came Charlie again with the full breakfast: scrambled eggs that became famous in our group, crisp bacon, sausage, toast with jam, and fresh-squeezed orange juice. I was delighted with myself, the country mouse, for getting exposed to such rarefied treatment. Breakfast on Fifth Avenue, with a butler in white shirt, white jacket, black trousers, and black tie.

"And where do you hail from, Mr. Noonan?" Charlie asked.

"Please call me Billy—I'm from Boston."

"I understand, Billy. I mean where are you from in Ireland?"

"Oh. From the west, in Mayo."

"Ah." Then he was gone again.

Must be from Dublin, I thought. *They think they're the only ones who matter.* I sat and read the papers for a while—still no John.

Bang! "Another breakfast, Billy?"

"No thanks. I'm just waiting for John."

"Good luck—that boy sleeps until noon."

Off he went, before I could thank him properly—but I was *not* going behind that screen to do it, not without John. I had the sense of a full-scale operation back there, with half a dozen cooks and steaming pots and orders being barked (though I couldn't hear anything), all at the ready of the household.

John's large bedroom was in the back of the apartment. It was loaded with Kennedy memorabilia, including that famous picture of him as a two-year-old under the President's desk, smiling, as his father and presidential aides stand in a group; a picture of his father and German chancellor Konrad Adenauer holding John; a framed letter that JFK had penned as a young boy; and a large highboy with his father's initials and a presidential seal. The highboy would eventually survive the first round of auctions, as I remember it in John's apartment years later on North Moore Street, but not the second round, after John's death. Hanging from the ceiling in his bedroom were Air Force One models, regular Revell planes that John had put together, and *PT-109* replicas. Yet the most intriguing thing was the scrimshaw collection. I had been a fan of scrimshaw—whale teeth with designs carved into the enamel—since a camping trip to Nantucket, but this was something else, something that deserved to be on display in a museum, with intricate scenes of whaling ships and nautical adventures. I knew that the collection had been his father's, since I'd seen pictures of it on his desk in the Oval Office. John had twenty-five or thirty teeth—and a bill from a narwhal, now near extinction, about eight feet tall and standing on end. Just a typical fifteen-year-old's bedroom.

When John woke up—sure enough, it was practically noon—he found me in the library trying once again to figure out how to turn on HBO. I told him about my experience with Charlie and the great meal.

"You had breakfast in the dining room? Mummy must have told them to do that to make you feel comfortable," he said.

"You mean you don't eat like that every day?"

He laughed. "No. We eat in the kitchen like everyone else."

"What about Charlie?"

"What *about* Charlie? Isn't he something?" According to John, Charlie was not really just off the boat—he'd been with the family for at least a decade. Apparently the secret to his longevity was never letting anything bother him. They'd once had a Chinese butler who would get so upset he would swear at Jackie, but because of his accent she did not pick up what he was saying, except that he called her "Big Lady"—she thought that was a sign of respect. Charlie, however, informed her of exactly what word he was putting in front of "Big Lady," and that was the end of him.

We, too, called her "Big Lady," a code when we were around nosy people or in public. John got a kick out of giving people nicknames or landing on catchphrases and then beating them to death. For a while he called me "Chopper" and then "Sylvester"—part of the point, of course, was to label you with something vaguely embarrassing. A good nickname for John would have been useful, especially then, because he was on the cusp of being recognized. Starting the previous summer in Hyannisport, when I first got my driver's license and a car, we had started roaming more, going to parties. "John Kennedy" was always a showstopper with girls, but not in the way he'd want—it would ruin the moment. We never came up with a good name for John. We tried "Sparky," which sounded stupid, and "Spanky," because he was the runt of the crowd, but that was even worse. He hated "John-John" for obvious reasons. So he'd typically introduce himself as John, which, when he still wasn't being recognized, came off sort of flat. As in:

"Hi, I'm Billy Noonan, nice to meet you."

"Hello, I'm John."

John. . . . A moment of silence. Just John? Or sometimes, especially in Hyannisport, that would be the tip-off that would start a buzz when all we wanted was to have a good time and meet girls like everyone else. Timmy would later tell a story of going down to Panama with John. One night they went to a disco, and John was wearing a raspberry-colored shirt with his initials on it, also in raspberry, that somebody had given him for Christmas. He and Timmy were introduced to two girls, and one of them caught the monogram. Timmy could see her eyes getting bigger and bigger, and finally she elbowed her friend, who said, "JFK—isn't that an airport?"

It became a standing joke for the next few years: It was impossible to meet girls when you were with John, because he got all the attention. Which just got crazier and crazier the older he got.

THAT FALL AFTERNOON in New York, Jackie wanted to take us to the American Museum of Natural History. I was up for that because I admired Teddy Roosevelt, the founder. But John quickly shot down the idea; he took me to Forty-second Street instead, trying to show me the gritty New York he loved. To me it was nothing but a mess of people grabbing me and trying to sell me things. I was sure I was about to get mugged. No Secret Service in sight, though I knew they were there somewhere.

Jackie took us out to dinner that night at Patsy's, a midtown Italian restaurant where Aristotle had taken her. It was always interesting to watch the reaction Jackie got in public. Or didn't.

For example, our cabdriver, with a cigar hanging out of his mouth, dropping us off at the restaurant: "That'll be four-fifty, lady."

Jackie handed him a ten, got out, and walked away. He had no idea. Then, suddenly, a smile of recognition creased his face.

But she wasn't sure we were at the correct place. "I *think* this is where Ari took me," she said, looking through a window. A crowd immediately started forming, watching her, gawking. Then the maître d' popped out. "Hello, Mrs. Onassis. It's so nice to see you again." He gave us a table directly behind his little stand. I wondered, Had she made a reservation? *Did* she make reservations? Or did she just show up?

The maître d' insisted on creating a special meal for us and selecting the wine; he was definitely looking out for us. New York is so accustomed to celebrity that you can be famous and left alone, although Jackie would prompt pointing and staring; she just looked right through it and spoke to us as if nothing else were going on.

As we ate and chatted, a classic "big, brassy broad" arrived, making a scene at the door by kissing everyone and speaking loudly. She strutted in, her hair all done up, too much makeup, wearing a big mink—she was a caricature of herself, a wannabe from North Jersey right out of a Woody Allen flick. Suddenly, though, she got the sense that something was amiss here; she stopped to take inventory, laser-beamed around. There, on the other side of the room, sitting with two teenage boys, with a sable slung over the back of her chair: Jackie. "Oh, my God!" she let out, covering her mouth, gasping for breath as if she'd been punched in the stomach. The maître d'—smart man!—seated her as far away from us as possible. John and I found this pretty funny, John because it was yet another moment in the carnival of going out with his mother, and me because it was all brand-new. Jackie just grinned, as if to say, *Oh, my, the poor thing.*

When we left, Jackie marched right out into the street and stuck her hand up to hail a cab, like any other New Yorker on a Saturday night. Without missing a beat, she turned around and told the agent, who she knew was within earshot, that we would be going home.

"Right," he said. "Back to the nest." Government precision.

At 1040 an agent asked John if he was in for the night or going out. We were going out. We cabbed up to Mike Malkin's on Seventy-ninth Street, a hangout for Upper East Side kids. Just as we were paying for the cab, a guy a little older than us and two girls came flying out of Malkin's, with a few Eighty-fifth Street gang members pounding him. It was ugly—they were throwing this guy into a newspaper stand like a rag doll.

Suddenly a Secret Service agent appeared. He told the punks to get lost.

"We'll cut your fuckin' throat," one challenged.

"Get the hell out of here," the agent commanded, and, lo and behold, they backed away and left.

"I knew it!" I said to John. "It's kill or be killed in this city. I'm not going in there."

"Oh, Billy, come on. . . ."

"No way. Let's go home."

"It couldn't be any safer now."

We went over to the agent. "What would you do if they pulled a knife?" I asked him. "Would you have pulled out your gun?"

"You never pull out your gun unless you're going to use it," he answered coolly.

Inside Mike Malkin's the walls were lined with photos of the mop-top Beatles hanging out there, after *The Ed Sullivan Show* back in 1964. John had obviously been here before—he knew a lot of the other kids. We checked out a back room, replete with black light and pre-disco funk; we sat at a banquette in front. Every time I finished my beer, another would materialize, without my asking; they wouldn't let us pay.

A Secret Service agent sat at the end of the bar the whole time, sipping 7-Up. A new agent appeared at midnight to baby-sit us until we were ready to go home, a guy about twenty-five, in shades. It was absurd, but that, of course, was his job—to watch John and make sure nobody got any stupid ideas. I don't think Jackie had a clue what we were up to, though, as I'd learn, she was very good at walking the line between reining John in and giving him freedom.

Early that morning the agent drove us back to the apartment. This was his first field assignment. Luckily, the night ended more quietly than it had started.

5

Arts and Entertainment

ONE EVENING in the summer of 1977, at dinner with Jackie and John at the President's house, John put me on the spot. "Tell Mummy about what you studied in Ireland."

I had just returned from six months of studying ancient and modern Irish history and literature in Dublin but was unsure where to start. Jackie had been aware of my interest in Ireland, since a maid had come into their living room one day two years earlier to tell us that Eamon de Valera, president of Ireland, had died. Jackie immediately left the room and went upstairs; she must have placed a call to Dublin. (De Valera was an American-born Irish patriot who'd fought for Irish independence from England. While he was in jail, his associate Michael Collins signed a treaty with England releasing all but six northern counties to a new Irish government. Once de Valera was released from jail—his release was a condition of the agreement—he returned to Ireland and began a civil war with Collins. After Collins was assassinated, de Valera became president of Ireland.) He was president when President Kennedy visited Ireland in 1963. Kennedy addressed the Dail—the Irish parliament—by saying that if Mr. de Valera had never left Brooklyn and Kennedy's own grandfather had never left New Ross, they might have each other's jobs. It was a humorous juxtaposition, but the truth went beyond that, since it was de Valera's American citizenship that had saved his neck from the gallows during Ireland's fight for freedom. The Kennedys still had a dog named Shannon (and now some of its puppies) that had been a gift from de Valera.

I was aware of all this as I started telling Jackie about the great writers I had studied: Beckett—a favorite of hers—Yeats, Synge, and Joyce. I told her I was sure that Joyce's writing had been drug-induced, which got a laugh.

Jackie asked me whether I'd studied Irish painting. Yes. We discussed Sir John Lavery—who had painted his wife, Lady Hazel Lavery, a Chicago native whose face adorned Irish currency—and Jack Yeats, W.B.'s brother. Did I know, Jackie wondered, that Iron and Bronze Age Irish artifacts were leaving Ireland for the first time to come to the Met in New York?

I did—my professors were the ones cataloging and documenting them; this would be the first time they were shown out of Ireland. *But how did she know that?* I wondered silently. I should have known better, as Jackie was fascinated with the arts. She had taken John and me to see a Russian exhibit the Christmas before at the Met. Afterward she walked us through the impressionist gallery, filled with throngs of astonished art admirers. She moved with incredible speed and dexterity, and when someone approached her to ask if Jackie were really Jackie, she moved right by without acknowledging the person. (What could she do, engage everyone? It would have created a riot.) John rolled his eyes as she explained Renoir's use of small strokes on a girl's sock; when we stood back, it was simply a perfect sock, which of course was his genius. The crowds ebbed and flowed with her movements, and then we slipped out, back across the street to her apartment.

"That was the quickest tour of a museum I've ever been on," I told her.

"The only way to go to the museum is quickly"—on that point John certainly agreed with her—"because it gets so boring and overwhelming when one dawdles." Dawdles?

That night the following summer at the President's house, after our literary discussion, we took our green tea by the fire in the living room.

Jackie produced small booklets from her trip to Ireland in 1967 with John and Caroline; they were filled with poetry and prose, perhaps thirty pages long, and were published every few months by an Irish literary guild, with short pieces by obscure writers, some of whom later became famous. A few happened to be my professors. She brought out a big book, given to her by Aer Lingus, with great flowing script commemorating her trip. It included pictures of the university where I'd studied, and some of my professors were in photographs—I was pleased to connect with Jackie on this level and gained new insight into the breadth of her knowledge and curiosity.

John had two memories of the trip to Ireland. One was "Up with Nelson," a song memorializing the day when the IRA blew up a pillar in Dublin; the pillar celebrated Lord Nelson's victory at Trafalgar, and blowing it up celebrated, in turn, the fiftieth anniversary of the Irish uprising of 1916. John's second memory was of Irish government drivers telling him that the only way to catch leprechauns was with pints of Guinness, and if he happened to produce a few pints, they might be able to snag one. So John secured them a few glasses; the next day he noticed there were empty glasses, and no leprechauns. At six years old, he'd had his first taste of Irish blarney.

That summer had started out at a much more frantic pace. After my return from Ireland in June, I visited John at Andover. It felt odd to be back. We went to the Andover Inn and I had a beer in the basement; the band Boston had made the national charts in my absence, and the album *More Than a Feeling* was playing every five minutes on every radio in New England. One of the songs, "Rock and Roll Band," referred to "dancin' in the street of Hyannis."

"What is this?" I wondered.

John laughed—he was used to the strange sensation. "It's called culture shock, Billy."

"What's that mean?"

"It means you're overwhelmed and confused about what's going on because you've been wrapped up in another culture for a while."

Then he told me that he had a girlfriend now and that the three of us should drive down to Boston. Meg Azzoni was eighteen, a senior—John was only sixteen, so this was a real coup—and I liked her immediately. She was pretty, with curly hair and a raspy voice she used for comic effect, the perfect girl to take road trips with. We jumped into my Cougar and headed to the city.

Instead of a debutante or typical graduation party, Meg Azzoni and a few friends had convinced their parents (or maybe it was the other way around) to have a black-tie extravaganza on Long Island. "You should come down to my party, Billy Noonan," she said.

John liked this idea, since he wouldn't know anybody there except Meg Azzoni. A groundbreaking ceremony for the Kennedy Library in Boston was coming up at the end of the month, right around the President's birthday; John invited me to that as well. But before either Meg's party or the library groundbreaking, we had to empty out his dorm room and get his stuff to the Cape. We'd put it in my mother's garage in Osterville and he could retrieve it in August, when he came back to the Cape after traveling in Africa. If there was ever a person for whom moving around like this, living on the fly, was second nature, it was John.

Even at sixteen, John had an exotic collection of stuff, like the silk robe with MUHAMMAD ALI stitched on the back—it was from a title bout. This wasn't something John had hanging up to show people; he wore it to the shower. He also had an Andy Warhol lithograph of Chairman Mao that the artist had inscribed "To John Kennedy Jr." It was in one of my apartments for a long time, for some reason, and when I moved, it got lost. No problem—he got another from Warhol.

Since staying at my mother's house was a little too supervised for us, after unloading his things we headed off to see some Cape Cod friends who had rented a house in Edgartown for the summer. I had spent the previous summer working on the Vineyard, so I knew my way around. We got off the ferry and hitchhiked in the rain. John had brought a sleeping bag but didn't get much sleep—there was a pesky girl from Hyannisport who wanted to climb in with him. At this point he had a full head of hair, almost like an Afro; he hadn't morphed into Mr. Heartthrob-with-No-Shirt quite yet, but he was an attractive kid now, and increasingly recognizable. I had a talk with the girl, since I knew her better. She said that she just couldn't help herself. After a couple of days of very little sleep, we decided to head back up to the Cape and stay—safely—at my mother's. From there we'd go to Boston for the groundbreaking ceremony.

In our absence Jackie had called my house to check in with John and remind him of the dates and his responsibility to attend the event. My mother finally had a chance to speak with Mrs. Onassis, and they had a lovely chat, as she pointedly told me. She had also obtained an invitation to the ceremony.

The night before the ceremony, we had no place to stay in Boston, and in those days kids didn't have credit cards. (It was typical of John to forget to bring cash as well—I was always loaning him money.) And he had lost his checks. After we picked up Timmy Shriver at the airport, John asked me the name of the second-best hotel in Boston, since he knew that his mother always stayed at the Ritz, and he wanted to avoid the pomp of the place.

The concierge at the Park Plaza, however, was not exactly enthused about renting a room to three longhaired teenagers trying to pay with cash. Like any ready-to-rumble kids, we found this highly annoying. *Unlike* most ready-to-rumble kids, we had a handy solution. John went to the bank of public phones to make a collect telephone call to his mother, still in New York, who was flying in the next day.

"Mummy, I'm here with Billy and Timmy in Boston, but the hotel won't take our cash and I don't have any checks." The name on the check, of course, would have gotten us in. "What should we do?"

She asked if he'd gotten the name of the guy at the desk. Yup. John gave it to her, hung up, and said, with cat-that-ate-the-canary glee, "Let's go back to the desk to watch this."

The concierge took a phone call. "Yes, this is Robert," he said. He listened for a moment.

"Yes, I see the three boys." Then his eyes snapped wide open. "Can you repeat that? . . . Oh, my God, yes, of course we can. . . . Yes. . . . Of course."

He started waving as if to fan himself. "Would you mind holding the phone, madam?" Immediately the busboy bell was ringing like an alarm. "Oh, my God, this is so freaky!"

An older, clearheaded Irish bellhop appeared. "Please take Mr. Kennedy and his friends up to their room." Then he peppered Jackie with a few apologies and assurances.

"You really got Robert going," the bellhop said, laughing on the way up in the elevator. "He'll be talking about this for months."

When we went to tip him, he said, "Ah, no, it was a pleasure, now. Good luck tomorrow"—he knew why we were in town—"and do a good job."

We thanked him, then collapsed on our beds and laughed like the kids we were.

The next morning John discovered that he had left not only his sport coat in my closet on Cape Cod but his shoes as well. So had I. We rushed around Boston looking for dress shoes; Jack Walsh, the former head of the Kennedy Secret Service detail, from South Boston, was able to procure shoes for John. I was left to fend for myself, as usual, and ended up in old boat shoes.

John had begun acknowledging his family publicly by going to Kennedy events, so he knew the lay of the land—meaning a lot of photographers would be snapping away. We gathered behind the "Big Lady" as she walked down a long plank that had been set up—it was like a runway on Oscar night. The point, of course, was the photo op; she was not averse to that, just paparazzi. John was happy to remain behind her, in the background, though within a couple of years that was going to change.

My mother had come in a new outfit and had brought one of her friends; she was in her element, talking with her old friends, drinking white wine, and testing the appetizers. At one point, she told me later, she was in the elevator with Mrs. Onassis and told her how wonderfully John had behaved while staying with her earlier that month, though she had told *me* that he'd eaten her out of house and home and had made a big mess.

A few days later, I met John in New York. I rented a tux and we drove out to Long Island for Meg Azzoni's big graduation/coming-out bash. On the way I double-checked with him to make sure the Azzonis knew I was coming.

"Oh, yeah, sure. I told Meg, and she told her mother. It's cool."

Then, of course, we arrived to discover that her parents had no idea what I was doing there. Typical John. I had already developed a theory that he was sadistic—he clearly enjoyed a certain level of confusion and ad hoc planning (or no planning). He liked to create a little trouble and make a splash. His attitude was, just show up, it'll work out. For *him*, sure.

Anyway, Meg had me spend the night in an apartment over the garage with some friend of hers who had a Volvo with a NO NUKES sticker on the bumper. A Birkenstocks fellow. Just my type of guy.

Friday night arrived, and off we went to a party under a big tent at someone's house where everyone was dressed in country-club-casual cocktail attire. I started talking to an older group of men while John was ganged up on by smiling fathers and gushing wives—the sort of fanfare he would soon get good at dealing with. Now it made him uncomfortable. I, on the other hand, discovered that I'd gone to the same prep school as one of the men I was chatting with, and another guy asked me if I was by chance related to a Harvard football player from the late forties, a guy named Jimmy Noonan.

"Yeah, I'm his nephew."

The guy gave me an isn't-this-a-small-world smile. "I just saw him in San Francisco at the Top of the Mark." (Jimmy would confirm this a month later.)

I made a big impression with these fathers, which I tend to do— sometimes good, sometimes not. This was a good one.

The next night people were flying in from everywhere for the main event; we put on our tuxedos and headed to an even larger tent by the sea. I was not there long when I started dancing with a beautiful girl, and we ended up going for a walk in the moonlight, and . . . well, suffice it to say we were gone from the party for a long time. Meg's parents were worried, probably because the girl's date was annoyed and no one could find us. John assured the hosts that I was okay and that everything was fine. Eventually the girl and I returned to the party, and Meg's father promptly gave us a ride home.

I woke early the next morning—I always wake up early—in the loft above the garage, the room I shared with the NO NUKES guy, who was sound asleep. I was still in my tuxedo. I got up, went down into the kitchen of Meg's parents, and opened the refrigerator, which was packed with plates covered in tinfoil, stuff like deviled eggs—it looked like if you touched one thing, everything would come tumbling to the floor. Dying of thirst, exhausted, I grabbed a beer. As I was slugging it down, I turned around and saw Meg's mother, Mrs. Azzoni, standing in the doorway watching me. I quickly made myself scarce.

I roused John and suggested we get out of there. I'd been on the road with him—Andover, the Vineyard, New York, the Cape, Boston, here on Long Island—for the better part of a month since returning from Dublin, and I needed to get organized. He was headed to an Outward Bound program in Maine. On the road again.

When I saw him in Hyannisport that August, John had a number of photographs of me and the girl—and stories of my behavior—from the party. John the storyteller felt the need to regale our crowd with what had happened.

"So Noonan shows up at this party. We're with all these proper people, he's over in the corner with these sixty-year-old men, throwing back the drinks with them, yukking it up with the guys, and I'm over here meeting Meg Azzoni's aunt—I gotta meet the whole family—and Noonan completely stiffs me, he's over there yukking it up." And he went on to say how I disappear with this guy's date, and everyone's wondering where the hell the two of us are, until we *finally* appear, Meg's father drives us back to their house and . . .

"So the next thing he does? Here's the icing on the cake, as if he hasn't done enough already, here's what he does next: He comes down in the morning, still in his tuxedo, opens up the fridge, and Meg's mother is sitting there. 'Billy,' she asks, 'can I get you some orange juice? Would you like some scrambled eggs?'

"'Ah, no thanks. I'll have a beer—'"

"Wait a minute," I interrupted John. "It didn't really happen like that. You're embellishing."

"Then how *did* it happen, Billy? Were you drinking beer in the morning or not?"

"Yeah, well, I was thirsty, there was beer. . . ."

John got a "case closed" look. But I had an answer for him:

Earlier that summer John had left his sport coat—the one he was supposed to wear to the library groundbreaking—at my mother's house, and when she found it and went to send it to the cleaners for him, she found not only his checkbook but some cannabis. Actually, it was a bunch of seeds. John got the idea he'd grow some pot in a cutting garden on the compound. But to my mother—the daughter of a jurist—the bag of seeds was marijuana.

"I took John's coat to the cleaners, and I found pot," she'd told me.

"Oh?" I responded nonchalantly. "What did you do with it?"

"I threw it away."

"That's fine. Don't worry about it."

"He shouldn't be bringing pot into my house." She warned me again about the bad behavior of those Kennedy boys and the possible consequences if somehow I was involved.

So I began to tell the same audience about how John had brought pot into my house and got bagged, which shut him up about my high jinks at Meg's house. I feigned real annoyance—hey, it's one thing to get caught with your own pot, which never happened to me, and quite another to get caught with someone else's. John was more than quiet. He was mortified.

The next afternoon I saw him in Hyannisport, and we went out waterskiing. Afterward he said to me, "You know, your mother really is something else. Now I see where you get your sense of humor, Billy."

"What are you talking about?"

"I called your house this morning and talked to your mother. She asked me about Outward Bound, told me how much fun she had at the groundbreaking ceremony, and then she says, 'Oh, John, you left a sports coat here last spring.'"

Silence on John's end of the conversation.

"I was sending it out to get it cleaned for you," my mother apparently went on, "and you will never believe what I found in your pocket."

Pause. . . . John got his profuse apology ready. "What was that, Mrs. Noonan?"

"Your checks! I found some of your checks."

"Oh. Thank you so much! I've been looking for them."

"Come by and pick up your coat and your checks sometime."

"I'll do that! Thank you!"

She knew, of course, that I had told him she'd found the seeds. And she got a big kick, my mother, out of having him by the scruff of the neck. And then letting him off the hook.

"She is so fucking funny, Billy. Your mother."

Later that summer John asked his mother if Meg could visit him in Hyannisport. Jackie was delighted; remembering how significant her own first visit to the compound had been, more than twenty years earlier, she said this was a red-letter day.

John suggested that Meg take the shuttle to Boston from La Guardia and that I drive Jackie's new BMW up to collect her—Jackie didn't want John to drive but trusted me. I was dying to get behind the wheel of that car. Back then most preppies were driving the 2002, a two-door coupe; we called them "radical preppies," kids who would keep their albums in peach crates. But this was a serious car; only a limited number of this model had been made.

Off we went to get Meg at Logan Airport. In those days state police were all over the Cape, pulling over speeders at 56 miles an hour. But once we cleared the Sagamore Bridge to the mainland, John said, "Come on, step on it. Let's see how fast we can get this baby going." This is why I was driving instead of him.

"Do you think it's broken in?" I asked. "It only has a few hundred miles on it."

"Yeah, yeah, we take it to New Jersey on the weekend"—to their house in Peapack—"but the traffic is so bad, we never get above sixty."

And this is why I shouldn't have been driving it either. Down went the pedal, up went the speedometer: 100, 110, 120, 130, 140 miles an hour. Not shaking a bit.

"Like we're on the Autobahn, Billy."

"Yeah, well, we're not helping the gas crisis much." Later we found out that this model had an alternate engine that engaged at a certain speed, with the main engine shutting down.

After we brought Meg down to the compound, I hit the road for a few days. I knew what was going to happen—there would be great intrigue over John's having a girlfriend visiting, and I didn't want to be around for it. Sure enough, they went off to the RFK tennis tournament in Flushing Meadow, and a week later there he was—JFK, Jr., and his girl—in *People* magazine. In a way, that was the end of his childhood; I knew he would never get a break from the paparazzi after that.

AFTER LABOR DAY, that summer of '77, most people had gone home. The first two weeks in September and the last two weeks in June are always the best times on the Cape. I was still waiting to start school, and John and Anthony hadn't gone off to school yet either—prep schools started much later in those days. We spent a lot of time, with Jackie, at the President's house late that summer.

Just after Labor Day, we were rocked by the death of Kenny O'Donnell, who'd been President Kennedy's right-hand man and one of my father's best friends. I had seen his son Kevin at a party in the compound on

Labor Day, and he told me his father was in the hospital and not doing well. "He'll be fine," I told him, with every ounce of Irish denial I had. "He's tough. He'll pull through." I had seen Kenny at the library ground-breaking in Boston; he'd seemed maudlin, but he always did at such events. The truth is, Kenny had never gotten over what happened in Dallas, or to Bobby, and the solace of whiskey eventually caught up with him.

Kenny was buried in my family's plot, next to my father, partly because his second wife didn't want him buried next to his first. His death brought my father's passing, six years earlier, right back to me. At the wake in Boston, I couldn't look at the O'Donnells; all I could do was cry. I thought about how he had sat with me at my father's wake when I was inconsolable. At the funeral home, I had seen him hugging Uncle Jimmy and crying in the room where my father lay, unrecognizable to me. Then Kenny sat next to me, put his arm around my shoulders, and told me all about my father, how Kenny had called him "Blue Eyes" and "a stout Cary Grant." He told me how much my father had done for him and for Jack Kennedy, and about the President's plan to make him ambassador to Ireland.

"I'll tell you what," Kenny had said to me. "Tomorrow is the Princeton game, the game your dad and I would go to every year. Junior Carr [the third of their trio] and I will pick you up after the funeral, and you'll come with us. Your father would want you to get on with your life."

Now, at his wake, I thought about how he had helped me take the first step forward after losing my father. It was terrible now to lose him, too. At the cemetery in Holyhood, the funeral director escorted my mother, my sister, and me to the side of our plot. The O'Donnells buried their father while news photographers stood on headstones to get a better angle. Jackie came and stood next to me. Seeing how upset I was, she said, "Don't be so sorry for Kenny. He is at peace and in a better place." I sobbed. "He's not just burying Kenny," my mother said to Jackie. "He's burying his father again." Jackie looked at me with sad eyes and kissed me—she knew too well, of course, what it was like to see these lights go out. (A month earlier, when Meg was visiting the compound, a group of us went to see the James Bond movie *The Spy Who Loved Me*. I sat next to Jackie, and when in one scene the camera panned to an assassin, she muffled a scream and grabbed my arm.) When I think back now on all she had been through, her strength was remarkable.

That September—as John, Anthony, and I were still on the Cape—the season's change felt like a life shift for me. My mother had retired to the Cape and Florida; I was now officially out on my own, making runs back into Boston looking for an apartment. It was a difficult time. My friendship with John was a way station; we spent a lot of time exploring different parts of the Cape, not something that's easy to do in the height of the season. We'd decide, for example, to head up to Provincetown, a fishing village that had turned into a gay community, to eat kale soup at a Portuguese restaurant.

John would wonder, "How are we going to get there?"

"My car."

As he well knew. But it was a moment to have sport with my Boston accent: "We're gonna go in yawh cah." John would get a line in his head and then hit you with it for the next twenty years: "God love ya, I knew ya fatha. How's ya lovely motha?"

Or some days that September, we went waterskiing or listened to music in John's room. We went four-wheeling on Sandy Neck, on the north side of the Cape. John had a motorcycle for a while that had belonged to Alexander, Aristotle Onassis's son who died in a plane crash; somehow John got it from Greece to my mother's garage, where he was hiding it. But then Jackie found out about it, and that was the end of the motorcycle.

Sometimes we'd escape up to the widow's walk of the President's house to have a beer. John was never much of a drinker. He wasn't a good drinker—he tended to get drunk fast, which he didn't like, and he hated hangovers. If we'd go out for a beer, he'd have one and then order a Sprite. John's father didn't drink much either, and I think that influenced him. Neither was his mother a drinker—she'd take a mouthful of wine at dinner. John told me once that after his father's assassination she drank a great deal for a while but then stopped when she realized it could become a problem.

Other times that September, we would ramble along with his mother, who liked to go antiquing on 6A, the Old King's Highway in the oldest part of the Cape that was dotted with little shops. The road is full of dips and bends, as it was originally a cow path and later a coach path to Boston. One day Mrs. Onassis came around a corner with a little too much speed—as I've said, the BMW was just begging to go—and there sat a state trooper. He pulled us over.

Dressed in knee-high leather boots and jodhpurs, with a black leather strap across the chest, the troopers were an intimidating presence. As the trooper walked up to Jackie's window, John turned to Anthony and me in the backseat. "Watch what happens now."

Nothing annoys Cape Codders more than New Yorkers in large, expensive, foreign cars who are speeding. We do not have much in common with them, given how they put tomatoes in their clam chowder and root for the Yankees.

Without peering below the roofline, the cop barked, "License and registration." Jackie was already looking through her purse; John found the registration in the glove box. The officer's gloved hand snatched the papers.

There was a moment of silence while he read them.

Suddenly the trooper doubled over as if he'd been punched in the gut to stare in at the driver, who was now grinning shoulder to shoulder with a "Yep, it's me, I'm embarrassed" look. The trooper's eyes darted around the car. "That's your son! The President's son! Is that a Secret Service agent in the backseat?"

"No," Jackie said, "that is a friend of my son's."

"Who is the other guy?"

"That is my nephew."

Trying to regain his composure, the trooper straightened up, deepened his voice, and said, "You know why I pulled you over, don't you?"

"Yes, I was speeding. You see, it's a new car, and I'm not quite used to it yet."

No doubt the trooper was wondering why she was driving at all and where her protection was. But Jackie never wanted to be protected; she was happy driving herself around. Her life was not all champagne and limousines, especially not at this moment on the Old King's Highway.

The trooper coughed and told her in an official tone, "I guess we can let this go. Please try to slow down."

"Yes, Officer."

With that he stepped out into traffic, raising his hand in a halt, which scared the hell out of an oncoming driver, who screeched to a stop. Then the trooper waved us back onto the road. The three of us boys laughed like hell. Jackie kept her eyes on the speedometer and checked the rear-view mirror—"Okay, enough, you guys," she chided gently—as we headed back to the compound.

Another tragedy marred that Indian summer on the Cape—this one was far away but still profound. John had been in South Africa that summer, and it wasn't his first visit to the continent. His interest in the emerging nations there was deep-seated: It was an exotic pursuit, and it connected to his father's acknowledgment of African independence, his interest in civil rights, and the creation of the Peace Corps. John had met leaders of several nations. Fresh from studying in Ireland, and as a student of Britain's colonial past in Africa and other places, I shared with John an interest in fights for self-government and economic control. I had long been a supporter of the IRA in Ireland, though I'd soured on their methods. An IRA bomb, in fact, had exploded near Caroline that year when she was studying in London and staying with a member of Parliament, who was the target. "Hey, your boys almost blew up my sister," John complained to me. Imagine how the American funding for IRA activities would have been slashed if it had really happened. We talked about Africa's emerging nations for hours, especially apartheid in South Africa, Nelson Mandela, and Steve Biko. Jackie was impressed with John's knowledge and passion.

When Biko died while being detained and interrogated that September, I came to the house with the news. John told me to hold my tongue, that Mummy, who was upstairs, had heard and was not taking it well. When she came down, her hair pulled tightly back, she said hello and took her spot on the patio where she spent most of her days, sipping iced tea and eating carrots and speaking on the phone. The profundity of the loss was thick in the air. I noticed her mouth. It was long and thin, as if the bun in her hair were too tight, contorting her mouth like a sad painted clown's. We left her there with her thoughts, and when we returned for dinner, Biko's name never came up; clearly his death had touched a nerve. We discussed instead our coming academic years.

6

"The Billy Noonan School of Diplomacy"

IN THE FALL OF 1977, we all returned to school. I had rented an apartment in Brookline and was finishing my courses at Northeastern so I could return to Boston College. Anthony was off to Choate; John started his second year at Phillips Academy.

One Friday evening I was walking with a friend through the recently renovated Quincy marketplace in Boston and heard Irish music. Since I was just back from Dublin, I stepped in, and almost immediately I was approached to work the door for a private concert of the group De Dannan. I jumped at the chance, since I was very familiar with their music. The next thing I knew, I was working at the Black Rose every weekend night, checking IDs and quaffing pints. I loved it—the Black Rose was the first Irish pub in Boston that played traditional Irish music.

John would often come into town on weekends. Caroline was at Radcliffe, and some of his cousins were at Harvard; the Kennedy School of Government building was under construction. We would hook up and play touch football and go to Harvard football games. At night he and Caroline and a group of their friends often came to see me at the Black Rose. There was always a healthy line waiting to get in, but I could get them in the back door and put them at a table with some people who would look after them. Naturally, the management was delighted to have the Irish royalty in the house.

It was the beginning of a tough period for me. Since my mother had sold our family house in Boston and my much-older siblings lived in the suburbs with their own families, I was on my own for the first time. I dealt with it by keeping busy; that winter I began campaigning for Ed King, a dark-horse Democrat who was opposing the incumbent, Michael Dukakis, for governor. Dukakis was a Brookline native, like myself, but was a complete bureaucrat who thought that all problems could be cured by government, which had put the commonwealth in serious fiscal peril; King unseated him in '78. This end of politics was not a place where John and I saw eye to eye.

Politics, in fact, was a tough thing to discuss with John. Even at seventeen, he was very sure about his opinions on public service and campaigning. It was not just that he seemed to know more than most of us; he seemed to employ a better understanding of the mechanics of politics, as if he had an alternate book on the subject. Maybe it was his mother's influence, maybe it was growing up in a family of politicians, or maybe it was simply in his blood.

Having an interest in history, being exposed to politics and studying it in college, I considered myself worthy to joust with him. We started getting into it a good deal over President Carter. John was all for Carter. I called him a liberal.

John informed me that Carter was building up the navy to a post–World War II height. "So how can you call him a liberal, Billy?"

"Only a liberal would give away the Panama Canal, which we've protected for a century."

"That was the original deal—to give control back—when Teddy Roosevelt seized the land to build it in the first place."

"How can we maintain the greatest buildup of a two-ocean navy since the war if we don't have access to the canal?"

"If we have to take it back, we will, since we're subsidizing their economy."

We'd go around and around like that. I'd push the envelope by saying how liberals wanted to give everything away.

"You know, you're the kind of Democrat my father used to rail against," John told me once. "You got a few bucks in the bank, you forget where you came from, and everyone else is a freeloader." Ouch.

So I'd take him to the international front. "The Soviet Union is a farce. Look at medical care—even bad medical care in the U.S. is better than excellent medical care in the Soviet Union."

"How do you know that? Have you ever been to Russia? I was just there." Now, *that* was a low blow.

"Why, then, did Brezhnev send his daughter to America for a breast-cancer operation? Isn't that an indictment of socialism?"

"Why shouldn't he? Wouldn't you want the best treatment for your daughter?"

"Sure, but why criticize us as capitalists and then come running to capitalism for medical assistance?"

"Why doesn't capitalism provide equal treatment for all its citizens, then?"

"Let's keep this international."

"No, Billy, let's keep it real. You're right that we will overpower Russia eventually, but you also have to be open-minded enough to understand that we have to lead by example, rather than just antagonize them with comments like what you read in *Newsweek*."

Shit. He'd read the same article.

As part of my work for Ed King, we staged events with signs at Red Sox home games; I must have gone to some thirty or forty games in 1978. Which happened to be the year the Red Sox had a fifteen-game lead over the Yankees on August 15, a lead that the Sox spent the next several weeks losing. At the end of the season, the teams were tied.

Anthony had moved to Boston in September to attend Boston University, and when it was announced that a one-game playoff would be played at Fenway, he ran a mile down to the park to get two tickets. It was the infamous game where Bucky Dent of the Yankees . . . Never mind.

Something else even uglier happened. Anthony, the little Polish prince, now an ardent New Yorker, had insisted on wearing his Yankees hat at Fenway. In the men's room, he was accosted by some Boston fans who didn't appreciate his allegiance. After they'd punched him and thrown his hat in the urinal, Anthony followed the boys out and reported the incident to one of Beantown's finest.

"Officer, those boys there, those bullyboys," Anthony said in his slightly formal way, "they punched me and threw my hat in the urinal. I would like for you to apprehend them. I plan on pressing charges."

The cop took a good look at the freshman with the British accent and asked why something like that would happen.

"Because I was wearing a Yankees cap."

The cop snorted. "Serves you right, then," he said, walking away.

Poor Anthony. America never entirely made sense to him. The two princes in the Kennedy family—Anthony with the Polish lineage, John, of course, with the uneasy mantle of Camelot—viewed their lots very differently. Anthony had grown up used to the pomp and circumstance of England, and he never completely assimilated here or quite got over what he'd lost. When he moved here in 1976, Jackie took him in and got him into Choate. John, on the other hand, rejected what everyone tried to give him, the keys to the imagined kingdom. He had no respect for assumed position.

That same fall I moved with a bunch of guys into what quickly became a quintessential Animal House. I was back in Boston College at this point, which was good; working at a bar and living at party central didn't work. It was the kind of house where sex, drugs, and rock and roll were constants. Strangers were in and out all the time; I'd come home to ad hoc parties at any hour. We all kept our bedrooms padlocked. I lasted six months there—at the end we called it the Fall of Saigon. Eventually three of us moved to a Victorian in Brookline that used to house the Church of Scientology, a place with big fireplaces and some semblance of sanity.

Meanwhile John had finished at Phillips and was living in the Bowdoin Street apartment in Boston that his family had held since the 1940s.

It *looked* like the 1940s—yet when I asked him if he wanted to live with us in our Victorian, the answer was succinct: "No way." Though he *would* come to our parties from time to time or drop by to watch sports.

But I'm getting ahead of myself. First there was an infamous birthday party for Caroline and John—she turned twenty-one that November, John eighteen—that ended up making the pages of *Life* magazine. I got in there, too.

JACKIE ONASSIS INVITED about a hundred people to a private club— called, simply, "Le Club"—on Fifth Avenue to celebrate the combined birthdays of her son and daughter. The invitation came as any invitation might, though on this one, above the printing, an angel announced the importance of the occasion by holding a pair of torches aloft—as in torches being passed. It was scheduled for the Sunday night after Thanksgiving.

I came down from Boston on Friday with a girl I was dating, and we headed over to 1040 on Saturday; it was cold and snowing—so cold that the snow, even as early as late November, was sticking. Jackie's apartment was a beehive of friends and presents, including a Monopoly-like board game someone had made that was all about Caroline and John. John had a beautiful new girlfriend, Jenny Christian.

Jackie had invited her friends, her children's friends, her extended family, and the president of the United States to the party. (Secretary of State Cyrus Vance stood in for Jimmy Carter.) There were celebrities, financial barons, the writer Pete Hamill, and Ted Kennedy—all the Kennedys, in fact—and loads of young college and prep-school friends of the celebrants. It was an amazing mix. Most of John's friends gathered around John Perry Barlow, once a Grateful Dead lyricist and a friend from when John had worked on Barlow's Wyoming ranch the previous summer. I chatted with Pete Hamill, who'd been Jackie's boyfriend for a while; he had come up to the Cape a few times, but he was like a city kid who doesn't quite know what to do with himself—falling off sailboats was not quite Hamill's thing. He spent his time sketching on the sun porch of the President's house, a room I don't remember anyone else ever using.

After dinner Senator Kennedy gave a short, understated toast, something to the effect of, "I shouldn't be doing this tonight. By rights it should be the father of these two children. Young John and Caroline bring new life to the family." He was wise to keep it short—for obvious reasons Teddy can't get too deep into moments like that without becoming upset himself; his toast came off as just the right touch.

Then the inevitable happened. The older folks at the party started to leave. It was, after all, the Sunday after Thanksgiving, and they were exhausted. For the rest of us, though, the party took off, and we were intent on staying into the early morning. I wasn't going home to Boston that night, so what was the rush? John's mother departed at about midnight; we were pretty young and inexperienced to be left on our own, but the party went on. We drank Hennessy stingers out of wine goblets and smoked; it was the height of disco, and we danced around a roaring fire that was just off the dance floor.

Suddenly it was 4:00 A.M.

Club management told us they had to shut down for legal reasons, though they were probably getting the idea we'd go on until noon if they let us. As we got ourselves together, Gustavo—the son of Provi, Jackie's longtime housekeeper—looked out a porthole in the door to check for the cabs that management had promised were coming; no cabs yet, only a group of paparazzi assembled underneath the awning. "Galella," he hissed like the name of the devil incarnate.

"Who is Galella?" I asked.

"Ron Galella is the bastard who keeps following John, Caroline, and their mother around. He's supposed to stay a hundred feet away from them, but he never does."

Long before I heard his name, I knew there were some paparazzi that used to dog Jackie, not just in New York but all over the world. She'd get on a plane here, fly to Athens, get off the plane, and there he'd be. She would be on the *Christina* and maybe go waterskiing, and he'd be snapping pictures. She'd cruise to Sardinia or someplace like that, and he would be there. She'd be walking down the street in Paris, and there he'd be *again*—it went on like that for quite a while, with him following her around the globe. Jackie took him to court because she was really worried that he'd chase Caroline and John in New York and put them in a dangerous situation—that John, say, would be on his bike and take off from him into traffic. So she got a restraining order to keep him 150 feet away from her and 100 feet from her children; Galella then went to court and got the distance reduced. He used to show up sometimes with a tape measure, to taunt them. To him it was a hunt, a game.

And that frigid night in New York, I was about to find out what it felt like to be prey.

"Yo, John," Gustavo called to him, "you're never going to believe who's out there."

John peeped through the porthole in the red leather door and then did an about-face, heading back to management. He was looking for another way out, but there wasn't any, only this door that dumped into a side street. Meanwhile the photographers—there were four or five of them—could see us checking them out. They crushed their cigarettes, pulled their jacket hoods back up, and got their cameras ready for the ambush.

So there we were—kids—left to our own devices. "Can we take them?" I asked Gustavo.

He nodded, though clearly we needed more brawn. Among the fifteen of us left was John's roommate from Phillips, John Pucillo, a wrestling star. He would help.

"Okay, here's the plan," I told Gustavo. "I'll take that guy in the green—"

"I want Galella," Gustavo said.

"Fine, you take Galella, and, Puce, you take that other guy. We'll charge out, tell them to get lost, and John will run up to the corner behind us and grab a cab. Then we'll meet back at 1040."

I popped my head out the door. "I'm giving you fair warning," I said to the photographers. "Don't start any shit."

John donned a pair of sunglasses—at four in the morning in November? That's how unprepared we were. But out the door we went, Gustavo, Pucillo, and me heading to our assigned photographers. John was behind me, with Jenny Christian. I told my snorkel head to back away.

"Fuck off, fat boy."

Oh, not the thing to say at that hour to someone who doesn't easily take physical threats. As I went after him, John held me back and tried to put his hand over my mouth, because I was screaming at the guy.

"Hey, get your hand off my mouth!" I told John. "I didn't start this!"

As others trying to leave the party stood back watching, Gustavo pushed Galella away, but they came at us again. I stood my ground, and John sensed his moment and bolted up the street with Jenny. My photographer ran past me to chase John and tackled him; he went down between two parked cars.

Now it was a donnybrook. A group of paparazzi that had been parked across the street, staying warm in their cars, raced out to get their shots. Bulbs flashed, and we all started swinging away, except John, who was trying to reason with the guy who'd knocked him down, to just let him get out of there. The guy said he thought it was me he was chasing.

John pointed out the obvious. "He's twice my size, asshole!"

It was mayhem. John managed to run with Jenny to the corner, grab a cab, and head back to 1040, with the photographers in full pursuit.

We bodyguards were left behind as if, suddenly, nothing had happened. The whole thing took probably thirty seconds.

We gathered back at 1040—what an awful climax to a wild night. I slept for a few hours; when I got up later that morning to head back to Boston, I felt bruised inside and out. But that was hardly the end of it.

Late Tuesday afternoon, when I got back from class, my roommate was reading the *Boston Evening Globe*, which included a picture of me trying to get at the photographer and one of John sitting on his butt after he was knocked down. Well, I thought, at least no one read the *Evening Globe* anymore. Then the phone rang.

"Did you see the six o'clock news?" my sister, who lived in a Boston suburb, wanted to know.

"No. Why?"

"Was there a fight in New York, Billy?"

My stomach sank. "Uh, how did you know that?"

"It was just on the news. With a picture. What happened, Billy?"

I tried to explain that it was not my fault, that they were like jackals—but it was no use. There I was in full fight mode, caught.

Then the *New York Daily News,* the *National Enquirer,* who referred to me as the "beefy buddy," and more phone calls. I escaped to my mother's house at the Cape that weekend; luckily, she was in Florida. What, I wondered, was I going to do when she saw it? I knew the button she'd push: "If your father . . ." The guilt would be unbearable. All I could do was feel sorry for myself and think how the road to hell is paved with good intentions. I called John.

"What are we going to do?" I asked him.

"I think it's kind of funny."

"You do?"

"Yeah, but . . ."

Oh, no, worse than my mother.

"Mummy is not happy. I tried to explain it to her, but I think you should write a note."

I wrote a long, apologetic letter to Jackie to say how sorry I was about what had happened. These photographers, if they'd been at home in bed with their families at four in the morning, it never *would* have happened—but I was sorry. I knew that it might appear to be my fault, since I was the focus of the picture. If anyone would empathize, it would be Jackie.

Apparently she did, because I was invited to attend her Christmas party. I demurred—New York and I, I decided, were not compatible. Furthermore, I wasn't interested in hearing the New York slant on the event. I was getting enough of the "beefy buddy" stuff at home in Boston.

Between Christmas and New Year's, my roommate and I were at a party. Someone had brought the new issue of *Life,* now a monthly. He was paging through it, and when he came to the last picture, captioned "Coming of Age," he said, "Hey, this looks like that guy over there." All heads swiveled in my direction.

My roommate grabbed the magazine, and found it hilarious that I had made *Life,* and even funnier that it was a photograph of me in a grand moment of clearly screaming the worst word any of us could think of back in elementary school. (John quickly relabelled the picture "The Billy Noonan School of Diplomacy.") They asked me to sign the photo. When, I was thinking, was my mother going to see *this*?

About five months later, while sitting in a hair salon in Palm Beach, she happened to pick up an old *National Enquirer;* I could hear the hair dryers humming in the background when I answered the phone in my apartment in Brookline. "What the hell is going on up there?" she demanded. "Does Jackie know about this?"

"Yes, Mother. She does, it's cool. You are the last person on the planet to know. It's okay, I worked it out."

"Your father would be so—"

"I know, I know. No one knows that more than me. Listen, I've got to go to class now—I'll see you on Mother's Day."

It turned out that my mother tore the picture of her son the pugilist out of the salon's *Enquirer* and put it in her purse, to emerge at certain social events with the comment, "Here's my son Billy protecting John Kennedy from those nasty paparazzi. What a good boy."

The truth, though, was that it was embarrassing. I had a bit of a reckoning with myself over it, and I decided to avoid situations with John where paparazzi were a possibility. Even if it was down on the Cape, and he'd ask me to go for a long walk with his dog Sam, a German shepherd only he liked—nah, I don't think so. Too exposed.

John's mother brought up the incident only a few times, usually when John and I had on sunglasses. "Dark glasses," she called them. "Are you boys going out looking for a fight?"

~

IN THE WINTER and spring of 1979—after finishing his make-up work at Phillips—John lived in his family's apartment on Bowdoin Street and worked with juvenile delinquents at the Massachusetts State House, practically next door. He showed them the movie *Scared Straight*, wherein prison life is described in detail; John said it should have been called *Scared Shitless*, because his JDs were completely freaked out to see the reality of life behind bars.

The apartment—it was the address on his father's driver's license the day he died—was basically just a crash pad. I don't think it had changed for three decades. The kitchen had a deep, industrial sink with no dishwasher. A bunch of small international flags were lined up on the mantel above the fireplace, but there was nothing at all on the walls; you'd never know that a Kennedy had set foot in it. John brought his stereo, but the place never got homey, and since he was living on a big allowance, I don't think he ever attempted to cook a meal there.

We'd go out to the Bull and Finch, the bar that would later become famous as Cheers, or hang out at the Black Rose after going to the occasional political event or sometimes to movie openings—we both loved movies. On weekends John tended to get lost, either heading down to New York or hanging out at Harvard with Jenny Christian and his sister. But John had no interest in going to college there—as a Kennedy, and a Phillips grad, it was expected, which he felt was a very good reason *not* to go. When to ride the possibilities that his legacy opened up and when to go in a different direction—that was front and center for John now. He had decided to pursue another Ivy League college.

Sometimes Phillips students would come into Boston and hang out at John's apartment. One little group of three were nasty, privileged, dirty punks; they also had a really annoying the-world's-my-oyster attitude. John was comfortable with different sorts of friends—there I was in my khaki pants and a turtleneck, and Anthony, elegant and understated in his Armani blazer and crisp shirt. But we pointed out to John, privately, that these kids were jerks—not because of their appearance but the entitled attitude that went with it. They were sarcastic, dismissive, just plain mean.

"I was thinking the same thing," John said. "But I wasn't sure what to do."

Because his impulse was to give people latitude, to accept different types, John gave people an *incredible* amount of room to mess up. But he told these guys that they were acting like jerks, which only served to get them acting like bigger jerks.

"You know what?" John told them. "You guys can hit the road."

"You can't treat me like this," one of them sneered, claiming his father was the president of some nationally known bank.

Oh, boy—John was mad enough to bring out something I'd never heard from him. "Is that right? You know what, pal? My father was *the* President"—which, of course, they knew—"and no matter what your fucking problem with authority is, take it with you when you leave."

Out they went—and then John felt bad. "How are they getting back to Andover?" he wondered.

"If his father is president of some bank," I assured him, "I think it's likely they can afford a taxi. Let's go get something to eat."

"Yeah, okay." But he was bothered by his own reaction to them. Jackie's concern that too much Kennedy privilege could make John into a "screw you, Charlie" kind of guy had made him anything but, and he didn't tolerate arrogance in others.

That spring John had a graduation party at his house in Hyannisport. Everyone from his class was invited, but no one could sleep over, since there was not enough room. The upstairs was cordoned off, and a housekeeper assigned to keep control had her hands full. Jackie had barbecued chicken and hamburgers and hot dogs served—enough for an army, and there *was* an army. Teddy sent a case of Dom Perignon to toast the event.

They weren't *supposed* to sleep over, but sleep over they did: The next day neighbors found kids in sleeping bags in their sheds, backyards, empty swimming pools, and front porches.

John soon took off for Africa, where he spent a major part of his sum-

mer traveling and camping. One day at the end of summer, after he'd returned, we were out sailing and passed Teddy's sailboat. He shouted,
"John, I told the liquor store to send a *bottle* of Dom over to your house,
not a case! I've been drinking Miller all summer!" John loved that, the idea
of Teddy limited to a working man's beer.

Meanwhile my life had gone south, the inevitable fallout of working
in a bar and hanging with guys who lived to have a good time at the expense of themselves, not to mention everyone around them. I was in danger of becoming like that, too. As my older siblings were married and
raising children, and my mother spent most of her year in Florida, I was
trying to find my own way on my own. But I was lost.

That autumn I decided I'd had enough of Boston and headed west,
becoming a true rolling stone for the better part of a year. Late seventies
in America—it was the end of the era of hitting the road and finding out
what life is about, but I was determined to do just that. Substance abuse
was part of it. Suffice it to say that it was *not* a good time for me.

Movement—that was something John and I had in common, though I
was in far worse shape than I'd ever seen him in. John took road trips; he
traveled everywhere. It was his MO. He told me many times, "If I stop to
think about it all, I would just sit down and fall apart." He meant, of
course, what his family had endured. So we shared that, too, though I had
been able to know my father until I was thirteen. At any rate, I felt boxed
in by Boston, and I was tired of being a Noonan. The real point was that
I needed to come to terms with myself, with who I was. That, too, John
and I shared, the need for a reckoning with ourselves. First, though, I took
a self-destructive detour, into that next spring and summer.

But I came back to Boston in the spring of 1980 to celebrate the 350th
anniversary of the founding of the city. John and I went to various events
and visited my old stomping ground. The USS *John F. Kennedy* was in
town, and we were invited to a gala on board. Governor Ed King—my
guy!—reviewed the troops. King's politics had completely alienated him
from the Democratic Party, and, as Teddy was running for president, the

Kennedys did not want to get anywhere near him. My father always said, "Stick with the guy who brung ya." So I did, but King was still my guy.

John and I got a VIP tour of the ship. Slipping into a restricted area, our guide was stopped by a superior officer. "This is his father's ship," he explained. The officer snapped to attention and saluted us . . . well, John. When we moved into the officers' mess, the room stood at attention. We learned that when a ship in the U.S. Navy is given the name of an individual, it is literally considered his (or her) ship, which explains why the names are given only posthumously and why John was treated with such respect. The ship's size was staggering: It could carry five thousand sailors, who ate fifteen thousand meals a day. We learned of the myriad floors and stations between keel and tower—it was a floating city.

The ship's commander took us to his private quarters. He had a painting of President Kennedy and an exact replica of George Washington's sword, down to the gram; John's father had had these replicas made, in a limited number, as gifts for foreign dignitaries, and only a few remained. The admiral took particular pride in possessing a direct link from the first commander in chief to his vessel's namesake.

Disembarking, we were given ship's hats. Insignia baseball-style caps now are common but were rare then—though it seemed, that weekend, as if everyone in the city were wearing one. John's had "scrambled eggs"—the gold laurels reserved for high-ranking officers—on the visor. When he wore it into town, every sailor that we'd come across from the ship would turn to him, stand at attention, and salute. It did not take long for John to want to lose the hat. It quickly became my prop.

The next day he took me down to Brown in Providence, Rhode Island, where he was finishing his freshman year, and showed me around. I felt like the big brother on family weekend: "This is the cafeteria, over there is the library. . . ."

"Great, John. Let's get something to eat."

He was a celebrity at Brown, full-fledged JFK, Jr. It was both amusing and daunting to see. And he was about to stop being my little brother.

THAT SUMMER, 1980, I came home. And home now meant that I lived
two weeks with Timmy Shriver and his family and then a week with John
and Jackie. I needed them. I was still seeking stability, a center, and I
needed to recover from a period of crazy living. The connection I felt to
both of them—John and Timmy—had everything to do with how gen-
uine they needed their friends to be; they were both, in turn, utterly loyal.
I had never actually *lived* in Hyannisport since I was a little kid. With my
own room at the President's house for my week there, having all my
meals with them, my clothes washed, and invited as their houseguest to
whatever Kennedy fest was afoot felt completely different.

People came and went all the time in the Kennedy orbit; years later
John and I would sing the Rolling Stones' "Star Star" when we'd sense
somebody trying to wedge in for the wrong reasons: "You're a star fucker,
star fucker, star fucker, fuck a star . . ." What I needed from him, and
from Timmy, was friendship. They delivered in spades.

John was out of the country during the Democratic National Convention that summer, as Teddy challenged a sitting president from his
own party; Jackie and Anthony were there. John worked for Teddy locally
but not nationally. Teddy gave an impassioned speech at the convention:
"The hope still lives, and the dream shall never die. . . ." John's moment
would come eight years later.

I struggled that whole summer with my next move. I decided to return to Boston, and, living with an aunt, got a job through Governor King
as a welfare caseworker. It gave me a good look at people out of a job,
falling through the cracks of society, and some who didn't have the energy or ambition to take care of themselves.

I calmed down; I was regaining a foothold. The stability of a job that
had a point helped immensely.

Then, one day in late 1981, a slow, barely perceptible change in my
plumbing became obvious, and dealing with it became unavoidable. I
called a doctor. His diagnosis was testicular cancer. And now my friendship with John was about to shift again.

7

Reality Sets In

MY MOTHER—who was great in a crisis—returned home from Florida to oversee my medical care that December. I had a tumor removed at Massachusetts General Hospital posthaste. Cancer was not taken lightly in my family; it claimed the lives of my father, two of his siblings, and my cousin.

There was a fierce snowstorm in Boston, plus my sister-in-law was giving birth at another hospital across town, so I was left alone to get the bad news as the family trudged home in the snow, visiting the new baby along the way: I had embryonal cell carcinoma, which is a very rare cell in this type of cancer and spreads fast. The prognosis was not good.

I called Timmy at Yale. He was the logical guy to talk to first, because Timmy was the pragmatist, a man of action. I knew that John's reaction would be, *Oh, my God, Billy.*

At first Timmy didn't believe what I told him. In fact, he made me hang up and called me back to confirm I really was in Mass General. Then he started calling me at all hours of the day or night; he would call from a party and put friends on the phone, trying to cheer me up. His parents, Eunice and Sarge, were in constant contact with me, my mother, and my doctors.

After the initial surgery, I had to come back to the hospital to have a CAT scan and other tests to determine whether the cells had spread. I was officially a cancer patient now.

I was put on a cancer ward, a large room with five other cancer patients. One was in an oxygen tent, staring at me with death in his eyes, and then—this seems, looking back, too awful to be true—an alarm went off, and nurses and doctors came running. . . . One of the other patients had died before I'd been in there ten minutes.

I made a beeline out of there, back to the admitting attendant in the lobby. "How could you do this to someone my age?" I yelled. "I am trying my hardest to keep my shit together, and you put me in a cancer ward?"

"Mr. Noonan, you are a cancer patient, so you need to be where you can be properly evaluated."

"What I need is someone who has a brain and maybe, just maybe, a heart big enough not to send me to a room with dying patients."

Liaison staff appeared. They took me to a different room.

After a clean CAT scan, I was on top of the world, as if everything that had gone before had all been just a bad dream. Then I was told I needed follow-up surgery to remove my lymph nodes, because if the cancer had spread there, it would then travel to my lungs and brain, and that would be fatal. To me it seemed like a chance worth taking, but my mother wasn't having it. "I watched your father die, Billy. I am not planning on watching you die, too."

I was terrified. This second surgery meant that my rib cage would be broken, a lung collapsed, my diaphragm punctured. The incision would run the width of my torso—this was a major procedure. I yearned for divine inspiration or intervention. Was this it? Was this my last Christmas? I needed to be alone.

Driving to the Cape, thinking about all this, I was overwhelmed. I felt cheated, and I started pounding the dashboard of my Olds so hard that the radio skipped stations. It was surreal: from somebody speaking Portuguese to some sappy song to Mozart. I'd reached the point where hitting a bridge abutment seemed like a sensible possibility. I checked the speedometer: 140. If it was going to happen, it might as well happen right now.

And then I called out, "What do you want from me? If you are there, now would be a good time to come." With that, the Olds started slowing down, back to normal speed. I suddenly felt calm. The radio was quiet, a low hum between stations. With surprising suddenness I felt serene. I had reached a point where the only possibility of going on was through faith.

I had an image, then, of a cottage, a sweet little thatched-roof place on the west coast of Ireland. It occurred to me that if I died from the operation, or from cancer, all my problems would be over and I could live in that cottage forever. Fear slipped away. The abutments kept passing me by until I arrived in Osterville, safe. I don't care if this sounds unbelievable or maudlin. We all find what we need in our own way, and sometimes crisis does it. Faith had arrived.

Still, there was a harsh road to travel.

When I checked in a few days later for the big surgery, I was welcomed with an enormous basket of flowers from Jackie. And a load of attention: The nurse looked at me like, *Who* are *you?* She asked if there was anything I needed, and I said I would like to see a priest. One was making his rounds; when he arrived, I confessed my sins and received Holy Communion. I was ready.

Then the nurse came in and said that I had a visitor.

"The priest just left," I told her. "I'm not expecting anyone else." Besides, it was past visiting hours.

I went out to the waiting room, which was dark. John was standing there. His head was nearly bald, and he was wearing a multicolored sash.

"What are you doing here?"

"Billy, I couldn't sit in Providence knowing you were up here by yourself."

"Is that why you shaved your head? Is that some sort of artistic sarcasm about what I'm going to look like if I survive and get chemo?"

No—it was for the role of Big Al in David Rabe's play *In the Boom*

Boom Room. John had gotten into theater at Brown. And the sash was something he'd brought back from Africa.

We sat and talked; I told him about the flowers his mother had sent.

"Listen, I know you're reluctant to do this," he said. "Mummy knows lots of people who have had this and are still alive. Frank Church had it, and he's a senator. You still have a future."

"In the Senate?"

He laughed. "Maybe. So . . . what's this like?"

"I don't know," I said. "I feel like I'm sitting in God's waiting room. My family's been great, but what's the point, if I don't have the possibility of a family of my own? Maybe I *am* better off in another world."

"Billy . . ."

"John, you and I are holding out for a better life and the other world." Back to the most basic challenge we shared: growing up without fathers. "I know it and you know it. What would *you* be thinking?"

"There are other things to do in life, Billy."

"Yeah, like what?"

"Well," he said with a smirk, "there's always the priesthood."

"The *priesthood*? That would be more for Shriver, not me. You know about me and institutions."

"Billy, don't give up—I need you, we all need you. What would we do without you?"

"I know, I know, but I'm tired of what is written in this book. I want a new book."

"We all do, Billy. But we'll get through this together. Mummy says that she'll use any of her influence to assist, in any way."

A nurse appeared, tapping her watch face. After-hours limits applied even for John Kennedy.

The next day I woke—following a six-hour operation and six hours of being unconscious in recovery—to blinding fluorescent lights and a sweet voice saying, "Chuckles . . ." It was a high-school nickname.

Huh?

"Do you remember me, Chuckles? I'm Michael Grace's sister, Sally."

Oh, an angel to slip a tiny lollipop inside my mouth. I'd known Michael when we were kids on the Cape, and Sally, it turned out, was my recovery-room nurse. "I'll be looking after you, and you'll be fine." The voice of an angel.

For three days I lay in excruciating pain. Shriver said that this was my three days of passion, and all my sins would be forgiven. I hung on to that. John called every day, just to check in. I was released Christmas Eve. Then I sat at the Cape for two months, slowly getting my strength back, taking baby steps to a new life. It was two weeks before I was able to walk the quarter mile to Nantucket Sound and another week before I could make the return trip.

The New Year brought good news. There were no cancer cells in the lymph nodes. I had been to the mountaintop. Weeks later, after a shower and peeling off the last butterfly strips, I joyfully went downstairs to play Trivial Pursuit with visiting friends. I knew then that John was right, that I would be okay.

OVER THE NEXT two or three years, John and Timmy and I moved on with our lives. My bond with both of them, after what I'd been through, was now deeper; they felt it, too. We had endured this together. It was not just parents who could die—we were all vulnerable. Years later, when Anthony got sick, also with testicular cancer, John talked about how rocked he'd been by my illness, how shocked he was at the possibility of losing a friend.

John no longer seemed like a younger brother; we'd bridged the two-year age difference. Part of that stemmed from my vulnerability in getting sick, and then we ended up graduating college at the same time, in 1983.

In the meantime John helped me recover. He invited me down to stay with him at Brown during St. Patrick's Day in 1982; he gave me his room, and he stayed with his girlfriend, Sally Munro. I couldn't really go out—my rib cage was still healing. I was determined to get healthy. I'd stopped drinking, I didn't smoke or eat red meat. I suppose I wasn't much fun to be with, but that didn't matter to John.

Not that it changed how he talked to me.

"Hey, oddball, you want to play some Frisbee?"

I'd give him a look, and come back with, "That's not funny. Don't you realize I could have died?"

"Yeah, but you didn't. Come on. Let's go."

That was very Kennedy: You survived by counting your blessings, which means that you soldier on. "We have to soldier on"—that was a special phrase to Jackie and her children. As a survivor, too, I now had a better sense of what they felt, how important it is to count one's blessings. I could now taste things, hear things, see things that I had never experienced before. Life seemed to slow down. Timmy and I had many spiritual discussions about life and faith. We had deepened our triumvirate.

Once I was up and around, I grabbed my bicycle and headed off to Nantucket to work for a friend who was opening a bar there that following summer. The island was a natural place to ride and get healthy. John was something of an expert on bikes, not just as an enthusiast but because his were always getting stolen—he could easily go through a dozen bikes a year. John was infamous for it; he'd drop fifteen hundred bucks on a Univega at some New York shop, tool around that afternoon, stop somewhere for coffee, get lost in a magazine, some kid would eye the bike. . . . A few minutes later, John would come out and look around: *Where the hell's my bike?* I mean, the guy could *literally* buy a bike in the morning and manage to have it stolen that afternoon. So here was his advice to me on bikes, left on my answering machine one day:

"A Univega is the right bike for a guy with a uniball. Okay, chowderhead? Bye!"

What a reverent SOB.

Yet I can see now, looking back, that John, Timmy, and I were looking for the same thing, though in different ways. Timmy's Catholic faith was deepening. For John what began as pure adventure and escape—hiking, biking, skiing, kayaking, jumping out of airplanes, *being out there and doing it*—shifted to traveling to exotic places. Exotic places—especially Africa—were an escape for him, too, and, as I've said, if he kept moving, he didn't have to think about what he didn't have, what, in sad fact, he'd really never had. Sometimes he'd walk the break wall in Hyannisport at night, and when he'd come back, I'd ask, "What the hell were you doing out there by yourself?"

"Pondering."

Now, as he kept moving, he found, within that, a way. He found direction in nature. He found healing in nature. Hiking in the woods, sleeping under the stars, started as a lark and turned into something else: reaching out to reach in, to who he was.

Because ultimately, of course, there is no escaping, and for John that truth could take on absurd proportions. He told me once about being shown into a hut somewhere deep in Africa, and there, on the wall, in the humblest of homes, was a picture of his father.

John began to try to understand his father. The following spring Anthony, Timmy, and I went to Providence to see the budding thespian as the bad guy in *Short Eyes,* a play about doing time in prison. Later, when we went back to his apartment, I noticed some additions: He had not only one of his father's rocking chairs but also a framed picture of him giving a speech and books about JFK. It was more than personal; he'd sent away for official presidential speeches, proclamations, bills signed. John had started *studying* his father.

As John and I finished college, he prepared for a yearlong visit to India. This was an important step for him. The world's most populated democracy, with all its struggles of poverty and lingering colonialism, was a perfect subject for postgraduate studies. It was also another way to get closer to his father's legacy. JFK had considered India a crucial country in the East-West balance; it was a huge territory to maintain as a democracy, and he had made John Kenneth Galbraith, his friend and professor at Harvard, ambassador there. Jackie had many contacts in India, having visited as the wife of a head of state, and she had a great deal of Indian art in her apartment, including some randy poses from *The Kama Sutra*. Going to India also meant John would be far away from what he called "The Day," the twentieth anniversary of his father's assassination.

A bunch of us got together at his mother's apartment for a send-off. Timmy and I sat in the corner and watched the craziest display of post-punk haute couture we had ever been privy to. Timmy himself dressed like a janitor, buying only utility clothes at Sears; this was another scene of John the collector of eclectic friends. (There was something to be said for Timmy's humility. His mother once told me that, at a private audience with the pope, Timmy was the only one the pontiff spoke to. Eunice thought it was his lack of fashion that caught the pope's eye; Timmy believed that the pope sensed his spirituality.)

A girl in black-and-white, pinto-horse-spotted, knee-high boots had added small red flashing bulbs to them. Timmy and I challenged each other to see who would ask her how they were powered. I lost. I wasn't quite sure how to put the question, so I just asked.

"Batteries."

"Uh, where are they located?"

She wouldn't say.

Our night went on like that, Timmy and I amused by John's friends. Jackie was at her Peapack house, which was a good thing, as there were minor laws being broken in the presence of busts of Greek philosophers. We ended up going to a disco, and the night became morning. Bob Brown, the director of the summer program at the University of Connecticut, where John had worked the year before, had driven down from New Haven with Timmy and lost his dove gray '65 Mercedes-Benz, with original leather interior, to a car thief. Wrong part of town—a brother should have known better.

John came back from India in the spring of 1984. He talked about meeting Mother Teresa in Bombay and how she spoke to the poor. She was very direct, almost matter-of-fact: *Get off the street, you'll get run over. I talked to you about this yesterday—you know better than this.* John was amazed by her bluntness. He had a lot of crazy photos from Calcutta,

Bombay, all over. He had a picture of himself and Mother Teresa that he gave Timmy, the spiritual one, for his birthday, just to taunt him. India was eye-opening. John had discovered a mix of culture and abject poverty in an edgy democracy—it both jazzed him and gave him deeper pause, I believe, about how the world's riches are parceled out.

Back home John went to work for the Forty-second Street Development Corporation for a few months. It was a time of professional awakening for all of us. I was training to become a stockbroker, Anthony moved to New York to work in TV journalism, and Timmy was getting his master's in education at Catholic University, to pursue his goal of teaching inner-city youths.

In the fall of 1985, Timmy was adamant about having me come down to Washington for his father's seventieth-birthday party. I didn't understand the importance of my being there, but Timmy, it turned out, had a big announcement, the reason he wanted John and me present: He was now engaged to Linda Potter, whom he'd been dating for seven or eight years, since he started at Yale. It made sense; the most directed and sure-footed of us was going to go off and get himself hitched.

John, as usual, snuck in on the last Saturday-night shuttle. Someone remarked that it was Washington's "other" list at the Shrivers'. President Reagan was entertaining Prince Charles and Diana, Princess of Wales, at the White House that weekend, and all the important Republicans were there, while all the exiled Democrats were having more fun with Eunice and Sarge.

Later that night John and I found ourselves walking in Georgetown, down a wobbly brick sidewalk on Dumbarton Avenue. It was a nice, crisp autumn night. Some of the backyards of these brick Georgian places are the size of football fields; some of them have orchards. We came by a big white house and could see through a fence to a backyard that was lighted by torches, with a bartender in a white shirt and bow tie, and pretty young girls. It could have been a senator's house; maybe it was his daughter's coming-of-age party. Maybe it was an ambassador's place.

"I could use a beer," I told John.

"But we don't know who—"

"That's the fun."

In we went,

John and I headed right to the bar, ordered beers, and started talking as we always did, which was pretty animated, no matter what we were discussing. It could have been about how debutante parties had fallen by the wayside, it could have been some debate about Ronald Reagan (John liked to accuse me of being a closet Republican). Whatever it was, people left us alone, thinking maybe we were heatedly debating Sino-Soviet relations, all the while getting a read on what was going on around us. This party was a pretty fancy-pants affair—our guess was someone's twenty-first-birthday bash.

Pretty soon some girls came up and started talking to us.

"Where are you guys from?" one asked.

"I'm from right here," John announced. "I used to live in this neighborhood." *Attaboy.* In Washington, like New York, power is omnipresent and control an attribute.

She started squinting at us—or rather at John. "This is a joke, right? Are you here for the party? Are you, like, some Kennedy look-alike?"

Silence.

"How do you know Donna?"

We laughed. "From school."

The girls moved away, but we could hear a rumbling: *Those guys over there, I think that's John Kennedy. Did Donna go to school with him? What should we do?*

Of course they weren't going to throw us out. We departed on our own, leaving behind a gaggle of openmouthed coeds and hip brat packers. Just a little Billy-and-John fun.

The next day John went off to Paul and Bunny Mellon's farm in Virginia for a luncheon hosting Princess Diana. Later I bumped into him at the airport and asked about her. "She has the most unusual upwards glance, really seductive," John reported. I asked if he broached my concerns about IRA prisoners in Long Kesh with Prince Charles. He laughed. "He wasn't there."

But Diana had "the most unusual blue eyes."

FORMAL FESTIVITIES at the John F. Kennedy Library in Boston began that autumn. It was the twenty-fifth anniversary of the President's election, and the entire Kennedy family showed up for a fund-raiser. John invited me to be his guest, and he escorted his mother. Jackie moved effortlessly through the room, mingling and talking, much to the delight of the local contributors and especially their wives.

Just shy of his twenty-fifth birthday, John was growing into his public responsibility; he actually admitted to me later that he enjoyed the event and got a big kick out of the white-haired Boston Irish ladies coming up to him with, yes, "God love ya, I knew ya fatha." He enjoyed their zeal, and he knew that if it were not for people like them, there would be no legacy and certainly no library.

He also pointed out that most of the wealthy contributors were in fact Republicans, even in Boston, Kennedy country. Welcome to the changing atmosphere of America.

8

The Pivotal Years

WE WERE BEGINNING to come into our own during the mid-1980s. Some of our contemporaries were getting married and launching careers in politics, law, finance, acting, and the media.

It also felt as if the country itself was changing under Ronald Reagan. Jackie and John and I had several discussions about him on their patio in Hyannisport; they had a much different reaction to Reagan than one might expect. Reagan was actually older than President Kennedy would have been, if he were still alive; they had lived through the same midcentury American challenges. And Jackie believed that Reagan was building the first formidable administration since her husband's, with an agenda based on sound principles stemming from his life experience.

Sociologists refer to this as social filtering. Living through the Depression and World War II, the atomic bomb and then the Cold War gave Presidents Kennedy and Reagan a different slant on the world and America's role in it from that of my generation of Baby Boomers. Conservatives hailed the return to American values; my mother viewed Reagan's administration as a Hollywood stunt. John admired him. He believed in free markets and capitalism, and he believed in sticking to your guns. He liked the idea of challenging the Russians; as he had predicted years before, it was only a matter of time before the Soviet Union collapsed. Meanwhile Uncle Ted had branded the military policy that caused the collapse "Star Wars."

In January 1986, when the *Challenger* blew up, I read about it on the Dow Jones news wire at Smith Barney in Boston, where I worked, and ran to the conference room to watch the remnants of the *Challenger* streaming to earth. A few days later, President Reagan assembled a national tribute to the fallen astronauts and to science teacher Christa McAuliffe. There at NASA headquarters, in the front row next to Reagan, were Jimmy Carter, Gerald Ford, Richard Nixon, and, in the last two seats, Caroline and John, children of the first president to dare the nation to put a man on the moon. It began to dawn on me that President Kennedy would always be a great influence on contemporary American history and that John would now represent that influence to the country.

Back home, more personally, 1986 was a summer of weddings. A former Austrian bodybuilder-turned-actor and box-office sensation was marrying Timmy's sister. Arnold Schwarzenegger first showed up on the Cape in the summer of 1977, right after the RFK tennis tournament. Maria Shriver, who had invited him, was giddy with her new infatuation. Everyone, of course, was impressed with this guy's size and physique. We asked him the obvious questions, like what he ate for breakfast: "A dozen eggs." We looked at one another in disbelief. "Raw," Arnold added. We watched out the windows as he did his calisthenics on the Shrivers' tennis court, then later attempted to emulate him. Believe me, bending your knees while you keep your back straight, taking a step, straightening, bending, then taking a step with the other leg has your thighs begging for mercy in about twenty seconds. When we went sailing with Arnold, we asked him to drag, which means hanging off the stern with a line and getting a quick swim; Arnold nearly brought the boat to a full stop.

Maria, not quite knowing what to do with Mr. Universe, asked me to entertain him. I took Arnold and a few others to play miniature golf in Hyannis. The little putter in his massive hands looked like a toothpick; remarkably, he made a hole in one.

"Nice shot, Arnie!" I was thinking, of course, of Arnie Palmer.

"My name is not Arnie," I was informed. "My name is AAAAAAAh-nuld."

I had this image of me in a tree trying to unbend a putter from around my neck. "Everyone see Arnold's hole in one?" I said. "Great shot, Arnold. You sure you haven't played before, Arnold?"

I tried again, taking him to the Foxhole, a local bar—everyone in the place stared, wondering who was this enormous guy with Billy Noonan. Why, isn't that . . . ? No good.

The next day I took him to the health club at Dunfey's Hotel, a place where I worked out and thought he might feel more comfortable. This was better; Arnold was gracious, answering questions and making recommendations. The only problem was, I'm sure there was a rash of hernia operations at the Cape Cod hospital over the next few weeks, because every lifter was adding weight to his workout to impress Arnold. That was enough for me—I left the rest of his entertainment up to the Shrivers.

Obviously it worked, as Maria was now planning her wedding for that April. Timmy's would be six weeks later.

Maria's wedding drew guests from television, the movies, and politics. After a full Catholic mass at St. Francis Xavier in Hyannis, Oprah Winfrey, then a relatively minor personality, gave a reading. We headed back to the compound for a gourmet meal and music; Andy Warhol and Grace Jones showed up at the reception together, all ten feet of her unraveling out of a little Volvo. Warhol with his white wig carefully in place took Polaroids of everybody. Grace quickly hit the dance floor. Everyone stared; like Arnold, she was impossible not to watch, though I don't think the bride had danced yet, and it felt as though she was upstaging Maria on her special day. Somebody told her to knock it off.

I spent most of the reception at the raw bar, sucking down fruits of the sea. Sargent Shriver had had special Austrian beer imported, which assisted me in sliding down dozens of oysters. A life-size statue of Arnold in lederhosen, holding his bride in his arms in full wedding attire, had been sent by Kurt Waldheim. It stood, absurdly, in a huge box on the dance floor. Waldheim had just been elected and was under scrutiny as a former Nazi. Arnold—loyal to a fault—had defended him as his "main man."

At one point I witnessed a slightly intoxicated movie mogul standing over a seated Jackie. He was tall and thin, gray, very distinguished, though he looked like a cobra ready to strike. Sitting on a white folding chair, she looked very small and vulnerable.

I watched from a distance, waiting for her to give me a sign that she needed a distraction. After a few minutes, I approached them, presenting myself silently as a possible means for escape. No sign was given. So I asked.

"Is everything okay, Mrs. Onassis?"

Oh, the look she gave me, something I'd never seen before. Did I think for a moment that she wasn't in complete control of the situation? Did I think that she needed me to get her out of a troublesome spot? Certainly not. The idea was laughable, of course, once I thought about it. This was a woman who had handled de Gaulle, Khrushchev, and various other world leaders with grace and elegance. She was in complete control. I made a mental note never to make that mistake again.

Timmy's wedding, six weeks later, was in Washington at the Georgetown University chapel; his bride, Linda Potter, had gone to school there, and her parents lived in Washington. John and I were in the wedding party, and he had arranged for us to share a room in Georgetown for the weekend. I should have known better.

After the reception at Linda's parents' house, a group of us headed back into Georgetown for an after party. I was having the time of my life when John vanished. Which wasn't unusual; John really wasn't a late-night guy, and once he'd had enough—gone. I was still in my wedding tux, hanging with the other twenty or so groomsmen. Eventually I bummed a ride from Kara Kennedy, Teddy's daughter, who dropped me off at my hotel on her way home.

Walking into the hotel lobby on top of the world, I explained that I did not have my key to the room.

"What is your room number, sir?"

"I don't really remember, but it is under the name John Kennedy. We're both registered."

"Oh, Mr. Kennedy had arranged that room through Senator Kennedy's office, who informed us it was only for one night."

"Great, we'll straighten that out in the morning when we check out and I get my credit cards." My wallet was in the room.

"Well, I'm sorry, Mr. Noonan, but we don't have any room for you."

"Well, where is Mr. Kennedy?"

"Oh, he encountered the same situation and left for another hotel."

"Which one?"

"I don't know."

"Okay . . . where are my belongings?"

"The maid secured them for you, and you'll be able to pick them up tomorrow."

That set me off. I demanded my wallet and a room.

"Sir, I do not want to call security."

A moment of clarity: In my state, arguing over a room rented through Senator Kennedy really was not the smartest thing to do. So I shut up, called a cab, and actually found a sympathetic cabbie who let me forgo the fare. Rescued again by an angel, screwed again by Kennedy. Typical John: Sometimes he'd invite people for the weekend at his place in New York and forget to leave them the key. There they'd be, left on John's stoop, fending for themselves while he was off who-knows-where.

A FEW WEEKS LATER, I received a thick envelope addressed with extraordinary calligraphy and a stamp honoring the French designer of the Statue of Liberty, which was being rededicated. When I opened it, there was that special address: 1040 Fifth Avenue. Inside was a series of cards inviting me to Caroline's wedding to Ed Schlossberg in late July, including a picture of the President's house on the Cape, another of Our Lady of Victory Church in Centerville, and a painting of Ambassador

Kennedy's house, now jointly shared by Senator Kennedy and his ailing mother.

Once I responded, I received two acknowledgment cards; the second was for a date. Since I was not dating seriously, I had no intention of bringing anyone; that would make it a day of introductions, followed by speculation. Also, I'd learned a lesson from the past: You could never be sure how someone new to the Kennedy orbit might react within it. So I chose to go it alone.

The thought of an unused invitation to the President's daughter's wedding, however, was too much for my mother to accept. A month or so before the wedding, I was at a dinner at her club when a beautiful girl walked by to use the ladies' room; my mother excused herself and a few minutes later returned with the girl, whom she had promised I would escort to Caroline's wedding.

The girl was stunning and definitely game, but the only place I escorted her to was her seat at this dinner. I explained that my overzealous mother was using this extra invitation as bait to get me a steady girlfriend so I would settle down, and in fact she was misinformed about the extra invitation. I returned to my seat, and explained to my mother that bringing any girl, especially a blind date, to the wedding was not the proper thing to do, and that if she pulled something like that again, I would disown her.

On the day of the wedding, my mother emerged from her bedroom with her hair done and wearing a new dress.

"What are you up to?" I asked.

"Well, I was thinking that if you're not going to use that ticket, I should go to the wedding as your date."

"*Ticket?* It's not a ticket, it's an invitation, and I am *not* taking my mother. Forget about it."

"Listen, Billy, your father was part of that administration, and I knew Jack Kennedy. I will know everyone there, and your father would want me to go."

Great, bring up the old man, stab me in the heart with Irish Catholic

guilt. I reminded her of a story my sister had once told me. In the summer of 1963, she was at a coming-out reception with my parents in Hyannisport; Ted Kennedy happened to be there, and just as the party was
getting into full swing, the President drove by on his way to Squaw Island;
these were the days when a president could still drive himself around.
Teddy whistled and called out, "Hey, Johnny!" The President stopped,
and the entire party emptied onto the front lawn to say hello.

Everyone, that is, except my father. After the President drove off, my
sister found my father sitting on the front porch alone. She wondered
why he didn't come down to greet his friend.

"I'm socializing and on vacation," he told her, "which is exactly what
the President is doing—vacationing. Why would I go out there and
bother him? He is my boss, you know."

My mother didn't appreciate hearing this story—away she went to
sulk. Then I could hear her on the phone ranting about my selfishness.

A half hour later, she reappeared with my eldest brother, Tommy,
who said, "Why won't you let her go to the wedding if you have an extra
ticket?"

Again with the ticket. "It's not a ticket—it's an invitation to a wedding, and she is not going to crash it. It's not going to happen."

"How about if I just go to the ceremony?" she pleaded.

My brother said he would drive us in her near-limo-size Olds 98. Now
double-teamed, I couldn't take any more. "Fine, you can come to the ceremony, but not the reception. Deal?"

"Deal." She was delighted.

My brother, former federal agent and Barnstable cop, pulled right up
in front of the church and started chatting with the local police who were
controlling traffic. My mother would not budge—she wanted to see
everyone arriving. I finally got her into the church just ahead of the bride,
which, of course, meant that Jackie saw us, exactly what I didn't want to
happen: Billy Noonan bringing his mother to the wedding because he
couldn't find a date. I was livid.

After the ceremony I was one of the first out of the church. Saying hello to friends, I spied my mother talking with someone, kissing cheeks. This wasn't good. John came over to rib me. "What's the matter, Noonan, couldn't get a date for the biggest event on the Cape?" Before I knew it, an usher was assisting my mother up the steps of the bus for the reception. I ran over. "Oh, no, Annabelle, we have a deal."

"I just want to see the tent and the appetizers. Tommy will come get me in an hour."

"Oh, Billy, let your mother come for a little while," Provi and Marta chimed in. "Madam won't mind, and we would love to talk to your mother."

"Nope, a deal is a deal. Good-bye."

Grudgingly, she stepped off the bus, got into the backseat of her car, and my brother chauffeured her home to the phone and her circuit of inquiring associates.

The reception at the compound was unreal. Hanging inside a huge tent was a fifteen-foot-wide orb chockful of flowers, perfuming the enormous dance floor. Outside the tent, umbrella-protected seating areas were scattered all over and white boxes filled with ferns and ficus had been placed around. Two bands arrived, one formal, one for rock and roll later.

Senators, former cabinet members, and myriad celebrities were among the crowd, but the first person I saw at the reception was a now-elderly man named Jack Dempsey, still an imposing figure, very tall and strong, with a shaved head. Dempsey had been a state police lieutenant and a confidant of Joseph P. Kennedy's. During the Kennedy administration, he was the top cop in Massachusetts and had remained friendly with the family.

He asked about mine; I told him the story of my mother and the ticket. Dempsey had once been an aide to my mother's father, a superior court judge. They used to ride horses, early mornings, before court was in session, and Dempsey was still close to my family as well. "It doesn't surprise me one bit!" He laughed. "She's some gutsy gal."

Later John, the best man, welcomed Ed into the family. He presented one of the George Washington swords, like the one from the USS *JFK*, to his new brother-in-law, and said, "It's been the three of us alone for so long, and now we've got a fourth."

WITH THE WEDDING of his sister, the expectations for John himself were naturally getting stronger. Christina Haag, a former Brown house-mate, was his steady girlfriend, and he was planning on starting law school the next year. John's slightly older cousins were building their ca-reers: Joe Kennedy would run for Tip O'Neill's congressional seat (once JFK's). Chris Lawford was seriously pursuing acting. And Maria Shriver was an anchor on television.

Law school, for John, was inevitable. Jackie thought a law degree was the postgraduate step to take. The connection to politics was obvious. Caroline had passed the bar a few years earlier. To John, going to NYU was merely fulfilling an obligation. He was a natural debater and theo-rizer, but the minutiae of law really didn't interest him, and he had never been a very good student; plus, he didn't have the concentrated patience to sit at a desk and dedicate himself to the ins and outs of legal briefs.

Furthermore, in his mid-twenties, he had no intention of settling down, or even acting his age. The summer of 1988, John showed up on the Cape with an orange Karmann Ghia convertible. *Orange*. On its last legs. He tried to generate enthusiasm for this purchase with a stoned hip-ster falsetto. "Yeah, dude, I saw it on my street in New York with a For Sale sign in the window, so I called the dude up and paid him cash. Pretty cool, huh?"

"What the hell are you going to do with it?"

"Drive it until it dies, then sell it for parts."

We took it to a car-stereo place in Hyannis and got it wired for sound. John's taste in music was getting heavier: the Who, Led Zeppelin, and Aerosmith—he'd told me I was nuts when I had listened to Aerosmith in the seventies, which I pointed out to him.

"Just catching up, I guess," he explained in this new dude voice.

John was merely fooling around, of course, but that Karmann Ghia represented his refusal to grow up on anybody's terms but his own. He had called his mother and told her he was coming home with a big surprise. To Jackie this could mean only one thing. She shared the news with Marta, her personal assistant, who bought a new dress. Then John arrived in an orange Karmann Ghia.

"Isn't it great?" he said to her. "Don't you just love the color?"

"John, I thought you were coming home with important news. I even went to the safety-deposit box" to retrieve her diamond engagement ring. "And this is your big news? This garish old jalopy?"

John was crestfallen. And embarrassed that she thought he had intimated impending matrimony. Nothing could have been further from the truth.

John did truly like and understand women—which I think was the result of growing up largely with his mother and sister. At the same time, the possibilities were limitless for *People* magazine's "World's Sexiest Man," and John played them out.

He was on a roll. John had finished his first year at law school, spent most of the summer in L.A. working for a prestigious law firm, and had addressed the Democratic National Convention. He was also sleeping with every hot chick on the planet and getting dangerously close to getting caught by Christina, still his girlfriend.

He would call my apartment in Boston during the workday and leave a message. Telling me to check out the cover of a certain magazine, John would proclaim, "I banged her last night. Just thought you might like to know." I would run down to the newsstand in my lobby and check out the babe on the cover, call him up, and get the details of how it happened.

One day at the Cape that August, John called his apartment in New York to retrieve messages. I was flicking through the sports pages when I heard him say, "Oh, my God," and start laughing and grabbing his manhood. He was grinning stupidly. "Billy, come here, you have to listen to this."

He rewound the message, stopped, and reconsidered. "No, never mind. I can't."

"What is it?"

"You won't believe this. Listen to this. No, I can't do it—yes I can, what the hell. I have to enjoy this with someone, so it may as well be you. Just listen to this."

I grabbed the phone, and a familiar voice was on his answering machine, calling him "Kennedy" and moaning about being drunk and in Rome and describing exactly what she wanted to do with his plumbing and how it was all going to come, quite literally, to a climax. Who *was* this?

I sat down and asked him to play it again. I am no fan of pornography, but I had never heard anything quite like this. I listened again—*who was this?* I knew her voice.

John was laughing quietly so that I would not miss any of the hushed adjectives.

I hung up. We laughed like hyenas.

"Who is that?" I pleaded. "I know that voice."

Laughing so hard and grabbing himself in a sort of weird pantomime of her suggestions, he couldn't speak. He just nodded.

"Where did you come up with her? How do I know that voice? For fuck's sake, tell me, I can't stand it."

Finally he looked at me, calmly, like it was nothing. "Madonna."

"You are banging Madonna? How do I not know this until now? Call back—I want to hear it again, now that I know who it is."

He declined, shushed me up, and told me to come outside. He was so full of himself I could have kicked him, but I didn't want to drive him underground into silence.

As we smoked, John told me that they worked out at the same gym and shared the same trainer. "You can't believe how small she is—she's, like, tiny. Let me tell you, she's a sexual dynamo."

Later, after a game of touch football, John, still full of himself over Madonna, told me he had another story. Teddy was trying to fix him up with a certain woman, the stepdaughter of a big contributor to the DNC: Daryl Hannah.

"Oh, come on, this is really lopsided and unfair. Why can't *I* date Madonna and *you* date Daryl Hannah? And by the way, where's Christina in all this?"

Oh, yeah. His girlfriend.

"She hasn't a clue." John told me how one day he arranged to meet Madonna in a hotel suite for a matinee, then had to race to meet Christina. When he arrived late, as usual, she asked him about the unusual scent in the air. Without missing a beat, John said that he was walking through a department store and had stopped to find perfume as a gift for her, but there were too many testers and he was creating too much commotion, so he bagged the idea.

He grimaced when I asked if she really believed him.

Probably you won't believe *me* when I tell you this wasn't typical John, acting out, lying to his girlfriend. But it was certainly him then.

At the same time, John's involvement in politics was growing on the heels of his speech at the Democratic National Convention, which the press played as his political coming-out party. We had pretty healthy arguments over Gary Hart and Michael Dukakis. In 1987 Hart had visited the Kennedy Library to watch films of JFK so that he could emulate his mannerisms. I thought the guy was an impostor. John liked him. Naturally we had discussions about whether the press's prying into his sex life was fair; I argued that Hart had asked for it, since he baited the press to see what they could dig up. John thought that we should hold politicians to the same standards of anyone in, say, business, where one's private life is exactly that. I believe that an elected official should tell the truth. I believe that everyone should tell the truth, which is unrealistic. But those seeking office, especially higher office, where the direction and safety of the country are at stake—to me those people must be above reproach.

John bemoaned Hart's withdrawal, blaming the pressures of private-life scrutiny. "But he got out too early," John believed. Hart would realize this, throwing his hat back into the ring, but it was too late. I didn't feel sorry for the guy. This was just something John and I weren't going to agree on. Yet I understood his position; he defended Hart because he'd become, in the face of his scandal, the underdog, and that was always appealing to John.

The longtime gossip about JFK's extramarital dalliances was the elephant in the room as we debated. My own view was that it was just that—gossip—and I didn't dignify it even privately. John and I certainly never talked about that. Over the years I've heard and read that John was occasionally asked about his father and women, especially when he was running the magazine *George* during the Clinton-Lewinsky scandal in the nineties. That strikes me as laughable. If he actually was asked about his father's sex life—if a colleague or reporter really did broach the subject—I'm sorry I missed it. Because the fur would have flown, I can assure you. I doubt anybody ever had the guts to confront him that way.

At any rate, John's point about Hart was really about a certain post-Watergate atmosphere that had taken hold in Washington and in the press, which he was fond of calling "the unbridled fourth estate." Every politician was under the microscope now. The collision of culture, sex, and power fascinated him; the genesis for *George*—which he would conceive to ride the tension between politics and pop culture—had begun.

Before the election that year, John met up with Michael Dukakis and his wife in New York to campaign for him. John told me how they sat silently in a car as they made their way from one end of Manhattan to the other, stopping at rallies.

"Nobody spoke, Billy. It was strange—just silence in the car. Like the guy has nothing to say."

"That's because he's a fraud. He has no vision and no message. The 'Massachusetts Miracle,' which he's claiming, was all accomplished by Ed King"—my guy, the previous governor. "Dukakis inherited it. Furthermore, he's a wimp. He's a shinkicker."

"What's that mean?"

Dukakis, from Brookline, my home turf, was a guy who'd never held a job outside the public arena. I told John a family story. In 1958 my father was running his medical-supply business, working Brookline for JFK's Senate reelection, and serving on the board of selectmen. On Election Day, stressed out and tired, he went to a polling booth to see how a precinct was doing; some old ladies approached him and asked advice on certain candidates. My father advised them "to vote the ticket."

With that, Dukakis, all of twenty-five years old, went up to my father, explained that he was a town-meeting member and that my father was in violation of election laws.

My father asked him what he was talking about.

Dukakis explained that it was illegal to campaign within so many feet of a polling booth.

My father tried to ignore him; Dukakis claimed he was going to make a report to the state's campaign election panel.

"Is that right?" my father said. "Well, you better know what you're up against." Then he physically removed Dukakis from his path.

I once asked my mother about this story. "He had a lot on his mind and lost his cool," she told me. "But nothing ever came of it." Kenny O'Donnell, Jr., had a more annoyed take. "Can you believe this little punk going up against your father—a physically imposing guy—and the town's leading Democratic politician, who was heading to the White House?"

John's response to this story was beautiful. It also annoyed the hell out of me. "I admire Dukakis for going up against the local ward boss," he said.

"John, my father was working for your father and in a seat your father had encouraged him to pursue. How the hell can you think Dukakis is one of us?"

"He's going to win in November, Billy."

Boy, was his radar off. We bet a hundred dollars on the election's outcome.

The twenty-fifth anniversary of the President's death fell later that month. I watched some of the documentaries with a friend; they included clips of campaign speeches I'd never seen before. I remember one analyst commenting that to be Irish is to understand that the world is eventually going to break your heart. We shook our heads, thinking how different the country would have been if JFK had served out eight years. I wrote John a letter telling him I saw his father kicking Nixon's ass on television and what a shame it was that the nation, the world, and he—especially—had lost such a wonderful guiding force.

The following weekend, I went to New York to help John celebrate his birthday, jointly with his friend Santina Goodman's. We had dinner at his apartment—Ethiopian food—then headed downtown to the big party. I hadn't seen him since the election, and before the night got crazy, I reminded him of our little bet.

"Oh, Gawd," he moaned. "If I welsh on this bet, I'll never hear the end of it."

He had our limo driver pull over at an ATM. As he withdrew money, I told him that I'd recently seen Dave Powers; Powers told me that if Dan Quayle had not been on the Bush ticket, Dukakis would have won even *fewer* states.

"Pretty savvy guy," John said. "Most people dismiss him now as an old storyteller, but boy, does he know his shit."

The next words out of his mouth will always be important to me. As John was putting five twenty-dollar bills in my palm, he looked up at me and said, "You know, Billy, of all the people I know and all the friends I have, I received only two notes about my father's anniversary—and you were one of them. I really appreciate that."

I didn't know what to say, so I mumbled something like, "Isn't that what friends are for?"

"Yeah, sure. But only you two had the balls. Let's go."

Within the next year, as Massachusetts sank to the second-worst debt rating in the nation, a cartoon in a Boston paper showed Dukakis sitting at his desk in the Massachusetts State House with a cake and one candle, floating in a sea of debt; an aide says to him, "Congratulations, Governor. One year ago today you won the Democratic nomination." I sent a copy to John, with a note: "I hate to tell you I told you so. . . ." (By the way, the state hasn't had a Democratic governor since. Chalk one up for the big guy.)

Never heard back on this one.

THE FOLLOWING ST. PATRICK'S DAY, I went to New York for the big parade, which was a more-or-less annual event for us; plus, I was dating a girl who lived there. I met John in a bar near his apartment, where he was sitting in back, with Daryl Hannah.

I liked her immediately. She was tall, willowy, dressed in ripped jeans and army boots—the grunge look before grunge, but Daryl made it work. She was smart and well read, very interested in social and environmental issues, with a counterculture point of view. In many ways she was John's equal, with fame and money of her own and a famous boyfriend in Jackson Browne. She didn't need John for status and had no agenda in seeing him. Many other women were different. Some listened to John as if, when he spoke, his parted lips would yield golden honey. John could sense control, when his soliloquies about politics or music or anything could alter people's opinions, and when he was on a roll, he took every inch of rope they would yield.

Daryl could not have cared less. She had her own ideas. Sometimes they came off as flaky because of her appearance, her connection to liberal Hollywood, and her apocalyptic approach to issues, but she could hold her own.

All this would emerge as I got to know her. At the moment John and Daryl were kissing and cooing in a back booth. My date met us. She knew some people, so we talked to them, because John and Daryl kept right on necking. Then John left to meet Christina. Daryl remained, another friend of mine showed up to join us, and in the celebrity culture of Manhattan, Daryl fell in with the three of us easily.

John knew I'd watch out for her. She took us to see some grunge band she liked from California, at a downtown club. I looked at her profile in the backseat of the cab—she was beautiful, with large features, yet you would not believe she was a starlet; she belonged in *Vegetarian Times* rather than *People*.

My friend was a little confused about the arrangement and later said, "When I asked for you to set me up with a date, I didn't think you would come up with Daryl Hannah."

The next day Daryl, John, and I went to JFK Airport to pick up some errant piece of Kennedy luggage. While we waited, she had John paged as "Helmut Head"—a nod to his sculpted, Brillo-pad hair. The airport employees were giddy with the exchange; they knew who she was and clearly who *he* was, in the airport named for his father. This sort of thing—creating scenes, acting like blithe flower children running around as if the rest of the world didn't exist—was the downside of John and Daryl; they were really more competitors than complementary, and the relationship was doomed from the start.

For a long time, John struggled with what he needed in women, which came from Jackie's having to be both a nurturing mother and a strict father to him. I think he wanted something of each parent—femininity and toughness—from his women. It's a lot to ask, and it requires a unique chemistry. He hadn't found her yet.

9

Struggle with a Capital S

AS WE HEADED INTO the 1990s, there appeared to be a geologic shift, as if our lives weren't quite in our control. But first there was another health crisis. This time it was Anthony Radziwill.

In the summer of 1989, I received a call from John at Jackie's behest. Anthony had been diagnosed with testicular cancer, and John asked if I would give him a call to discuss the operation and different postsurgical options. Immediately I got on a shuttle and headed to New York to see him.

Anthony had changed. Uncomfortable living in America, without a real home here, he had moved back to London, trying to connect with his heritage, without success. Then he had bounced back to New York, and as a reporter for NBC Sports had covered the Seoul Olympics the year before. Traveling on his own with a crew and seeing different parts of the world had opened Anthony up; he was finally coming out of his shell. He had begun religiously working out and running marathons, of which he was quite proud, though John was fond of telling him that exercising as much as he did was a sign of latent mental illness. That drove him nuts, which was, naturally, the point.

But now this—I knew all too well what he was going through.

One of the possible complications of testicular cancer is, of course, losing the ability to have children. In Anthony's case, with a direct, five-hundred-year line to an aristocratic family—the sort of family that had on their walls etchings of Mozart entertaining their ancestors—the threat of being the end of the line made his illness that much more daunting.

When I got to New York, John was holed up studying for the bar exam. Anthony and I talked for some time about the diagnosis and what he could expect. He was scared; I remember him taking a long drink of some Polish vodka before he checked in to Sloan-Kettering for his surgery.

After leaving the hospital that night, I walked for blocks, not knowing where to go or what to do; usually when I was in New York, I was with John, and he'd have a plan. It was almost unbearably hot—the kind of New York summer night when you can fry an egg on the sidewalk—but I just walked and walked, heading back to Anthony's apartment on the Upper East Side, thinking, silently praying for him.

I noticed a crowd outside a restaurant, looking at something in the picture window. I stopped, and there, about a foot above the sidewalk, facing out, sat Jackie and Maurice Tempelsman. I almost burst out laughing: They were perched like mannequins in a department-store display. I knocked on the window, something a cool New Yorker would never have done. The crowd looked at me like, *Who the hell are* you? Jackie and Maurice, who'd been at the hospital earlier, glanced up and waved me in—the crowd looked at me now wondering, *Who the hell are you?*

I joined them at their table, perspiring. Immediately I shared a glass of pinot grigio, and Jackie showed me how to apply a wet napkin to pressure points on my wrists to cool off. She thanked me for going the extra mile in coming down to the city for Anthony. I told her I could never have just sat up in Boston, just as John could not stay in Providence when I was going through the same thing; plus, her kindness to me back then had been an inspiration.

"I can't keep what you did for me and not give it back," I told her. "It needs to travel."

Jackie said she had never heard that before and thought it telling.

The next morning John met me at Anthony's apartment, and we walked over to the hospital. It was still ungodly hot. As we walked, whenever a door opened and a blast of air-conditioning shot out at us, I'd slip inside for a moment.

"What the hell are you doing?" John demanded.

"I can't stand this. You're used to it—you grew up here. But to me this place is like the Mojave Desert."

At one point we walked by a veterans' hospital. Guys in wheelchairs sat out on the sidewalk under a canopy; cool air was blasting from the open doors. I sat there with them for a moment. "Gawd Almighty, this is heaven," I told them. "All we need is a case of beer." I stayed for a couple minutes, and we chatted about weather, whatever. John watched.

When I joined him again, he said, "You know what, Billy? You should be a mayor. You can talk to anyone, from the pope to the plumber."

"Yeah, well, let's get to the hospital before I drop."

Anthony, who'd had his operation, looked awful. John went to him, held his hand, massaged his shoulder, and told him it would be all right. But it didn't appear all right. Anthony gazed up at us like, *Oh, my God, what did they do to me?* "It'll be okay, Ants," John told him.

For me, as soon as I saw his face, it was too much. I had to get out of there. John called a limo service for me, and I went home to Boston.

THESE WERE TOUGH YEARS. My mother was diagnosed with a degenerative brain disorder, and my sister had a recurrence of colon cancer. One of my brothers was in Singapore, another in California, and the third was emotionally distant. I moved to New York to get away from the sort of fatal-attraction women I kept getting hooked up with and to jumpstart my career; but I arrived in New York on Friday the thirteenth, the very day the market bottomed out in October 1989. It was all downhill from there, and I'd go home to Boston within a year.

I felt generally out of sorts, overwhelmed by what was expected of me. The harder I tried, the more desperate I was becoming. It seemed as though I were out of sync with the natural development of a thirtysomething. I started dating a more "appropriate" girl—a debutante, who I would become engaged to, but I was having a tough time wresting happiness from anything.

John, too, was struggling. He flunked his bar exam a second time, and of course it was impossible to avoid the "Hunk Flunks" media noise. The world seemed to have one question about him: Was he stupid? There was only one way to deal with that. Ignore it, soldier on. And hit the road.

In the summer of 1990, John called me right after he'd taken the bar exam for the third—and final—time. He said a nun had passed him a note saying, "We are all praying for you," so he was confident that divine intervention would see him through. "Let's take a road trip, Billy," he suggested. "Just you and me."

We headed up to Cape Cod in a rented car. We stopped at a little park somewhere in Connecticut to throw a Frisbee around, but some girls recognized him—"You're John Kennedy!"

"Let's get out of here," I said. "Let's get out of Connecticut." We were still too close to New York.

We drove up I-95, stopping a couple of times to visit people we knew, went into New Haven and split a pizza, then got back on 95. Since John had gone to Brown, he said, "Let's go to this bar I know in Providence." Fine—I was up for anything. That's what it was like, freewheeling on up toward the Cape, taking our good, sweet time. So we stopped off in Providence, had a couple of beers, hit the road again. We had seventy-two hours to kill, and it was just the two of us. Although he was nervous about it, John was relieved to get the bar exam behind him again.

Coming out of Providence, we saw a young couple whose car had broken down on the side of the road. They were just standing there. "Look at those poor sons of bitches," I said.

"Should we help them out?" John asked. He pulled over, backed up the rental car to them. They were maybe seventeen, eighteen years old and had borrowed her father's car, an Olds Delta, but it had died. They were just kids out on a date, hamburger-and-a-shake kind of kids, and they didn't know what to do.

So we gave them a ride. John started chatting with them. We introduced ourselves by first name and asked them where they lived. "Warwick," she said, although she pronounced it "Wahwick." And her boyfriend, from the same place, of course, chimed in. "Wahwick." Tried-and-true New Englanders.

She leaned forward, chatting with John, discussing Wahwick or what school she was going to go to or something, John talking to her in the rearview mirror. He loved this sort of thing, just getting out on the road and mixing it up. I was inwardly laughing: Here we were, Fear and Loathing in Wahwick, Rhode Island.

Then she said, leaning forward, "Can I ask you a question?"

"Sure," John said.

"What's your last name?"

He didn't miss a beat. "Noonan."

So she asked me my name, and I was on the spot. It's not like you've got time to think of your name. "Flynn." Flynn was my mother's maiden name.

She sat back, and we could hear them muttering. Then she said, "You know, this is really weird. Something really strange is going on here." We got to the girl's house, and she invited us in. So we went in—it was a typical Rhode Island rancher—had a glass of orange juice, and used the bathroom. And then we chatted for a couple of minutes more and left.

That was in August. In November, Patrick Kennedy was running for the House of Representatives. A girl at some event of his went up to Patrick and said, "You know, your cousin John picked me and my boyfriend up when our car had broken down." She went on to say that he had her vote and the votes of her whole family. Patrick, naturally, thought this was great, as now all of greater Wahwick would likely be pulling the lever for him.

John's reaction, when he told me that Patrick had called to tell him that, was pretty funny. He pretended he was pissed off. "Here we were, just helping out these kids, just being Good Samaritans, and it gets Patrick all these stinking votes." Truth be known, he was happy that he'd inadvertently helped get Patrick elected.

IT'S NO SECRET that trouble ebbed and flowed in the Kennedy family—and this was definitely a flow time. Divorces were rampant, there was general confusion over who was dating whom, the Senator was still rumored to be a big-time carouser, and on Easter weekend in Palm Beach in 1991, when I was down there visiting my mother, whose health was deteriorating, things went haywire.

Walking down to the beach from my mother's club, I bumped into William Smith, one of John's cousins. I knew him a little bit from the Cape; he would usually show up in August. William asked me to give him a call or come by for a drink, and I gave him my number. On Good Friday, the holiest of days on the Catholic calendar, I went to St. Edward's Church with my mother, a daily communicant, for the Stations of the Cross. Afterward we went to dinner, the one meal you're allowed on Good Friday, and returned home. It was still early. A message from William invited me to come by the Kennedy home for a drink. I planned on doing so, but because of a sunburn and the fasting, I fell asleep watching TV with my mother.

The next day was more of the same—swimming, lunch, dinner with Mom, then the vigil. This was a very religious woman, and it was a very religious weekend. I stopped by the Kennedy house that night, Saturday. The Smiths and the Edward Kennedys were there with a former FBI guy named Barry. He had these three or four really big sons—it was a weird combination of characters, and I felt funny being there without John or Timmy.

I left before they sat down for dinner, but it was clear that something had happened, and it wasn't good. William had whispered that they'd gone out the night before and brought some girls back, who had stolen a cachepot of some sort; I ignored it as typical high jinks at a Kennedy house.

Next day I had Easter brunch with my mother, flew back to Boston, worked all day Monday, and when I got home, John called me.

"Hey, Billy, were you in Palm Beach this weekend?"

"Yes I was, to see my lovely motha."

"No, really, Billy—were you there?"

"Yes, why? What's the problem?"

"Were you at our house?"

"Yeah."

"When were you there?"

"What's up?"

I could hear him move, shifting the phone, changing position.

"Were you there Friday night?"

"No, I was going to go over but fell asleep. I was there Saturday night. What's wrong? What happened?"

"Have you seen the news?"

"No."

"Go turn on your television."

I did so while he was still on the line—right to a tabloid shot of the beachfront home.

"Billy, are you sure that you weren't involved with any shenanigans?"

"Why are you accusing me—*what* is going on?"

"I'm not accusing you; I'm trying to get to the bottom of this. Some girl that they picked up is claiming that she was raped, and I can't get a straight answer from anyone about what happened."

"Oh, God. I was aware that something happened, but I wasn't involved and never heard exactly what went on except that someone stole a pot or something. Who did it—it's not the Senator . . . ?"

"No, I think it's Willie Smith, though I think there's more to the story, but no one is saying a word."

"What are you going to do?"

"I think I'm going to go outside and address the media by saying, 'We have put up a warning sign at the Palm Beach estate proclaiming, NO TRESPASSING: VIOLATORS WILL BE VIOLATED.'"

"Be real." I laughed, though neither of us thought this was funny. But that's how he coped—making light of a situation that would drag his family through the mud.

William, of course, would be acquitted of the charge. But it took a toll. The house in Palm Beach went on the market once the media circus subsided after the trial.

John stuck up for William not just because he was his cousin and friend but because he knew the foibles of celebrity and believed that William was innocent, even though there was plenty of smoke. When accusations like these came up, John would invoke a line from the film *Dead Man Walking*: "A person is not as bad as his worst deed." The long view—that was part of being a Kennedy.

IN THE SUMMER of 1991, my mother was seriously ill. Her disease was progressing at an accelerated rate. It was like a cyclone, with increased intensity as it progressed. Mary Ruane, the nanny who had raised me, had retired to Ireland, my sister was still battling cancer, and my mother was literally deteriorating in front of me. Faced with no female presence in my life, I was rushing to get married before my mother died—partly to please her, and partly to fill the void. But those are not very good reasons to take a mate for life.

My fiancée's family had no religious affiliation; she'd never been baptized. This was a problem, given that my background and especially my mother's devotion and piety were never going to allow for a nondenominational wedding. I pressed to have the wedding on the Cape.

So up to the Cape came her parents that August, to survey the situation. Our church was willing to accommodate this union, our country club would as well, and a private yacht club had agreed to permit the wedding reception as an extension of goodwill. While we were making the rounds, however, my prospective in-laws wondered why we had to get married in a Catholic church.

I pulled the car over and pointed out, as calmly as I could, without going into Catholic history, that as a Catholic I was required to get married
in a Catholic church by a priest.

We returned to the farmhouse I was renting that summer just as Hurricane Bob began to blow. Restaurants and markets were closed; we hun-
kered down with whatever food we had, candles, gas grills, and liquor,
and invited the tenants in the converted barn next door to join us. My
would-be in-laws had intended to go on to Nantucket, but as no ferries
or planes travel in a hurricane, here they were.

Finally the storm passed over us, and neighbors began driving around
to check on friends and family. Also to survey the damage, but as there
was no electricity, it was difficult to see the extent of it.

Senator Kennedy had left the compound to visit his mother at Cape
Cod Hospital, which employed generators when the power went off. On
his way home, he decided to stop in to see how we were doing, the
thoughtful act of a neighbor, a friend, and an elected official. He was also,
unknowingly, about to help save my life.

In my time as a Democrat, a liberal, and a Kennedy supporter from
Massachusetts, I have had to deal with some pretty contentious discussions defending policies and, especially, the Senator's high-spirited behavior. But my prospective father-in-law took Kennedy bashing to a new
level. He disliked politicians, liberals in general, limousine liberals in particular, and bad boys; he told me that if he ever encountered Ted
Kennedy, he would share his feelings about the Senator directly.

So here was his chance. Teddy stopped in, said hello, shared a drink.
Not a peep from my future father-in-law. Nothing. Nada. The Senator's
neighborliness gave him quite a thirst, and he went back to the kitchen to
help himself to another scotch before heading home.

My future father-in-law certainly deserved a drink himself, on the
heels of the Senator's departure. But when he went to the kitchen to retrieve his bottle of scotch, the bottle was bare—Teddy bare. Oh, this was
too much for him, and it set him ranting anew about the Senator. Sure,

now that he was gone. I loved the irony of Teddy drinking the man's last mouthful of scotch when *he* so clearly needed it, after not having the guts to utter a word.

I offered him some Irish whiskey, but he turned his nose up at that. He and his wife left for a hotel.

In the morning the bridges off the Cape were jammed with workers returning to their jobs. When my fiancée started yelling at me about the traffic, I felt as if I were now being blamed for the weather; perhaps hurricanes were an Irish thing. I told her to go off to Nantucket with her family and leave me and my family and friends alone.

In fact, canceling the engagement was the springboard to turning my fortunes around, to stop wallowing in my problems. I needed, once again, something of a reckoning. An aunt of mine had been fond of saying that if you're on a dead-end road, stop, turn around, and get back to where you need to be. I arranged for my mother to have full-time care, I let the doctors determine the fate of my sister, and I realized that Mary Ruane and her husband needed to live out their days in Ireland (though they would come back to America in March '92, because Irish weather proved too brisk for them). I was learning to accept what I couldn't control; it was time to sit back and watch the river flow.

John was highly amused by the Hurricane Bob story when I saw him at his house later, on Labor Day; he also claimed that he had my wedding in his sights all along. "We never would have let you marry her, Billy."

"Oh, yeah?"

"You have too much spirit and imagination to get stuck with those WASPs."

"Why didn't you tell me that?"

"You had to figure it out on your own."

"Well, you let me get awfully goddamn close."

"Timmy and I knew you would bail."

"Yeah, but . . ."

"Come on, let's go throw the Frisbee around."

Meanwhile, John's relationship with Christina Haag was petering out.

His affair with Daryl Hannah and flings with other women, like Madonna, had been a strong sign that he wanted his freedom. Part of the problem was that John couldn't seem to make up his mind on women. With Daryl he kept at it for several on-again, off-again years. She'd show up in New York after a fight with Jackson Browne. John would be taking care of her one moment, and then you'd walk down the street with them and they'd start fighting about whether or not to go into some shop. A classic case, as John Perry Barlow said, of people who were lovely individually, but together completely wrong.

One night a group of us went out to Michael's Pub, a typically offbeat New York bar, the place where Woody Allen played clarinet one night a week. A zydeco band that encouraged audience participation played two sets, and John thought the early set would be best, so we could go somewhere else afterward. But there wasn't much of a crowd, no buzz; it was kind of a dead performance. Between sets we went to the bar for a drink.

That's when we got into it: the Daryl thing, the Jackson Browne thing.

"He's mean to her," John explained. "They've got a lot of problems."

"It's simple, John. She's codependent."

He stared at me. "What are you talking about? That sounds like psychobabble."

"Maybe. But it's something I've had to examine in the women *I* attract."

"What's that mean?"

"It's about playing Sir Galahad. It's this role of taking care of women, protecting them, when they really don't want to be protected—they want something else."

"Like what?"

"Like drama, or they've got a father complex going. It could be a number of scenarios, but it's all based on abandonment. I've really been looking at the sort of women I'm attracting—when they're the antithesis of our mothers, it's not such a good thing."

He stared, thinking. I suggested we have another drink if he wanted to get into it further. Instead he moved toward our group. I really hadn't meant to upset him, but I could see I'd hit a sore spot. John looked back at me as if there were a lot more to say—and how the hell did I *know* this?—but the timing was off. Or maybe he wasn't quite ready. Yet the Daryl situation, and sorting out who he really wanted to be with, long-term, was weighing heavily on him.

For me, at any rate, things were soon going to get a lot better.

THAT SEPTEMBER, T. X. Cronin died. He'd been a World War II naval officer, graduated from the Harvard School of Business, and made a fortune in electronics in the sixties. When one of his sons married my sister, my father and T.X. became business partners, and when my father died, he became a surrogate father to me, a man who would take me to communion breakfasts, to football banquets—things a father would do with a son. It was T.X. who had taken me to Europe in 1974 with his son Philip.

It's something John and I talked about. He once asked me, "How much do you think about it?"—meaning the absence of our fathers.

"Every day."

"When does it bother you the most?"

"Father-son events. When everybody else's father is around. . . ."

Loads of people, naturally, would have jumped at the chance to fill that role with John, but Jackie was cautious about letting anyone get close for the wrong reasons. Teddy, after Bobby's death, would have been the obvious choice, but he had far too many responsibilities as a senator and head of the Kennedy family to take on that role. Jackie turned to Jack Walsh, the Secret Service agent from Boston, a tough, charming ex-marine with a shock of salt-and-pepper hair—he was called the "Silver Fox." Mr. Walsh (Bobby Kennedy wouldn't allow him to be called "Jack," as that hit a little too close to home) would play the surrogate dad with John, who looked up to him.

Now Mr. Cronin was inadvertently going to help me once again. On the way to his funeral, I picked up Dennis Maguire, who was also close to the Cronins, at his family's plumbing-and-heating shop in Newton. His mother was there with his younger sister, Kathleen, who we used to baby-sit when we were in high school. My God, how she had grown up! I remembered a freckle-faced tomboy; now she was a long-legged marathon runner.

When I brought up how stunning Kathleen had become, Dennis grunted something about her dating some jerk and maybe I should take her out. A date? My friendship with Dennis went back to high school—I didn't think it was a good idea to risk that. Plus, I had just gotten out of a bad relationship and wasn't interested in rebounding into another. And with my mother sick, I had my hands full.

I few days later, I saw Dennis again. "Listen, Billy," he told me, "I cleared it with my family, especially my mother, who said that it was okay to take Kathleen out."

"Okay. Did you happen to mention it to *her?*"

Apparently she was up for it. I demurred. He called again.

On an October night, under a nearly full harvest moon, I called her, and we went out.

With the right person, everything becomes simple. She was one of my own. Hell, I once helped her assemble a maze for hamsters one Christmas a long time ago.

She invited me to a harvest-moon party two nights later. I explained I had a friend coming into town with his girlfriend and that we were going out to dinner. No problem, Kathleen said, they could come.

"But the friend is John Kennedy."

"That's fine," Kathleen said, suitably unimpressed. "He can come."

I was onto something here. We picked up John and Julie Baker, the model he was dating, with raven hair and the brightest blue eyes, at the Charles Hotel in Cambridge, and went for something to eat across the street at Charlie's, our hangout from fifteen years earlier; the photos of him and his family still hovered over us as we drank beer and ate burgers. Kathleen and Julie were getting along well.

At the party—in the woods in the western suburbs of Boston—most people did not look too closely, because most people don't expect to meet fashion models and famous sons of former presidents at harvest-moon parties. John and I slipped away to the edge of the woods to catch up; I hadn't really talked to him since I'd broken off my engagement.

A couple days later, there was John yelling into my answering machine, "I can't believe you, Billy. How'd you pull that off? Your lovely motha would adore her."

I called him. "Yeah, but she's Dennis Maguire's little sister."

"She's *what?*"

"I used to baby-sit for her."

"Does Dennis know you're dating her?"

"He arranged it."

"Great, then. If he arranged it, what's the problem?"

"John, I used to baby-sit her."

"Does her mother know?"

"Yeah, she's cool with it, although this all just started last week."

"Billy, she's great, and if your old friend doesn't care, go for it."

"Doesn't it strike you as strange? I mean, would you want me dating Caroline?"

"Yeah, having you for a brother-in-law would be fun. And I'm sure Dennis feels the same way."

With that my doubt disappeared. Though in a few months, Dennis would start wondering, "Are you guys really dating? I mean, *really* dating?"

"Now, Dennis, no regrets. This was your idea."

THE NEXT APRIL the inevitable happened: My mother passed away. No matter how prepared you think you are, losing your mother is a shock. It was not the shock I had when my father died. With him I was totally unprepared to lose, at thirteen, the man I adored—who I caddied for, who took me on trips, who let me sit in on business meetings. This was different. This was the spiritual cutting of the umbilical cord, with the woman who'd held my life. I once heard a man say, "Never underestimate

Jimmy Noonan and Jane Connors's wedding party, 1952. Back row, second and third from left, Kenny O'Donnell and Jack Noonan; best man Tom Noonan is to the left of the groom; Bobby Kennedy is at far right. A decade later Kenny would be JFK's closest adviser, Tom Noonan a director of the Small Business Administration, and Bobby Kennedy attorney general. (Photograph by Bachrach)

Selectman Thomas J. Noonan, publisher G. Russell Phinney, and Senator John F. Kennedy setting type at the Brookline Chronicle. *(Robert L. Marchione)*

JOHN F. KENNEDY
MASSACHUSETTS

COMMITTEES:
LABOR AND PUBLIC WELFARE
GOVERNMENT OPERATIONS
SELECT COMMITTEE ON
SMALL BUSINESS

United States Senate
WASHINGTON, D.C.

February 25, 1957

Dear Tom:

I saw in the paper today where you had
announced your candidacy for Selectman in my
native town of Brookline, and I am delighted
that you are going to run as I think we need all
the good men we can get in public service in
our State.

I have not had a chance to see you since
the election this Fall, but I want to tell you that
even though we were unsuccessful on the national
level, I appreciated everything you did. Best of
luck!

Sincerely,

Jack

John F. Kennedy

JFK:el

Mr. Thomas J. Noonan
408 South Huntington Avenue
Jamaica Plain, Massachusetts

*A letter from then-senator John F. Kennedy
to my father that Anthony Radziwill
showed to Jackie.*

*My father, Tom Noonan, seated at the President's desk in the Oval Office.
My mother, Annabelle, on the right with gloves, looks on adoringly. (Cecil Stoughton)*

At Red Gate Farm, Martha's Vineyard: me, a friend of John's from Brown,
John, and Sally Munro, 1982. (Provided by author)

Adonis at Red Gate Farm, 1982. (Provided by author)

John's eighteenth birthday and the donnybrook with paparazzi; I'm at center, Pucillo's making his move, and Kennedy's knocked down between the cars, dark glasses in hand. (Richard Corkery, New York Daily News)

My favorite picture of John. Catskills, 1987.
(Provided by author)

John and Christina Haag, cross-country skiing, Catskills, 1987. (Provided by author)

*John and me,
Palm Beach Club, 1987.
(Patricia A. Cronin)*

*View of the Kennedy compound and Hyannisport Harbor
from the widow's walk atop President Kennedy's house. (Provided by author)*

John and Daryl Hannah, Martha's Vineyard, Fourth of July, 1993. (Provided by author)

Twenty-fifth anniversary of the signing of the Nuclear Test Ban Treaty, JFK Library, 1988.
From left: me; John; Christina Haag; Dave Powers, special assistant to President Kennedy and later curator
of the JFK Library; Mrs. and Mr. Gerry Doherty;
McGeorge Bundy, national security adviser under JFK.
(© 1998 James Trafidlo)

Timmy Shriver at my wedding-rehearsal
dinner, Allen Harbor Yacht Club, 1994.
The shirt reads: "Big Bad Bill . . ."
(Kathleen L. Noonan)

Timmy Shriver, reverse of T-shirt:
"Is Sweet William Now."
(Kathleen L. Noonan)

Kathleen and me on our wedding day, July 16, 1994, with Timmy and John. (Patricia A. Cronin)

John at my wedding reception with a gag gift from the bachelor party. (Provided by author)

*Ed Schlossberg with son Jack, three ushers, Anthony Radziwill, Carole DiFalco,
John (best man), Carole's brother, and me. (Eric Weiss)*

John in the Hyannisport house, Thanksgiving 1997.
(Provided by author)

Carolyn and John, Hyannisport house, Thanksgiving 1997. (Provided by author)

Dog Friday, John, Carolyn dancing with me, Thanksgiving 1997. (Kathleen L. Noonan)

Me, John, Narciso Rodriguez, and Gustavo Paredes
in the dining room, preparing for Thanksgiving dinner, 1997.
(Kathleen L. Noonan)

Ariel Paredes, Gustavo Paredes, Kathleen, Kiely on her lap, me and TJ, John and Friday, and Narciso Rodriguez. Providencia "Provi" Paredes sits on the coffee table. Hyannisport house, Thanksgiving 1997. (Provided by author)

John and Carolyn in the dining room of the Hyannisport house, Thanksgiving 1997. (Provided by author)

John and TJ watching television at the Hyannisport house, 1997. (Provided by author)

*Carolyn with TJ as an infant, August 1996.
(Provided by author)*

*Carolyn with Kiely, three months old, at the
Hyannisport house, Thanksgiving 1997. See the
daiquiris on the table in the foreground?
(Provided by author)*

Kathleen pregnant with Kiely, TJ in her arms,
John in GTO at Red Gate Farm, July 1997.
(Provided by author)

the prayers of a mother. Only God knows when they will be answered, but they will be." That's always struck me as just right.

I called Kathleen first and then Timmy Shriver. I needed her with me, and I needed Timmy to remind me of what we believe in. Timmy's mother called, flowers arrived from Maria and Arnold. If you know one of the Shrivers, you know them all.

I felt a little better when I finally got my sister on the phone. She was with my mother when she died in Palm Beach, and it was quick. I would always remember her there: Still getting her hair coifed, a manicure and pedicure weekly. To St. Edward's for mass, playing bridge in her cabana, doing water aerobics in her pool, tipping everyone a dollar, sneaking through the labyrinth of shops on Worth Avenue looking for the latest fashions.

At her wake in Wellesley, the biggest bunch of lilies I'd ever seen (short of Easter at St. Patrick's Cathedral) was right up front. The card said, "With deepest sympathy, Jacqueline Kennedy Onassis." Annabelle had finally gotten an acknowledgment from her much-admired paragon of style and grace. She would have loved it. John arrived at the wake with Timmy Shriver and his wife, Linda. We hugged and prayed, but suddenly it seemed that everyone realized just who was there; the three of them quietly slipped away. Later Kathleen and I found them coming out of the Wellesley Inn next door.

"What have you guys been doing?"

"We went to heah our president," John said in his faux Boston accent. President Bush, Sr., had just addressed the nation; Los Angeles had been burning all week in the aftermath of acquittals in the Rodney King trial.

The next day at the funeral—late, as usual—the three of them had to sit in the back of the church. My mother's friend Father Jim Rogers asked us all to offer a sign of peace, which generally means, of course, that you kiss the person next to you if you're close; if not, you offer a handshake. John and Timmy galloped all the way up the aisle, then whacked me on the shoulder. We shook hands, and they galloped back. Never mind usual decorum. My friends had come, in the most literal way, to me.

Timmy and Linda left for a friend's wedding on the Vineyard. John rode with me to Holyhood cemetery. Our family plot is close to his; after burying Annabelle, we strolled over to say a prayer for the Kennedys.

"It's beautiful here," John said. The original plan, in fact, was for his father to be buried in Holyhood.

"Isn't there a baby buried here?" someone asked—referring to his brother, Patrick, who died in infancy when they were in the White House.

"No. They're all in Arlington."

He came back to my sister's house. Even then, in that context, mothers couldn't help themselves around John. "Oh, I have a beautiful daughter. . . ." Usually he'd just walk away. Now he calmly tolerated the attention in order to stay there with me, but soon made a call to have a car delivered. Then he drove home to New York.

It wouldn't be long before John had to confront the same loss.

10

The First Lady Is Gone

DURING THE WINTER of 1994, I came down on the train from Boston to meet with a private money manager at Rockefeller Center and to discuss investments with John. He was living in a hotel on the Upper East Side, since the loft he'd bought in Tribeca was being refurbished. When I got there, it was snowing like crazy. John said I could stay over at his suite, as he had a sleeper sofa.

"I didn't bring any clothes, John. Not even a toothbrush."

"Listen, stick around. I want to talk with you later. Besides, Anthony just had some surgery—he's at his mother's apartment convalescing. It will cheer him up to see you."

What the hell. I was in New York in a near blizzard, on business with John, Anthony needed a visitor, and I'd probably get an invitation over to 1040 for dinner. I went uptown to see Anthony, who was being attended to by Carole DiFalco, his girlfriend, who was a producer for ABC News. He seemed to be doing pretty well; later I'd understand that Anthony, always trying to get back to the gym to stay in great shape, had dismissed his own condition too quickly.

I caught up with John early that evening at his hotel, ready for a night of New York fun in the snow.

"Listen, Billy," he said, "I thought what we might do is head over to 1040 to see Mummy and have some dinner. Mummy said she would love that, and you know how much she loves you, but she isn't up to it."

"That's fine. What, then?"

"No, Billy—there's a lot more to it than that. Mummy is going through chemotherapy and is not feeling well. She's got cancer—she's got it good."

Oh, God. From Anthony to now this. I'd been in this spot before, with both my sister and mother gravely ill at the same time. I thought, *Okay, don't let on. Keep it upbeat.*

"I'm sorry to hear that." I'd try to deal with the medical rather than the emotional. "What kind does she have?"

It wasn't what he said, but how he said it: like throwing a cinder block on the coffee table, and it made a loud flat bang. "Non-Hodgkin's lymphoma."

Silence. This was not good.

"What's the prognosis? Is she responding to the treatment?"

"It's pretty experimental."

"Well, that's good." I remembered how, when I was sick, she had offered, through John, access to the best doctors in the world. I remembered how John had made the same offer when my sister was very ill. "I'm sure she's getting the best care."

The phone rang in John's suite. It was Timmy, calling from New Haven, where he was planning the Special Olympics World Games; I was sure this was a daily call, since Timmy would not just offer help but monitor a situation like this—he was the go-to guy in times of crisis. John did seem a little distracted as he listened to Timmy, though.

"Yeah, I know, I know. Well, you talk to him, he's right here."

I grabbed an extension at the desk. I figured I was either in some sort of trouble or about to be asked for my advice—it was usually one or the other.

"Billy, are you engaged to Kathleen yet?" Timmy asked. "Are you go-

ing to marry her? What's the holdup? You're not getting any younger."
Phew—this was a relief.

John piped in, "Billy, she's perfect for you. What are you waiting for?"

I looked out the window at the flying snow, down at pedestrians holding scarves around their heads bracing against the wind, jumping almost
suicidally into the intersections, trying to hail a taxi or get to a subway stop.
This is what John wanted to talk about—not his mother's or Anthony's illness, or investment ideas, but about me getting married. Timmy's call was
a useful coincidence.

"Look," I told them, "I'm just getting over all the bullshit of dealing
with losing my mother and closing her estate, my job is going well, I have
a good relationship with Kathleen—why do I want to screw it all up by
getting married? I tried this once before, and it didn't work so well."

"Listen, Billy"—always "Listen, Billy." I was always getting lectured.
"What are you waiting for?" John said. "She's pretty, she's fun, she has red
hair, she's athletic, and she's Irish! What else is there?"

"Yeah, I'm sure you guys are right, but what's the rush?"

"Billy . . ." If it's not "Listen, Billy," it's the dangling what-isn't-said.
Double-teamed. But I knew they were right.

That night John and I saw the Crash Test Dummies, who'd had a hit
the past summer and were getting radio time with a song called "Mmm
Mmm Mmm Mmm." (Someone had slipped us tickets to Conan O'Brien's
show, and, as he's a Brookline guy, I'd wanted to go, but John was afraid of
getting pulled out of the audience by Conan.) We had dinner late and
headed back to the hotel to watch the big news of the day: snow.

In the morning we finished our investment discussion. Then he asked
me a loaded question: "If you're given a bill that you don't think you owe,
should you fight it or pay it?"

"Fight it."

"Suppose it will bring you under scrutiny and cause you to expose
your financial holdings."

"Settle it."

John nodded, mentioning Howard Hughes's attitude toward an IRS audit: "Don't fight it. Pay it." It was better to avoid trouble than foolishly risk it over a principle.

He never told me, though, why he asked the question. Was it to determine my business acumen? Something going on with him? (He didn't say.) Was he just trying to get his mind around how high-profile businessmen think?

We started talking about making payrolls. John wanted to launch a business. In fact, he had started a company called Random Ventures that was looking for just that. One idea was to mass-produce handmade kayaks, a plan that ultimately fell apart because the concept is an oxymoron. But he was searching, meeting businesspeople, looking to find something to call his own. If you make a payroll, you're a businessman. It goes back to the philosophy of John Adams, something John embraced: A man should go into industry first, take the knowledge of what that entails, the way the world of business works, before he enters politics. *George* magazine was being hatched.

I WENT HOME to Boston with a plan: I was going to get engaged. I thought that St. Valentine's would be an appropriate day; this year it fell on a Monday. In Boston the first two Mondays in February are reserved for the Beanpot hockey tournament, which was now in its forty-fifth year. It's an elimination tournament between Boston College, Boston University, Harvard, and Northeastern. They square off the first Monday, and the winners play for the beanpot, which is a silver pot full of Boston baked beans that also includes city bragging rights. The tournament gives Bostonians something to look forward to in the dismal month of February.

I decided to take Kathleen to see the championship game, as we were both Boston College grads. Since the consolation game was played at five o'clock, there was ample time to get dinner, drink some wine, and pop the question before the big game.

Here was where I went wrong: My choice of a romantic setting was a fine French restaurant, Maison Robert, with a great wine list. I was such a regular at the place that I called it "Bobby's House."

But—completely the wrong tone for my girl: *Bonsoir, mademoiselle et monsieur.* Chestnut soup, rabbit, halibut, and the like. Not for Kathleen. She's a steak-spud-and-Bud type of girl. Kathleen ate a salad, poked at some chicken. Dinner wasn't a pop-the-question atmosphere.

We went to the old Boston Garden to see Boston College play Harvard for the Beanpot. They were tied after regulation, so Kathleen suggested we go for a drink, to the box owned by the *Boston Globe,* where she worked in advertising, since the concessions had stopped serving. Three overtimes later, nearly midnight, BC had won the game, and Kathleen, who usually held herself to two beers, had had about ten, with virtually no food and lots of excitement. We left the Garden jumping up and down, until she hit a patch of ice and landed on her butt; I piggybacked her the rest of the way to my car. Enough excitement. No engagement.

A month later I went to Connecticut to see Timmy. It was three nights of black-tie dinners surrounding St. Patrick's Day. As the man who was bringing the World Games to New Haven, Timmy was the keynote speaker at an Irish dinner. The next night we were the guests of the governor, who was entertaining Albert Reynolds, the Irish prime minister; then we went to a dinner for the John F. Kennedy Trust, started by Kennedy cousins in Wexford. As always, I was there for moral support.

The second night, following the Secret Service motorcade to the governor's mansion in a blinding snowstorm—it was one of the snowiest winters on record—Timmy had a question.

"So how did you do it?"

"Do what?"

"Get engaged."

"Oh, no, not this again."

"Billy . . ."

I told him the Beanpot tournament story.

He was delighted. "See, I told you she was perfect for you—beer, hockey, BC. Let's get it done."

After driving back to Boston, after the snowstorm, after the three black-ties, I got home exhausted. Kathleen was sitting there in her sweatpants.

"Let's get married," I said.

"Yes," she agreed. She called her parents, flew down the next week to Naples, Florida, to discuss plans, and we set a date for July.

THE MEDIA WAS REPORTING, that winter into spring, that Jackie wasn't doing well. I was a little distracted with planning my wedding and talked to John only sporadically. I assumed—as with all things pertaining to Jackie—that these reports were exaggerated.

Wild speculation about the Kennedys had been a press staple for a long time, of course. It was something John had dubbed the Face-lift Factor.

"Billy, if I tell you my mother didn't have a face-lift," he once said to me, "you'd believe me, right?"

"Yeah, why?"

"Because she didn't."

"Yeah, mine did. So what if she did?"

"Well, some tabloid reported that she had one—they had nothing else to print, so they decided to make something up."

"Yeah, but what's the point?"

"The point is that now, because she didn't refute it, a couple of news sources are reporting how young she looks with her new face-lift and there are even some Park Avenue plastic surgeons hinting that *they* did the procedure. It's taken on a life of its own, and it's not even true!"

The Face-lift Factor would hit John over a few Labor Day weekends, when there is typically nothing notable happening in the world, a time for the press to conjure up engagement stories about him.

Now I called him to find out if something was really going on. As we'd been doing since we were kids, John and I began every conversation with, "How are you? How's your lovely motha?"

"She doing all right," John would report. "She's hanging in there."

But then in May, the media reports of her health got truly alarming. I called Timmy's house in New Haven; his maid told me he was with John in New York, that Jackie was very bad. I called 1040, and Anthony got on the phone.

"Anthony, what the hell is going on down there?"

"Billy, she just passed away. Just as you called."

"*What*? I had no idea." I figured that if John needed me, he would have called.

Which he did the next day. "It's pretty tough," he told me. "Can you and Kathleen come down tomorrow?"

"Of course."

"Great. We'll talk then."

Kathleen was ambivalent about going—she knew John but barely knew his mother, and she didn't want to appear inappropriate. I explained to her that John would be in our wedding, along with Timmy and Anthony, and this is what you do when someone is an important part of your life: share their pain.

When we arrived at the block of 1040, the cabdriver said he could not drive to the front door because the street was blockaded.

"Look, I'm supposed to be there," I told the cabbie, then realized that's probably what everyone was saying. "All right, just tell the cop, or pull up and I'll tell him." Which is what I did. Before we got out of the cab, I told Kathleen not to look at any of the press or photographers, to keep her eyes in front of her and her ears closed; if she gave them a scent of weakness or curiosity, they'd pounce. I was glad to get inside. Sitting on the little bench in the elevator, heading up to the apartment for the last time, I didn't quite know what to expect.

The apartment was crowded. Attentive staff took our luggage and coats.

"Wow, Billy," Kathleen said, pointing to a note attached to a singular bouquet in the front hall. It was from President and Mrs. Clinton.

John looked as if someone had let the air out of him. We embraced— something we were not particularly prone to do. He was talking with Mayor Rudy Giuliani, thanking him for all the assistance he'd provided in the last few days. There in the corner, to the left of the fireplace, lay the coffin; John and I walked over to it together.

"This was Mummy's bedspread," he said. It was an elaborate gold fabric. "It was my idea. We needed something intimate to dress up the casket."

Kathleen and I said a prayer. When I opened my eyes, John was standing there looking at us, his head cocked to the right; it was a signal, from him, of appreciation, or fondness, and I think he might have been remembering, as *I* surely was, all the times the three of us—Jackie, John, and I—had spent together. She was a wonderful mother and wonderful, always, to me.

John, obviously in shock, had a funny take. "It's a strange procession: First come the doctors, then the lawyers, then the funeral director. It isn't simply a death but a series of steps in death."

Kathleen and I sat in the dining room next to Anthony. He rubbed my back and said how strange it was that I called the moment she died. It was incredibly hot, and I noticed how many *old* people were there, which seemed strange because Jackie always, to the last, seemed so young. Which is the gift, now that I think of it, of presence, of not letting herself get stale or old. But now . . .

God, I was starving. Little wineglasses of Perrier were being served, and watercress sandwiches. It felt like we were getting bread and water—I popped them like Triscuits. I would have preferred a ham and cheese sandwich and a glass of milk. Then Lee Radziwill walked in.

It was eerie. Jackie's sister looked so much like Jackie, and had her hair done like Jackie's, and dressed like Jackie, that for a second . . . I couldn't take my eyes off her.

When someone fainted, I took this as a sign to go; wakes make me edgy, and hanging around, I feel, is ghoulish. John sensed this and asked us to stay for dinner. The older people began to thin out, and the Kennedy cousins started to show up.

I knew there would be a rosary, a long and difficult ritual. I tried to stay out of the way, standing in the foyer.

The curtains were drawn, and the sinking sun through them changed the patina of the room from a bright white and blue to a warm yellowish green. Candles and incense were burning. As the priest began the rosary, which is meant to release the soul from purgatory, the surreal light caught people's bowed heads in profile; tears streamed down their faces. I knew what they were moved by. It was not just the death of Jackie but of a certain First Lady who had been through so much and meant so much. It was the passing of an era, and it was overwhelming. I moved to the library to be alone.

I looked down from the terrace on the fifteenth floor at throngs of people below, a perfect blend of New York and a cross-section of our nation and the world: black, white, Hispanic, Asian, old, young—many of them much too young to remember her in the White House. I wondered how many people had emigrated to America because of her, her celebrity, her warmth and welcoming spirit. There were probably thousands of people out there for her now, standing, waiting, praying, including security and scores of photographers.

The rosary must have been too much for others, because the library started to fill up. When it was finally over, I grabbed John. "Come on, let's go outside"—meaning the terrace. We had ritually gone out there, overlooking the reservoir that would soon bear Jackie's name, to watch the sun set. John used to say that after the sun had dropped below the horizon, you could see a green flash; we kept waiting for it to happen, and it never did, though it was always an excuse for a cigarette and conversation.

It was an amazing moment. Just the two of us, John and me, as the light faded. Not just on this day but on his mother's life. As we leaned over the balcony, looking down at the crowd, they screamed her name and their love.

"Can you believe this?" John said, incredulous. "They've been there for days. All for Mummy."

"John, she was more than a First Lady to these people. She was an icon. She was their queen."

He smiled—it registered. We went in to eat. The crowd had thinned

even more. Dinner was buffet style, plate-on-a-knee. Daryl Hannah arrived and sat next to Kathleen. Things were definitely frostier than when
we'd seen them a month before. For some reason only she could possibly
fathom, Daryl started talking about Jackson Browne, the other man in
her life, and how they met: He picked her out of the crowd at a Chicago
concert and asked her to dance onstage. I was hoping he was somewhere
nearby to do the same thing at this moment.

But Kathleen distracted her, and I was able to sit next to John by the
kitchen-door screen—the one Charlie the Irish butler used to breeze
through—to talk. Soon the wake was down to just a few people, and no
Daryl. John and I talked for a long time.

It's hard to know what to say—how much to say—at moments like
that, but I decided to let it rip, to share what I'd been through. Having
both lost our fathers early was the foreground; John, of course, had the
double impact of never knowing his father and dealing with his unreal
fame. He would not be able to come into himself until Jackie was gone.
He couldn't. Jackie was too strong, and there was too much at stake. So
he had lived, pretty much to this point, in line with what she wanted—I
didn't understand this when we were living through it. But now I did.

I told him what it had been like for me, losing my mother. I spent the
first six months, at thirty-five, holed up in a spider shack in the back of a
house in Centerville, Massachusetts, where I had lived ten years before;
that much John knew. Taking a break from my career as a stockbroker, I
grew tomatoes, listened to the Grateful Dead, and worked as a bartender
four hours a night—enough to keep me afloat. My life as I'd known it, a
certain way of life—all the privileges that accompanied my mother's
milieu—were now gone. No more rounds of golf at her country club, no
more lobster salad sandwiches poolside at her club in Palm Beach. I didn't
entirely regret losing that world, though it was a connection to my parents' lifestyle. But the point, of course, was that I was starting over. Her
health, her demise, had become my focal point. No more worrying about
my mother, no more worrying about her health, about where she would

die and with whom. She was gone for good. And that can be, in a strange way, liberating, which was the point I made now to John.

With both parents gone, there was no need to try to impress them. For the first time in my life, I was not someone's son, someone's namesake. I was going to garden and think, think some more, go to the beach with my dog, work, and see Kathleen when she came down to the Cape to visit her family.

When summer ended, I had no idea where I was going to go. Both of my mother's homes were rented, and the spider shack had no heat. But I was determined to do what I wanted. There was no one above me, no one below me, just me.

But John and I both believed in and took our Irish roots seriously. We were sons of prominent Boston Irish Catholic men. My father worked hard for his success, owned lots of real estate, and invested well and belonged to numerous country clubs—the whole bit, the Great American Dream. That was his life. I'm sure that he would have wanted me to be happy, in whatever life I chose. That was why he worked so hard, to give us more opportunity. So when I was finished mourning, I went back to work as a stockbroker, back to pursuing my own life.

"It's amazing," I went on, "what your mother accomplished. My God, look across the street—her legacy at the Met, at Grand Central Station, at the White House, at the Kennedy Library in Boston, at Harvard." On and on. John smiled, or tried to.

"And also you," I told him. "I mean, what's inside you. Now you can break out on your own, do what you want to do." I reminded him, as gently as I could—but of course I just said it—that he had achieved all that she had hoped, he was a good citizen, he didn't get into trouble, he made her laugh, he went to law school. And he finally passed the bar. She had given him the toolbox; now it was time to create something with it.

John nodded—he understood, even now, the day of his mother's wake, what it all meant. That though her death was as profound a loss as he could suffer, it could also be liberating. She had given him the experiences and knowledge of how to live a happy life. It was time for him to go do it.

THE FOLLOWING MORNING Kathleen and I headed to the St. Ignatius of Loyola Church to say our good-bye to Jackie. The streets were a mess, so we walked the last few blocks there. At least this time we had the documentation to prove we were invited.

Timmy met us at the door, gave us each a mass card with an embossed scallop shell and a poem by Sir Walter Raleigh, then escorted us to seats about five rows behind John. The person seated next to us was Lady Bird Johnson, cane in hand. How alone she seemed, and forgotten; Mrs. Johnson looked around, sniffing. I thought maybe she needed a man's support and asked if I could assist her. She demurred, and I remembered that moment at Maria's wedding, when I thought Jackie needed assistance in dealing with a leering movie mogul. Uh—*no*. But Lady Bird was, to me, a woman of equal stature historically to the one we were sending to God, so why didn't Mrs. Clinton, sitting in the front row across from John and Caroline, beckon Lady Bird to her side?

We watched the casket from 1040 come into the church, sprayed with lady's mantle, to the tune of "We Gather Together." It was a song I would decide to have played at my upcoming nuptials, in deference to Jackie. The presentation of gifts to the altar, often reserved for children, was handled by Marta and Effie, Jackie's personal assistant and butler, respectively— strictly speaking, they were her staff, but in reality they were, to Jackie, family. John looked around, smiling at the beauty of the moment.

One of the readings was from the Gospel of St. John: "In my Father's house there are many mansions." In his homily the priest addressed this reading, first by saying that with all due respect to the Kennedy family— and not to be misunderstood or make the idea trivial—the concept of Jacqueline Kennedy Onassis in God's house with many mansions was an enticing one—as if to acknowledge that even paradise would be a better place graced by the presence of her spirit.

Senator Kennedy gave, as is his habit, a eulogy with just the right touches; he mentioned the powder blue note cards, as thin as tissue paper, that Jackie would send people: thank-yous, remembrances, and so on. And how no one else wrote like she did, or spoke like Jackie, or acted like her. When she took on the challenge of saving Grand Central Station, those bulldozers should have just turned around and headed home. He also told a story about President Clinton coming aboard Maurice Tempelsman's yacht in Martha's Vineyard; Jackie told Teddy to go welcome the president. Teddy protested nautical decorum, that the owner or captain of the boat must greet the guests. Whereupon she said, "Teddy, you do it. Maurice isn't running for reelection." Teddy concluded with a brief remembrance of her years as a wife, mother, and First Lady. "Jackie was too young to be a widow in 1963, and too young to die now."

11

Moving On

THE NEXT WEEKEND was Memorial Day. John chose to come to the President's house on the Cape instead of to the Vineyard, where Jackie had built a house in the early eighties and where John had usually assembled his friends for that weekend of the year. The Vineyard was much more isolated and out of the way, but also so clearly his mother's home; he needed a different escape. When I stopped by, John was making a bowl of pasta, his eyes as big as quarters, like a deer caught in the headlights. He was still shaken. Daryl was there—that wasn't good either; you could feel the tension. I think he knew at this point that their relationship was too broken to fix.

I didn't stay long, and it was the last time I'd see Daryl, even though John had RSVP'd to say that she was coming to my wedding in July. Part of the reason she didn't show was that, in mourning, John needed to be as low-key publicly as possible and did not want to fuel more speculation, even with her, that their relationship was going somewhere. He certainly didn't want to re-create the celebrity spotlight they were under at his cousin Teddy's wedding on Block Island, and he certainly didn't want more questions about when he'd be getting married.

We started planning my bachelor party. It would be on the Cape, which was more our stomping ground than the Vineyard was.

The Thursday before the wedding, we chartered four sports fishing boats for about twenty-five guys and called our party "bachelor blues"— we went blue fishing. A friend who owned a restaurant in Hyannis provided enough beer and sandwiches for everyone, and we stayed out until everybody caught a fish.

The bachelor party was like all bachelor parties, with one exception. The less singular aspects included blacked-out windows so as not to besmirch the restaurant's reputation and party favors that John and our mutual friend Dan Samson had bought in Provincetown, including blow-up dolls and the like. The theme of the evening was "One-Ball Billy" (subtle, my friends), with plastic eggs hanging from the ceiling. There were many embarrassing anecdotes told. Timmy related my life story and seemed to leave out the high points and hit all the lows—I finally wrestled him off the stage. John told stories about our first encounters, including how, when he was thirteen, I got in his face and threatened to beat him up.

"Who knew that twenty years later I would be here sending him to the altar, calling him my best friend?" John laughed. Even my closest friends never realized how close we were. "You're his best friend?" marveled Marty Galligan.

Every time a waitress came to serve dinner, I would ask if she was the entertainment. It became a running joke. In fact—and this is how my bachelor party was unlike most—we had put the kibosh on girls. This was in deference to John, because bachelor-party high jinks were an all-too-obvious possibility for tabloid fare.

"Who cares about him?" I kept asking. "It's my party."

The truth is, John wouldn't have objected, but it was a better party without "entertainment."

The next day some folks tried to play golf, but it was windy and rainy; it was a generally terrible summer, weatherwise. I stayed in my cottage to lick my wounds and get ready for the rehearsal dinner.

The Allen Harbor Yacht Club is a quintessential old Cape Cod clubhouse, right down to the knotty pine and nautical charts and portholes. We gathered there for a long cocktail hour. I spied John in the parking lot, sitting in a car reading something with a bunch of guys; they were rehearsing. I didn't like the looks of that—my family and prospective in-laws might be exposed to some off-color humor. John and I both enjoyed Monty Python; was he working up some sort of skit?

Dinner came off without a hitch. Then John assembled a group that had donned T-shirts emblazoned with the infamous *Life* magazine photo of me screaming at the paparazzi outside his eighteenth-birthday party at 4:00 A.M., bearing the caption BIG BAD BILL. . . .

They turned around. On their backs was a wonderful picture of Kathleen and me having dinner in Palm Beach, and the rest of the caption: . . . IS SWEET WILLIAM NOW! It was a song my mother used to croon to get me to behave when I was a kid. Of course they had to perform it. Music by Ry Cooder, new words by John Kennedy: "In the town of Osterville / Lived a man named Big Bad Bill. . . ." A certain Kathleen got the credit for civilizing me. John brought the house down. Though it was a very pliable crowd.

Later that night, after picking up his groomsman outfit and hanging it next to mine at the cottage, he thought it would be amusing to move my wedding garb to another closet. I had assembled everything he'd require: pants, shirt, and tie. All *he* needed to do was come up with a suitable pair of shoes and a blue blazer. He managed to show up at Holy Trinity Church in West Harwich wearing shoes, but the blazer, part of the uniform of all prep-school men—no. A guest of equal size was requisitioned to give up his blazer for John. The story of his life: always someone there to straighten him out, fill in the blanks.

Timmy, Anthony, and John all had readings; John's was "Desiderata," Max Ehrmann's poem about living peacefully. Not only did it seem appropriate to hear it from him, but I'd selected it, in part, *for* him. With his friends getting married—Anthony's wedding was the next month—and on the heels of his mother's death, John seemed strikingly alone, on what turned out to be one of the nicest days of the summer.

At the reception John was more than cooperative in having his picture taken with my mother-in-law's friends. "Don't worry, Billy," he said. "It's a good vibe. God love ya, I knew ya fatha."

It was a summer of weddings indeed. I was invited to fourteen and made it to eleven (including being in four). John was at many of them. It was so busy that Kathleen was in her best friend's wedding on the Cape as I was in Anthony's wedding on Long Island.

Since John was Anthony's best man, he organized a bachelor party at the Downtown Athletic Club in New York, with an invitation headed "The Few and the Brave." John tormented Anthony by calling him "the prince" all night long in an English accent. Just to prove that marriage hadn't really changed anything, as I drove John and Timmy to wherever the hell we were going next, a riot broke out in my car. It was small and self-contained. John grabbed me, causing me to drive up on a curb. With my right hand, I blocked his next advance, which deflected off his arm and hit him in the face. He looked stunned. Timmy jumped in with, "Hey, you can't hit my cousin."

"Like hell I can't." I gave him a whack. So they both attacked me while I was still attempting to drive. I pulled over and started wrestling both of them on the sidewalk. We must have been some sight. One of them pushed me up against a plate-glass window, and it wobbled like a Wham-O bubble.

We froze, waiting for it to crash.

Finally it stopped vibrating, and we looked at each other like, *Whoa, that was dangerous.* We jumped back into the car and eventually got in way too early, with the sun already blaring in the very white apartment John was theoretically sharing with Daryl on Columbus Circle until his Tribeca loft was renovated. She was long gone, and the place was a mess.

John and I each took a long cold bath, trying to get the dust out of the rafters, then started arguing about having to go to Brooks Brothers to get our pants for the wedding. He insisted that the cream-colored pants from my wedding would do just fine. I told him that there are at least twenty-five different shades of cream.

"So what? Who will know? Besides, I don't want to go to Brooks Brothers—it's too hot. We'll just wear your pants."

"I don't think it's a good idea."

"Billy, trust me on this—everyone will be looking at Carole, not your fat ass."

"That's my point. Since *you're* the best man, *you* show up in a different shade of white and they'll think it's your uniform, or you're being artistic. *I* show up with the wrong shade and they'll all think I couldn't get the Brooks Brothers pants to fit."

I had never been to a Long Island wedding before, especially wearing the wrong shade of pants. The tent was set up as an Italian piazza, down to the faux marble floors. We danced and had a blast.

"A dreamboat adrift?" That was the moony question in *People* over John's continuing bachelorhood. The real answer was, not at all. John was remaining low-key and respectful to Jackie's memory during his mourning, which left a void in the tabloids. Time for the Face-lift Factor, wherein the media would make something up.

But John was far from idle. While the rest of us were getting hitched, he was launching a seminal project.

GEORGE MAGAZINE STARTED, in a sense, with Grandfather Joe Kennedy. The Kennedy family had promoted itself through the Henry Luce media machine from the time John's grandfather was sent by Franklin Roosevelt to Great Britain as American ambassador, before World War II. The toothy Kennedys did photograph well, and the outdoor family sports of sailing and touch football—and seeming to have so much fun just gathering together in Hyannisport—made for great photo ops, long before the term was coined. In a lot of ways, they deliberately exposed them-

selves to the attention that eventually became exploitative and overwhelming.

John had been in the news since before he was born. During his ac-
ceptance speech at the National Armory in Hyannis in 1960, Jack Kennedy's final words were, "Now we are prepared for a new administration
and a new baby." John was the only child ever born to a president-elect.

Jackie, of course, disliked the attention her family got. Once, when
asked what she was going to feed a new dog, she sent a one-word reply to
the press corps in the back of the plane: "Reporters." Jackie's relationship
with the press, though, was complicated, going back to her days as a society-
page photographer in Washington who did a *Life* magazine layout on
Senator Kennedy when they were engaged. Of course she understood
how powerful her image was in perpetuating the Kennedy political fortunes; she also ignored the press when it suited her. Though that wasn't
really possible, not with the cottage industry tabloid journalism became
over the last two decades of her life.

John's own relationship with the press was complex, too. How the media portrayed him was, inevitably, part of John's sense of himself from the
beginning. He also had endured, his whole life, accusations about his father's affairs. He suffered through the reenactment of his father's death
brought on by congressional investigations and conspiracy theorists, including the movie *JFK*. The "presentation" of the Kennedys was an ongoing tension between the family and the media; I remember visiting John on
the Vineyard in 1988 when the twenty-fifth anniversary of his father's death
was coming up. The networks were trying to involve the family in how to
present it. Caroline's husband, Ed Schlossberg, told John that one network
wanted to rerun the entire assassination coverage over the weekend, just as
it had dominated the airwaves in 1963. John didn't like that idea. He also
didn't like the fact that Ed was the go-between, and he stormed outside to
cool off. His annoyance was some combination of dreading the anniversary
itself, the press's eagerness to capitalize, and, it seemed to me, his sense that
Ed was trivializing the whole thing into a strategy.

He was outside banging a tennis ball against the side of the house as
if to beckon me for a game of wall ball. "What I don't understand," John
said, "is what the fuck this has to do with Ed. It's my father, after all."

John had a grasp of his father's personal side from his mother. But how
did he think, how did he make his choices? John's life and legacy were tied
directly to his father, by name and DNA. Yet he had to invent that relationship, to make it real for himself, and discard the "prince of Camelot" myth.

For at least a decade now, since he was at Brown, John had been
studying his father's career by reading his papers and books, by reading
biographies and history, by trying to wrap his hands around the ideas of
leadership, power, politics, and what it meant to be a Kennedy. In John's
view, that pressure didn't come from what he felt his *father* expected. "All
these people have expectations of me because of my father," John once
told me, "but I believe *he* would have wanted me to do whatever the hell
I wanted." (One time when we were kids, we ventured into his father's
bedroom, next to his mother's, in the Hyannisport house. It had not been
changed since the President had last used it. There were golf caps in the
closet, an old doctor's-office scale in the bathroom, framed hand-painted
birthday cards from Jackie to Jack, bookcases full of books and photographs, faded now by sun and time. There was also an old seaman's chest
there. John opened it: In the President's distinctive scrawl, on yellow legal
pads, were his notes, perhaps for speeches, and what appeared to be official documents. John had never seen them before and quickly shut the
chest, as if he had opened Pandora's box.)

John was becoming knowledgeable about power and leadership on a
personal level—that is, how a leader conducts his life and what the inher-
ent pitfalls are, when privilege and power collide with vast responsibility.

It was a tension that intrigued me, too. "It's all about booze and
broads," I said to him once. We were trying to figure out where it tended
to go wrong, how the ugly side of power generally manifested.

"That's it, isn't it?" he said. "Women and alcohol."

"They're not the problems themselves so much as the trigger, where
men get exposed. Corruption is simply the love of money and power over

concern for people. And womanizing is about power—the feminists have got that right."

"So that means to be powerful is to be evil? And to be honorable means you're a wimp?"

"Well, the meek shall inherit the earth."

"I'm serious, Billy."

"If you're truthful, there's freedom in that, and if you're honest, and you try your best, who can find fault with you? One might not make it in politics or the business world, but there are honest politicians and ethical businessmen. Maybe the idea is to find them and find out what makes them tick."

So much was percolating in John: his keen interest in politics, his family remaining under the microscope, and how they were mistreated by the press. (John used to call it "the Teddy factor": The press would build you up, build you up, get you to a lofty and comfortable plateau, and then, for their amusement and to sell copy, pull the rug out from under you.) The press was playing John, too, of course, with the "Sexiest Man Alive" nonsense. John also was bothered by the insular nature of politics and the media, how anything resembling the true nature of the way Washington worked didn't really reach much of America. More and more people—especially people our age—were tuned out to politics; we were tending to see it as boring or a dirty business (or both). Yet John understood that if politics wasn't presented in the usual way, as wonky agenda talk or as a scandal, but as a cultural phenomenon, as a cast of characters in heavy pursuit of something (sometimes with high ideals, sometimes not), then the perception of politics itself might change. The political world of Washington, he wanted to point out, was not just important, it was also interesting and fun.

After a few fits and starts with his colleague Michael Berman, the idea of a political magazine came to life. John's decision to launch *George* was a surprise to a lot of people, including Kennedyphiles, as he called them. That was one of the reasons he did it—not to annoy anyone per se but to stake out a territory that was truly his own.

I think the heart of the idea goes to John himself. He thought you could argue with people all day, disagree on every subject, disapprove of their lifestyles, and still enjoy their company. He saw politics at its best as people honoring their beliefs and pursuing their callings, meaning that fights were a natural part of the process. The press had lost the ability, he felt, to communicate the real essence of politics: the importance (and fun) in the fight over ideas, policy, initiatives—the *pursuit*. Too often the press seemed to present merely the fight, to flatten the calling of politics, and to batter the players into fools. We were the post-Watergate generation.

He knew, of course, that his goal was lofty, that changing the way the press presented politics was, as he half joked, "like turning around an aircraft carrier. It takes some time to slow down, then execute the maneuver, face in an opposite direction, and get up to cruising speed again. It could take a generation." But it was his generation he was trying to save. The point of *George* was to bring politics to those who had never spent any time paying attention to it.

Moreover, the ruckus *George* created suited John perfectly. He was always counterintuitive; John liked to dust up a situation by doing something completely contrary. He'd tell a dirty joke, take an extreme viewpoint during a discussion, defend the most radical of positions, poised between pushing the envelope and being obscene. That's why he brought Larry Flynt to the White House Correspondents' Association Dinner. Flynt was, of course, a pornographer, one who had challenged obscenity laws up to the Supreme Court; he had published nude photos of John's mother sunbathing in Greece. John's justification was that Flynt had just brought down a Republican Speaker of the House before he was ever sworn in, for sexual misconduct, which was Flynt's response to how the Republican Congress had chased President Clinton over Monica Lewinsky; John was juiced by Flynt's unrelenting idea of fair play and sticking to his own idiosyncratic ideals. For similar reasons John interviewed, and deeply admired, the Reverend Billy Graham, a man, he believed, of real and unflappable faith.

John would stir the pot again by putting Drew Barrymore on the cover of his magazine decked out like Marilyn Monroe with the headline HAPPY

BIRTHDAY, MR. PRESIDENT, which tweaked the absurdity of our—and th^ mainstream press's—addiction to alleged scandal. "If it doesn't offend me," John said, "why should it offend anyone else?" He defended his cousins in an editorial note as "poster boys for bad behavior." It was widely interpreted as being critical of his family, and his family took the bait.

John's cousin Congressman Joe Kennedy publicly quipped, "Ask not what you can do for your cousin, ask what you can do for your cousin's magazine."

John called him. "That's a great quote, Joe. What idiot on your staff came up with that line, or did you do it all on your own?" John couldn't believe that his family would turn on him when he was actually support- ing them, when it was clear that "poster boys for bad behavior" was the label put on some Kennedys, not his indictment of them. "But if they're too stupid to get the point," John told me, "who needs them?"

The Kennedy clan, in fact, seemed to be at loose ends—the fallout of divorces, scandals, infighting. Teddy tried to have a family football game as a photo op to show family unity, but someone twisted his knee and had to go to the hospital.

"It's just not working," John confided. He meant the smiling- Kennedys thing. John was happy staking out his own territory and cava- lier enough toward his family to walk right through the RFK yard to the beach without giving a damn. He complained about how Ethel had taken over the garage to his house decades before as quarters for hired help. Now that there was less help, he wanted the garage back, but she appar- ently threw a hissy fit. John just laughed and forgot it.

But he could be tough. John once had his Hyannisport house occu- pied by a friend who was trying to get sober. This friend wouldn't give the RFKs free rein over John's property. Furthermore, he had a nasty dog that looked like a pit bull; it attacked everything and everybody and did seri- ous damage to one of Ethel's dogs. When John was called about that, he told them they should have kept their dog off his property—not to create animosity but because he knew it would help his recovering friend to have the responsibility of running the house.

And now John, carving out new territory for himself both within his
family and professionally, was about to change his personal life as well.

When I'd come back from my honeymoon in July, *People* magazine
had exposed Carolyn Bessette's shapely and properly thonged derriere as
John steered his ski boat with the registration number MS 109 PT. Skip-
pering his own destiny. *Christ*, I thought, *I can't leave him alone for a week before he gets himself in trouble.*

It would be a few months before he'd admit that anything was up in
that direction.

12

The Girl in the Thong

ONE OF OUR ANNUAL RITUALS was getting together for Presidents' Day weekend, usually to go skiing. The following February we decided to go to Hyannisport, since it was a snowy winter and we'd be able to cross-country-ski on the golf course next to the Shrivers'. John chose to stay at his house on his own.

On Friday evening we gathered at the Shrivers' table for dinner. Timmy was just back from a tour of the Galápagos Islands after a Special Olympics event. John asked Timmy what it was like to experience evolution firsthand, a jab at Timmy's intense religious convictions.

On Saturday afternoon Timmy and I drove past John's house on our way to Dunfey's for a workout. We spied a limousine idling in front— John hadn't answered his phone when we'd called earlier; maybe he was conducting some business.

Later, when we were returning from the workout, the limo was gone. Curious. I decided to stop by, alone, to see exactly what was up.

First John made some noise about my weight. He said he was afraid I'd die at forty and leave everybody sad.

"John, I just came from working out—we called to see if you wanted to join us, but you didn't answer."

Silence.

"Listen, what's with the limo in your driveway?"

"I had a friend come in."

"Who?"

"You don't need to know that."

"Daryl?"

"No."

"Was it the one with the thong?"

He gave me a look, his lips pursed. "You're a pain in the ass, Billy. Yeah, she's kinda my girlfriend now. She comes up on weekends."

Later, when I thought about it, I realized John needed some privacy—to protect both himself and Carolyn—from the media. It was part of keeping his life under wraps in the aftermath of his mother's death. Even, for now, from friends.

But about a month later, he gave me a call—he wanted Kathleen and me to spend the weekend with him in Hyannisport, and to meet Carolyn.

It was a Saturday night when we got there. They were in the kitchen making dinner. They'd flown in that afternoon, and Carolyn looked like a waif. She had long, straight blond hair like corn silk, she had flip-flops on—it was March—and she was wearing pajama pants and one of his shirts. So they'd come in and had at it upstairs and then come down to make dinner.

She seemed a little pissed off about having to make food, because she would rather have gone out to dinner. John wanted a love weekend on the Cape. I took a good long look at her head to toe, and when I got to the feet, I suddenly noticed her toenails. They were alternating black and white. I asked Kathleen about that. She said, "It's all the rage in the fashion magazines." So I looked closer and checked them out, and—it's not like I've got a fetish or anything, but I was thinking, *Jesus, look at her toes. They're as long as fingers.* I stared at them, and all I could think of were Egyptian statues, where the man has one foot in front of the woman, and that shows that he's the man, and everything is sort of elongated. I was thinking, *She's like a statue.* Perfectly formed.

She was so waifish, and she smiled—not because I was checking her out. She was just being friendly. And she had a perfect set of teeth. Not capped teeth, not filed teeth. Perfect teeth. Now I was watching her make the food, and I was looking at her hands.

Despite all this apparent evidence to the contrary, I'm not especially stuck on beauty. My wife is a beautiful Irish colleen, and that's nice but not the point. And it wasn't really with Carolyn either, once we got to know her. But I was just meeting her. I was watching her work with her hands, and the fingers were like her toes, impossibly long and shapely, with perfect nails. Everything about her was physically impeccable—and this was Carolyn straight from bed. She was magnificent. That was my word for her. *Magnificent.*

We had dinner in the living room, with a fire going, and I asked them how they had met. Later, of course, there would be all sorts of speculation about that in the media. Carolyn told me that a mutual friend had introduced them. It was a guy named Billy Way, a friend of John's from Brown.

That's who introduced John to Carolyn, and now I had a little fun with it: Billy Way was close to a guy named Bobby Potter, whose sister is Linda Potter, who happens to be Timmy Shriver's wife. Since Timmy had not yet met Carolyn, when she and Kathleen left the room with the dishes, I began to tease John. "Wait until I tell Timmy that you couldn't get your own chick and that Billy Way had to give you one of his throwaways."

"Fuck you, Billy."

"Oh, this is going to be rich."

Our typical fooling around—and the thing is, right from the get-go I felt that comfortable with Carolyn, too. She fit right in. She told me, "You know, this is not my first time up here at this house."

"Yeah," I said to her, "the last time you came by limousine, didn't you?"

John looked at me like, *Billy, you asshole.*

But she was game. "Oh, that's good, Billy. Actually, I flew. The limousine was from the airport."

And she was checking me out, sort of getting into my kitchen a little. "You know about that going on, huh, BillyNoonan?" That she'd been up here a few times already. "I've heard a lot about you, BillyNoonan"—she said my name like that, first and last, like it was one name—"and you're pretty quick. You really are quite a character, aren't you, BillyNoonan?" It was strange—that was how Jackie always referred to me too, her whispery voice running my names together.

This just might work out, I thought.

"I like coming to this house," Carolyn said. "I went down to Palm Beach with John"—to his old family house—"and the place was creepy. There were too many ghosts down there."

I knew what she meant. The house in Palm Beach was like the hotel from *The Shining*—it felt like New Year's Day 1959, as if time had stopped. It had a lot of pictures of the Kennedys as a family in Palm Beach, as young kids at the pool, and playing touch football. Right up until Jack was president—and then nothing. It was a white elephant, a sad old home. And when she said that, I knew she was looking at being with John for herself, in the right way. She had a vulnerability—she wasn't comfortable in that house in Palm Beach, and she didn't want to be there. And she wasn't a Kennedyphile. God knows there are loads of Kennedyphile women. She knew what she was getting into, and she was going to speak her mind.

"I like this house," she told us. "This house has got a nice vibe to it, BillyNoonan."

I GOT A CALL from John right before Christmas—our year-end call, I assumed, or Christmas wishes. Instead he said he was driving to Boston to hear Teddy perform a Christmas reading at Boston Symphony Hall and then heading down to Connecticut to spend the holidays with Carolyn's parents.

"Getting kind of serious?"

"Yeah, I'm pumped. I got a new apartment, a new magazine, a new chick who I am really digging—all in all, it's been a pretty good year. We're thinking about stopping by to see you guys on our way back."

"That would be good. We're actually having a party, so we'll be up late. Come by whenever you can."

About eight I got a phone call. "Billy, we're stuck on the turnpike and we're never going to get to Symphony Hall in time."

What a shock: Friday night before Christmas and there were cars on the road?

"Can we just come over now?"

Next thing I knew, the front door flew open and John's dog, Friday, bounded in and jumped up on the couch, scaring half our party. John presented me with a *George* T-shirt: "It's an extra-large, and it better fit!"

I told him that Kathleen could use it. She was having a baby that summer, which was the point of the party, to announce the news to our friends and neighbors.

My neighbors . . . they were a little confused as these interlopers joined us in singing Christmas carols. "That guy looks a lot like John Kennedy."

13

A Secret Unfolds

IN AUGUST 1996, a month after our son TJ was born, John and Carolyn invited us to Hyannisport for a weekend. Carolyn spent most of her time working feverishly on a publicity project for Calvin Klein—or so I thought. Contained in a three-ring binder, it was cataloged and tabbed, like something she was coordinating, maybe a fashion show. She had a label maker and was busy making labels for everything. I was curious, having never seen such a contraption; she showed me how it worked and made a label for one of our son TJ's infant seats.

I didn't ask what she was up to, though. That was once a risky question in this house—privacy was imperative. I remember one morning, back in the late seventies, when I was staying there with John, I made the mistake of asking Jackie what she was working on, out on the patio most mornings after breakfast. She didn't mind the question. Au contraire— she suddenly had an interested friend. She explained that this was a work project she was particularly excited about, translating some old Russian fairy tales; she told me they'd been lost for something like a century, and now she was translating them from French to English. Then she asked me if I'd be interested in hearing some of them. Thankfully, John came down then, ready, as always, to eat. I joined him for a second breakfast. John jok-

ingly instructed me that before asking such questions of Jackie, I should
check with him first, as my questions might lead somewhere I probably
shouldn't probe or, just as bad, yield agonizingly tiresome answers. Jackie
had gone back to work, zeroing in on those fables out on the patio as if
they were some sort of Rubik's Cube. John and I escaped into our day.

But this late-summer weekend, I should have picked up that something was different. John had called me earlier that week.

"Hello, how are you? How's the lovely Kathleen?"

"Hey, John-John."

"Oh, don't start that shit with me"—the name he hated.

"All right, John. How's the magazine business, John?"

"Listen, Billy"—suddenly all serious, which was very unlike John unless something was up—"are you guys coming down to the Cape this
weekend? Can you stay with us?"

"John, I have an infant."

"No problem, there's still a crib set up in Mummy's room from when
Caroline's kids were small."

"Let me check with Kathleen."

Something was up. Including TJ, it would be just the five of us.

Usually John and I took care of a lot of chores when we all first
arrived—Carolyn and John from New York, Kathleen and me from
Boston—including checking on the boats, the cars, purchasing the beer and
wine. We'd note who was in town as we did the errands, sometimes stop
somewhere for a drink. John got a fairly wide berth in Hyannisport, at least
compared to almost everywhere else. I was still pretty well known down
here. We'd walk in someplace—"Hey, Billy." And I'd say to John, "You remember Barney Baxter." They'd say hello, Barney might tell him that he'd
seen him on television and he looked great, then we'd grab a little table,
and that was that. We could hang out, have a beer, they'd leave John alone.

Or John would go off with his cousins or sailing with Teddy. I had
fishing friends and family that Kathleen and I visited. We'd all reconvene
in the late afternoon for a swim. There'd be a game of Frisbee, a late er-
rand, maybe a cup of tea. John had really taken over. His specialty, now

that the house was his, was inviting a few friends for a weekend, where late dinners were a feast of both food and conversation; John loved to debate politics, history, what was going on in the world. He liked the theater of it. Once he came down to dinner dressed in Masai warrior attire. Why not? Just for the fun of it, a new way of addressing the table and to get things rolling.

The RFK house was way too chaotic for me, with all these people, dogs barking, and Ethel carrying on and firing cooks in the middle of dinner. Jackie would have never allowed that. She had plenty of guests, but there would always be candles at dinner. It was sociable yet reserved. You'd drink out of these amazingly enormous goblets—one was for water, one for wine. They held about twenty ounces; you would get a full glass of water but just a puddle of wine, as it would take a whole bottle to fill one of the glasses. The crystal was really fine, paper thin; John still used them, and sometimes they would break. But there were dozens of them, and John's attitude was that the house should be used, it should be lived in. John and I had a credo regarding things like wine goblets and other family possessions. Being Irish, our ancestors had come over to America, worked as domestics, and served meals on fine china. The next generation would save to purchase the item as a sign of prosperity, but never use it, just possess it. But John and I felt that it should be used; what good was it if not utilized? It had a purpose, after all, and if it broke, so what? We enjoyed it. The house wasn't a museum, even though it hadn't changed much since the President had died. When Jackie started over at the Vineyard, she didn't take one thing from this house. It was still the way she decorated it when the President was alive—filled with beautiful antiques, but very comfortable. There was never a problem putting a glass on the old coffee tables—that's how it remained, preserved in time. It was a charming Cape Cod cottage.

At our dinners as adults, John and I would really go at it, get into these knock-down, drag-out arguments. But it was just sport. We got a little more spirited if other people were there, just to see how they'd react and if they'd weigh in, too. But not this weekend. This weekend was just the five of us.

I was in and out on Saturday, but Carolyn seemed to be spending most of her time consumed by her three-ring binder, and she kept running upstairs to talk on the phone. There were phones everywhere, a holdover from the presidential days. They connected to the other houses in the compound. The list of exchanges was still there, in the pantry: Ambassador Kennedy's Living Room, 76—some number like that. Mrs. Joseph P. Kennedy's Bedroom. The Attorney General's House. The Attorney General's Bedroom. And then names of local places were added at the bottom: Baxter's Fish House, Mildred's Chowder House. There was another list, next to that one, of Onassis telephone numbers: New York Apartment. Paris Apartment. Athens Apartment. Skorpios. Olympia Airlines. The *Christina*. On and on, with secretaries' names and so forth, two eras side by side.

Everything changed on the Cape after Labor Day. John used to say that Labor Day dropped like a curtain. This was a beautiful summer Saturday, still warm, yet now, late in the afternoon, the light was beginning to get softer. John had gone off waterskiing that afternoon; I went fishing. Kathleen stayed behind with TJ. And now we reconvened on the brick patio on chaise lounges. There was a table with an umbrella where Carolyn was set up, still working away on that notebook, whatever the hell it was, and Kathleen had the baby out there. I'd just returned from a swim, to get the fish stink off me, when John got back from his day.

"What do you want to do about tonight?" he asked. "There's a cocktail party over at the Shrivers'. Do you want to go to that?"

"If Timmy's not going to be there, I don't really feel like going," I said.

"I feel the same way," John said. "But Teddy wants me to go over to his house. He's got some senator over there he wants me to meet."

"Well, do you want to do that?"

"No, I don't want to do that. But I probably should."

"I just want to stay here," I said. "I don't want to abandon Kathleen and the baby."

Before going up to take a shower, John got after Provi to make her famous daiquiris. She and John had this wonderful back-and-forth. Oh, she'd
get on his case. "Yahn, you get down here for breakfast! It's getting cold!"

Down he'd come, yawning and scratching, the original dark-haired
fair-haired boy.

He called her out to the patio—"Provi!"—pretending he was pissed.

"What? What is it now?"

"What do you think, Provi? Are we going to have some daiquiris?"
Pause. "Please?"

These daiquiris were long associated with this house. The President
loved them. Once Judy Garland had a few too many and had trouble
navigating a step heading inside from the porch. "I'll make them if Billy
Noonan got the Bacardi"—which Provi pronounced Bah-ka-DEE.

"Yes, Provi, I got Bacardi."

"Last time you bought the wrong kind of rum. It has to be white
rum. The other stuff's no good. Okay, I'll do that now. Okay. I got the
limes going. Squeezing the limes takes some time, you know? It's a lot of
work."

She disappeared. We heard the *whirrrrrr* of the blender. John gave her
a minute. "Those things ready yet?"

"You just quiet down out there!" Provi yelled. "I'm making the syrup
right now. I tell you, I won't make this thing, you keep bothering me."

When John finally went up to shower, I couldn't resist a visit to the
kitchen. "Aren't they ready yet, Provi?"

"Don't start with me! That's what I need, Billy Noonan on my case.
You guys drive me crazy!"

And then she came out and sat with us for a minute. Where the hell
were the daiquiris?

"They have to be in the glasses. The glasses have to be frosted." So we
waited while the glasses—Waterford goblets with the Kennedy crest, inscribed "John-John and Caroline," a remnant from a family trip to Ireland—
chilled on ice. "You can only do these things right once. You get it right
once and that's it."

John came back down. "What, no daiquiris yet?"

Provi went flying inside, muttering now in Spanish. And then back she came. Silent. A tray of drinks, the world's greatest daiquiris. They were as magical as always. With the sun going down, they were the perfect thirst quencher for enjoying the remnants of a lovely Cape Cod day.

John asked Kathleen and me what our plans were for the coming autumn and if we would be coming to the Cape. Simple conversation— John and Carolyn were really enjoying the house and the privacy of the compound, which felt even more secluded in the off season. They wanted to know if we would be hanging out with them. Sure—Kathleen and I loved autumn weekends on the Cape. We drank. Kathleen went in to put TJ to bed, Carolyn took her big notebook inside. John and I were silent. Provi poked her head out. "You need anything?"

"No, Provi, thanks. The daiquiris are great."

"Of course they are. What d'ya think?"

When the women returned—the sun was setting now—John asked us what we were doing next month on the weekend of September 21.

Kathleen and I thought for a moment, and then I remembered that I had some event down here on the Cape.

This was the right answer, because John was about to instigate trouble. He got this prankster-let-loose look in the shadowy light and said, "Well then, you have a problem."

I looked at Carolyn—she looked back at me with her chin tucked in and that smile, those perfect white teeth. And an "I've got your number, BillyNoonan" smile.

Kathleen and I realized it simultaneously—there was going to be a wedding!

It was both a shock and not surprising at all. It immediately felt like . . . well, of course. They'd been living together. They were clearly head over heels for each other. Kathleen and I had speculated privately, but until it happens . . .

Though it did seem like an odd way to tell us; it suddenly seemed as if the whole weekend had been leading up to this moment. As if it was all somehow orchestrated. So *that* was what Carolyn's notebook and her phone calls were about. She was working on arrangements, getting her people to hold that weekend.

With most of my friends, I had gotten used to *this* version of the announcement, a phone call:

"Hey, Billy, I did something stupid last night."

"Yeah, what was that?"

"Got engaged."

"Ah, good for you. Meet you in the pub this afternoon, we'll hoist one. Give her a hug and a kiss from me."

Instead, here we were hoisting daiquiris from Irish crystal. Of course it was orchestrated—this was John getting married. It was John F. Kennedy, Jr., getting married. And even as we interrogated them with all the obvious questions—"When did you decide?" "How did he do it?" "You're getting married in a *month*?"—it hit me how everything would be different for him, that his life was about to change dramatically.

As it all began to register, John suddenly held up a hand and stifled our raised voices: "Listen, you guys, this is a huge secret. Only about fifteen people know. You can't say anything to anyone."

"Well, we can ask *you*, can't we?" I said. "How long have you been engaged?"

For the moment they laughed me off. As the logistics began to surface—a small wedding, forty guests, somewhere far away—John and I looked at each other: His face was both impish and dead serious, if that's possible. There was a lot to talk about. We signaled each other—just a nod, really—and left the women to discuss the bride angle. John and I went up to the widow's walk on top of the house. It was our retreat, a place to smoke a cigarette and talk out of earshot. We'd been escaping up there forever—to light up a joint when we were kids, since it was the one place on the compound where you certainly wouldn't get caught—but mostly just to get some peace, to check out Nantucket Sound, to be together. It was where Jackie used to sunbathe. Though in many ways John was a reserved guy, a keep-your-feelings-to-yourself guy, he wanted to talk. The sun had set now.

I knew that this was monumental, but at first, up there, looking out over the compound, our old stomping ground, I still didn't quite get it. I kept asking him the questions—"When did you decide?" He'd given her a ring at Christmas. "Christmas! And you're just telling me now? Why didn't you tell me?"—the way you'd pepper a friend, any friend. He blew smoke rings; John generally smoked a cigarette or two a day, primarily, I think, to blow rings. I kept asking about details: How? Where? Who were the other members of the apparently short list? I would mention a friend's name, and John would say, "Nope, not going to make the cut. It's a *small* wedding." I would ask about an obvious friend—Timmy Shriver, say—and he would say yes, that person would be invited but hadn't been asked yet. "No one knows," John kept telling me—which was almost literally true.

"John, the wedding's a month away. How can no one . . . ?"

I kept focusing on the logistics and who was invited. But John wanted to talk about Carolyn.

"Yeah, well, we all love Carolyn, she's perfect for you. What about . . . ?"

He waited for me to catch up to his mood, to see that he really needed to talk. Finally I shut up and started to listen. I was there for a reason.

I'd become even closer to John—and at this point we'd been friends for more than twenty years—after his mother died. In fact, the conversation we had at his mother's wake, about how it was his time to move on with his life, had touched a nerve with him and made our bond even deeper.

"I wanted to acknowledge that now, Billy," he told me.

And then I understood. He'd made this decision alone. He had to. That was exactly what we'd talked about, at Jackie's wake: It was now his time to step up, to become fully himself. Her death, as sad as it was, offered that possibility. Obviously this decision was a big part of it.

Up on the widow's walk, overlooking the Kennedy compound, John pushed his hair back across his head as if he were trying to make a duck's ass or massaging the stress out of his head. "What we talked about, that really resonated with me, Billy," he told me, "when I was thinking this through."

John pushed his hair forward, spiking it. "I understand her. I completely . . . I really feel"—his voice went high, almost a falsetto, with the emotion he felt for Carolyn, and he squinted toward the water—"I just completely dig her."

I laughed. "Obviously."

We smoked and looked out at the Hyannisport break wall; at the end of it, there's a light, both a warning and a beckoning. The big question hung in the air: "Do you think she's the right one?"

There were two sides to it. It was obvious they were deeply in love. Kathleen and I had gotten close to Carolyn immediately—she had a way, with women, of boring right in, of touching and staying close and needing to know how things were, with TJ, with me, with everything. She had a way of getting rid of the men—"You boys go get the stuff for dinner. We're going to talk girl talk and have a drink." And of teasing me. And she seemed right for John (as John and Timmy had pointed out that Kathleen was right for me), partly because she wasn't going to put up with any crap from him.

I flashed back to Daryl Hannah—and how far he'd come. This was different, this was calm, and it felt right. Carolyn was defining John and illuminating the house, and both needed her.

The other part was that marrying John entailed a lot more than marriage itself. Was Carolyn the right woman to become Mrs. John F. Kennedy, Jr.? Was she up for all the attention that would come along with being his wife? Could she handle all the pressure of being a Kennedy?

I thought so, and I told him that. Carolyn was street-smart—she'd negotiated her way just fine around the fashion industry, and that is a tough world. She was the kind of girl, I told him, who could handle it.

John blew a smoke ring straight up, as if to say, *Okay, that's a good answer.*

But I wanted him to hear something that I thought was important. I started this way—and now I sound, to myself, like a weary pilgrim: "In my experience it's not just the decision to get married but *being* married that matters. It's not the people who make the institution sacred but that the institution itself is sacred, and it's important that the person being considered is capable of keeping it sacred."

He smoked.

"Anyone, of course, can get married—drunken strangers are getting married in tacky chapels in Las Vegas at this moment. *Being* married is a different story. It's a long-term thing. It's a commitment. The alternative isn't merely the splitting up of assets but a dividing of *yourself.*"

I went on like that; I was giving him a lecture, partly because John had always had this quality of throwing up a wall, of literally putting his head down and walking away, when he didn't want to deal with something. So I suppose I was, in a way, testing him, to make sure he'd really thought this through.

"If a marriage doesn't work," I told him, "there is danger done to the soul and the far-reaching erosion of confidence in marriage and family in general."

A wry smile had started to form on that impish face.

"That's exactly what I'm talking about, Billy." Leaning against the railing on the widow's walk, he turned and looked across the compound, to the RFK house. "It can't be like that." His cousins were having a tough time staying married.

"This has to be different," John said. "It has to work. You know, Carolyn looks at marriage like a man does, that it's not necessarily a lifetime thing, because of the way her mother got burned. It's made her cynical about marriage. Carolyn's father left her mother with three little kids.

"But this can't be like that, Billy," he said again. That's why Carolyn and John had lived together in New York—they wanted to see how it would go and how New York would react to *them*. He reminded me of the fight they'd had in Central Park, where she took the engagement ring off (I now learned) and he sat on a curb and sobbed, an ugly skirmish that hit the papers. "*That* can't happen again."

The First Family's legacy was important to him. Even the whole Camelot myth was important to him on one level: He would safeguard his parents' reputation. That reputation was especially powerful in the world where we grew up and were gazing out over now.

Good Lord, what a load. But I understood and agreed. It had to work. There was no way this marriage could fail. His legacy—John's sense, now, of what the legacy had to be—couldn't stand for it. "You know," he said, "I *really* had to think about this. I could take my life in a lot of different ways. I had to think about the consequences of getting married. How we were going to get married. How we were going to live. What was going to happen after we got married."

All very important considerations. They could have just continued living together in New York, at least for a while. But John wanted to shift gears, so he gave her the ring at Christmas. There was no dramatic moment, but the ring affirmed their future. Carolyn told him that she would think about it—not whether she'd say yes, because at this point they both knew they wanted to be together. But she'd think about when they should get married, and how. Would they live like Caroline and Ed, walled off, raise their family in private? Or like Charles and Diana, the most famous couple on the globe? Big public ceremony or small? Elope? Live in Europe?

These are not the kinds of questions that keep you and me up at night.

But don't misread the mood, the two of us up in our old tree fort, Nantucket Sound washing below. John was getting married, to a wonderful girl! I was excited for him. It was a big step, the most important decision, I believe, anyone will make.

Ultimately he was wrong about Carolyn. I was, too. I'm not blaming her. She did not come into the marriage as damaged goods. I'm not blaming John either. The pressures of the marriage were too much for her. He thought with all his great heart that he had the right woman. Maybe there was no such animal. Maybe he needed a stone-cold bitch-priestess who could take it all on—what was put on them, on her, as a Kennedy newlywed, the perceived heiress to Camelot, the next Jackie, the mother of JFK III.

But at the moment the decision was both considered and dramatic. And it was time for us to go downstairs.

WE WENT DOWN to see what Carolyn and Kathleen were up to and what Provi was making for dinner. I thought, *How are we going to get through the night without slipping up in front of Provi?* She had a sixth sense about matters of the heart. As it turned out, John had wisely bought two tickets to a nearby concert for Provi and a friend, so it was only the four of us at dinner.

When we asked where the wedding was to be held, John said, "You don't need to know. You'll know when you get there."

Oh? "So . . . if we don't know where we're going, how will we get there? Where will we stay when we don't even know where we're going?"

John, of course, loved this stuff—intrigue, an adventure, playing the Wizard of Oz, orchestrating trouble. "Don't worry about it," he said, as if he had it all figured out. Sure he did. John was the world's worst traveler. For starters, he was always losing his keys and his wallet. He was simply a mess on that level. He was always losing *everything*—Carolyn complained how long it took them just to get out of their goddamn loft into the day, because John couldn't find anything. That's why he had a Post-it note on his apartment door that read: "Bonehead, don't forget keys and wallet." He was great on the big stuff and terrible—and I mean terrible—on the little stuff. And since Kathleen and I might have to bring TJ, I was nervous about knowing nothing.

Attempting to be coy, I asked what kind of clothes we should bring. Not falling for it, John the editor deferred to Carolyn. "Think about panama hats, ceiling fans, no air conditioners, iced tea on the veranda," she said.

Oh. That certainly cleared it up.

Kathleen and I kept guessing as if it were a parlor game like Twenty

Questions, eliminating and excluding geographical possibilities. It wasn't the Caribbean. It wasn't Brazil. It wasn't, in fact, South America. It wasn't Africa. It wasn't—

"Okay, if we have to bring TJ, will I need to get him a passport?"

"No."

A big hint. The United States. Somewhere warm. Still trying to get my mind around the whole idea that they were getting married and how they were going to pull it off with unbending secrecy, I kept at them. They could trust us—at least to the extent of revealing that it was going to happen—but why hadn't he told, say, Timmy Shriver? "He's your closest cousin and one of your best friends, John."

"Timmy can't keep a secret!" John yelled in a high-pitched voice. "Those Shrivers can't keep a secret—if one finds out, the whole world would know!" He also loved keeping Timmy in the dark. But this wasn't about the tabloids. He respected the Shrivers—especially Timmy's mother, Eunice—and he didn't want to hurt anyone's feelings. But there *were* going to be hurt feelings, because the wedding was going to be so small.

I asked, as delicately as I could, which is not very delicately, "But how the hell are you going to pull this thing off with such a large family?"

John had it all figured out. "I decided to invite one member from each of my father's family. Teddy will serve as the patriarch, and that takes care of his brood. Timmy will represent the Shrivers. Bobby Kennedy, Jr., will represent the Robert Kennedys"—as I say, a good planner, absolutely horrible in the details. And I could hear echoes of Jackie in that: making sure each family was represented. Hell, it was very Kennedy as well. That's how it is when you have a hundred cousins.

John had grown close to Bobby Kennedy in recent years, in large part, I think, because Bobby, who'd had a heroin addiction, had overcome so much. And I'd been there myself, immersed in my own version of late-adolescent trouble. John hadn't struggled in that way—with drugs or alcohol—but he understood hanging in there. He understood coming back.

Anyway, Sydney Lawford and her fun husband, Peter McKelvey, were

coming. She and Caroline were close, and Sydney would be a natural re-
source for her in what would be a pretty charged atmosphere. William
Smith had been a classmate of John's at prep school in New York, so he
would be there. They were the sort of decisions everyone makes, though
when John was excluding somebody, that somebody might be a congressman. Anthony Radziwill was the best man, and that took care of his
mother's side of the family.

AFTER THAT WEEKEND, when John and Carolyn broke the news,
Kathleen and I had doubts about whether we'd be able to go to the wedding. TJ would be only two months old. We were going somewhere that
might be away from doctors and hospitals if anything went wrong. We
slyly asked his godparents, my brother John and his wife, Jeanne, to look
after him so we could have a weekend away. Jeanne, daughter and sister of
medical doctors, mother of three grown children, was concerned about
TJ's age and didn't feel comfortable. Perfectly understandable. We didn't
either.

I called John for more details. Reluctantly, finally, he told me we were
going off the coast of Georgia to some obscure island, but there would be
access to doctors and hospitals if needed. "So you're coming," he said.

I laughed. "I guess."

"Billy . . ."

"Okay. Georgia it is."

"You're a pain in the ass, Billy."

"*I* am? Listen, pal, it isn't always easy being your friend."

He laughed. "You seem to have figured it out."

The only way not to be distracted by what was happening was by putting it out of our minds. Sure. Charles and Diana getting married, just circle the calendar and show up. Any slipup, any mention of being out of
town on a certain weekend for reasons we then wouldn't explain—that
would be an obvious tell. It was no secret that Kathleen and I were close
to John and Carolyn; people were constantly asking us about them and

what they were up to, that they'd heard rumors, saw something on TV, read stuff. I had learned to keep things that pertained to John or his family pretty quiet. There were a number of reasons for that—one was that dustup with the paparazzi when we were still kids; another was that talking about the Kennedys meant defending all the supposed indiscretions, without knowing, myself, half the facts. Plus, why the hell was I defending them? They didn't need it, especially John. People got locked into their opinions about the Kennedys, for better or worse, and they weren't going to listen to me. John was a good instructor at this level: Just stay above it and enjoy yourself. Sounds a lot like Oscar Wilde, but it worked for us.

To John the fame thing was simply part of the deal. Even when it meant hiding his wedding from everyone near and dear to him until it was a month away or, in the case of some guests, mere days or even *hours* away. As in the case of Timmy—though he would manage, at the last moment, to catch a ride on Teddy's plane. There are worse ways to fly.

14

The Wedding

A WEEK OR SO LATER, John's assistant at *George* called to say the plane would be leaving from Teterboro Airport in northern New Jersey, apparently a well-known departure spot for high-end residents of Manhattan, and I had to be there on Thursday afternoon, September 19. Because it was a private airport, there were no commercial flights in or out; I had to rent a car and drive the three of us down from Boston. Life with John: planes, trains, and automobiles. Our return flight would be directly into Boston.

When we got to the airport that afternoon, there was no real indication of what was unfolding, no gawking or whispering employees, just very professional and direct service, almost military directives to the jet, the time of departure. Nobody told us where we were headed—maybe nobody knew. *My God*, I thought, *he's really pulling this off.* One of the world's most famous men was hustling forty people somewhere, out of sight. We assembled by the jet—just Kathleen, TJ, me, Robbie and Franny Littell (John's closest friends from college), and the best man, Anthony. No John. He was probably back in his loft searching for his wallet. We shuffled around, not saying much, probably because we thought the others knew what we didn't, which was where the hell we were headed.

Then John's limo came right up onto the tarmac, what I thought was some clandestine maneuver—you have to remember, the rumors were flying, any paparazzo getting the goods on this event would become a rich man. But John jumped out and ran past us into the terminal, then quickly returned. There was, in fact, no trumped-up secrecy. Nobody knew!

Very coolly, we taxied down the runway. With New York City on our left, we headed off to a destination somewhere south. Georgia. *Georgia?*

There were many things I knew about John, and one is that he was a guy who was very good at getting a private plane and very bad at remembering to pack shoes. But we were off, heading to the biggest event of his life. He was sparing no expense—when John zeroed in, he was a great organizer. He loved getting a lot of people in motion. The messy part—the missing wallet—he did to himself. Anyway, I decided to sit back and enjoy the trip. It was too late to worry.

Kathleen, on the other hand, was uneasy. As TJ had never flown before, let alone on a private jet, she was a little concerned about his ears and not being able to pop them. If TJ was going to have a tough trip, we were all going to have a tough trip. A lot was riding on him. Franny suggested giving TJ something to keep his ears open, such as a pacifier.

"Oh, no, it's okay," John told Kathleen. "Because we're in a private jet we're going to be flying at a higher altitude and away from the commercial planes, and we'll get down there quicker, so there'll be less time for the baby to have a problem."

"Oh, okay," Kathleen said.

I thought, *She just bought that line of crap?* "If we're traveling at a higher altitude," I said to John, "isn't that going to hurt the baby's ears more?"

He didn't answer. It made no sense, given that he hadn't even addressed the issue. It didn't matter. Logic didn't necessarily apply, but it worked on Kathleen, and that's all I needed. I doubt if anyone else could have gotten it by her so smoothly. And John—in his way—was right. Being right meant, *Don't worry so much. Go for it.* As it turned out, TJ was a trouper, not just on the jet but the whole weekend.

The rest of the flight was pleasant. We took naps, enjoyed some snacks. There was not a lot of chatter, as the engine was loud and everyone quietly rode the sense of anticipation: Where were we going? What, exactly, was going to happen when we got there? I let my imagination run wild. Then we arrived in Jacksonville. *Jacksonville?*

"What the hell is this?" I wondered. "I thought we were going to Georgia."

"Shut up, Billy," John said. "You'll see."

He was whisked away to the terminal, I assumed for some private jet documentation. Hardly. We could see him sitting, framed in a window, talking to a woman. He was signing his marriage license and getting his blood test—though I wouldn't find that out until later—under the cloak of Jacksonville.

Our luggage was picked up by a local driver in a red station wagon. We had been expected—the driver seemed to know John and, apparently, had been apprised of the plan. He was one of those laid-back southern guys who's not bothered by much, the sort of guy who is always a surprise to provincials visiting from the hopping North. When my family bought a winter home in then-unknown Boca Raton in the early 1960s, there were a lot of guys like him around. Not in any hurry, not at all. Still wearing jeans, plaid shirts, and work boots, like they were out of some Depression-era work project. This guy still had the Timex watch with a flexible wristband, as if progress had stopped right there. The only obvious difference was the graying crew cut (he really had been there, tossing luggage in a station wagon, thirty years ago). This definitely felt like the Deep South.

We were off to meet a ferry. The driver told us a little about the island we were headed to. I knew he was in cahoots with John—had John made a trial run down here and greased all these palms in secrecy?—because he would only give us a mysterious taste of the place. He told us there were tame boars that you could pet, armadillos, and other exotic animals.

"Oh, yeah, how'd they get there?" I asked.

He said he didn't know, but that no one would ever go hungry out there. All you had to do was walk up to a boar and hold out an apple to feed it, as they're so tame they would eat right out of your hand, and then you could knock them on the head with a hammer and cook 'em up.

"You're kidding! You eat wild boar down here?"

He looked at me the same way I would look at someone from Kansas who asked if I ate clams on the Cape. "Great eating," he said.

The ferry was a new twist: a spruced-up commercial fishing boat. Maybe they'd get married at sea, as if he were Ernest Hemingway. It looked like a lobster boat, seriously tricked out with twin diesel cats, a heating stack, and it was remarkably clean. I imagined the ad: WEDDING BOAT FOR THE INCREDIBLY FAMOUS AVOIDING THE PAPARAZZI. TAKE YOUR VOWS. REEL IN A MARLIN. I asked the captain about his vessel. He told me he fished all year and serviced the island. I gestured to the island off to starboard. "That's Amelia Island," he informed me—the first I'd heard the name of our destination.

"So that's where we're going," I said.

"NOOO!" I was still a dumb Yankee. "That's a resort island with golf courses and chain hotels."

Okay, so, really, where *were* we going?

"Cumberland Island."

"Is it like Amelia?"

John was standing there with the warm breeze raking his hair back, proud as a peacock. The captain gave him a look that said, *This guy is really so lost he's got his wife and kid with him and doesn't know where he's going?*

"Yup," John told him. "He's completely in the dark."

I'd have to see for myself. I was now expecting Ricardo Montalban, who played Mr. Roarke on *Fantasy Island,* and Tattoo at the dock, Tattoo shouting, "Da boat, boss, da boat!"

When we landed, I offered the captain a tip, trying to do something to chip in. "No," he told me. "It's all added in." Now I half expected that this would turn out to be a subterfuge, that a jet on the island would pick us up and take us to Monte Carlo. Just another Kennedy road trip, with John at his best: movement! The guy had ants in his pants; if he wasn't throwing a Frisbee or kayaking out on the sound, he'd go batty. Unfolding a grand plan and breaking his friends' balls simultaneously was John in his element.

After another short van trip through palmettos, we arrived at the Greyfield Inn, a hotel that was out of an Agatha Christie novel and already swinging. As if the jungle had opened and we'd landed in a colonial outpost. Now I felt stupid to have offered the boat guy fifty bucks—the rest of us make a date with a church and rent a reception hall when we get married. John had commandeered an entire island.

The Greyfield Inn was like a Clue game come alive, with graceful rooms and filled with unusual guests. Carolyn, her family, and some of her fashionista friends were already here. She greeted us with big hugs and kisses, with the exciting realization that her wedding weekend had officially begun. The groom, the best man, and John's oldest friend—that's how Carolyn introduced me—had now arrived. Arguably, no one else was really needed, except the priest, and even then we had the ferryboat captain if need be, so the wedding was going to come off. Since I was John's oldest friend, and with a baby in tow, Kathleen and I were given the master bedroom, with a crib for the babe set up in a sitting area.

After settling in, getting TJ into bed, and setting up the portable baby monitor, we headed back downstairs to the drawing room, which was the epitome of tropical Victorian elegance—with electricity. Walls of leatherbound books lined the large room full of sturdy oak furniture and desks, palm trees, bankers' lamps, and beautiful art. I was expecting Teddy Roosevelt to walk in with some dead animal slung over his shoulder, proclaiming this to be a "bully" weekend. It was a wonderful room.

We spent some time with Carolyn's family—her mother's mother, especially, was a real pistol—and her fashion-industry friends from New York. That is not a crowd I would normally take to, but this bunch I liked. I had met Gordon, a handsome young black man with a great sense of style, at the Cape. Narciso Rodriguez was the dress designer who introduced himself as "the other man," Julie an outrageous blonde who was speaking with an affected British accent—somehow she was funny instead of annoying. And Jessica, who was looking a little tired. They'd been there a couple days already, styling, having a blast—there was a lot of partying going on in this group—and primping for the blessed event.

Kathleen and I went outside for some fresh air and a swing on the hundred-foot-long veranda, which ran the entire length of the mansion. By this point it was dark. John came out and sat on a railing to smoke. Ah, the cat who ate the canary. Now he started telling us about the Greyfield Inn and the island. A horse let out a whinny from the darkness—suddenly it seemed like a vast and strange place. "The horses run wild here," John told us. "They've even evolved into a master breed."

"You've been here before, I take it."

John took his time taking a drag from his Marlboro Light; he blew a smoke ring. Then he told us that he had brought Carolyn here for a long weekend and she had loved it; when they started planning a wedding, they immediately agreed: This was the place. It had everything, all the grace and accoutrements and personal service they needed. And privacy. He told us about the history of the mansion, how it had been a Carnegie family estate and that Gogo Ferguson, an heir, had returned here with her mother to convert it into an inn.

Gogo and her husband, Dave, a pilot, enjoyed entertaining, so they ran the inn; in the dead of summer, when it was too hot for tourists, they came to the Vineyard.

"So that's how you heard about it?"

Another smoke ring—the guy was enjoying this a bit too much.

For a moment I thought maybe this place was well known only among the rustic elite, that it was a little secret passed among a select few.

"No," John said finally. "Christina Haag." His old girlfriend; Christina had found out about it somehow, and they'd come here a few times.

"Boy, is she going to be pissed," John laughed as we headed in for dinner.

Kathleen and I sat with Sasha, an old girlfriend of John's from Andover, and her husband, Phil. Sasha and Phil were bohemian artists living in New York, and Phil was very proud of the fact that when he told John he didn't have a suit to wear to the wedding, John gave him one of his to have tailored to fit. In fact, Phil had never owned a suit before. He opened his jacket to show us the label. "Giorgio Armani. Is that good?"

After dinner most people went to their cottages. John, pretty exhausted from his day of getting us here, went off to bed. Robbie and I went to the bar for a drink. It was self-serve, and we kicked back with a beer. Phil came with us and filled us in on other suits John had given him. Narciso came in after a while to tell us about his history with Carolyn, particularly the story of going to Paris with her to buy the material for her dress and have it cut. When she was spotted with him, the European news agencies surmised that she and John had broken up and she had run off with this "other man." Which was, to say the least, unlikely, and Narciso played it to the hilt, loving the intrigue, the deception, and even the possibility that he'd be mistaken not just for Carolyn's suitor but any woman's.

It was becoming a bachelor party—never mind that the bachelor had gone off. I searched the bar for something stronger. An employee showed up to serve us, and in a little while I asked if we could continue on as long as we used the honor system of adding the drinks to Anthony's bill. Sure. Before he left, the bartender asked if we wanted any champagne.

"Champagne? Do we look like a bunch of sissies from New York?"

"Hey, wait a minute!" Narciso protested. "*I'm* a sissy from New York."

"Fine," I said. "Then give us a bottle."

We were on our way.

THE NEXT MORNING a bunch of the early arrivers headed to the beach to swim and hang out. John disappeared with Anthony for a workout and a massage. We still didn't know anything about the actual ceremony, but that was fine—we were now content to roll through the day. It felt like what it was, the end of summer. After breakfast we toured the grounds; there was another Carnegie mansion in ruins, destroyed by fire. The windy beaches were bleached with fine sand; the water was turquoise.

Before long, TJ was ready for a nap, and we headed back to the inn. I had a small problem: I happened to have gone swimming with my security pass in my bathing suit pocket, and it was now part of the coastal surf. Kathleen still had hers, a small Greyfield Inn card with her name and a Buffalo-head nickel (the profile of the Indian faced out) and a penny glued on.

This was a whole different level of security from the Secret Service that once surrounded John; he had really taken the privacy of his wedding to extremes: The security guard radioed to some central command post, giving my name and physical description to get clearance. I wondered what they actually knew about the guests, the staff, the locals. Was there a mainframe on the island? I didn't think so, since there weren't any telephones, and even electricity was limited. Were there hidden cameras, or were we all being monitored by satellite? (I'm not kidding. Later I'd find out that John had spent three hundred thousand dollars on security *alone*. It was the difference between this wedding coming off privately or being a disaster of intrusion, with pictures beamed all over the world. Money well spent.) There was an electronic perimeter that had been installed—some sort of hidden trip mechanism that apparently surrounded the inn and cottages. No wonder this security guy wasn't impressed with my size, my designation as John's oldest friend—which I assumed they knew—or the fact that my wife and infant son had just gone ahead of me. This was not a setup to be fooled with. Once cleared, I made sure to have my pass and know the password of the day—I think it was "Deadhead"—going forward. As a matter of fact, I was comfortable knowing we were so well protected.

While Kathleen and TJ napped, I headed to the back of the inn, where serious dinner preparations were under way. There was a small inlet there and an outside shower that was surrounded by hundreds of monarch butterflies. The staff was eager to feed me and quench my thirst. I was happy to oblige. I imagined that this was what Eden would have been like, with ice cubes. They were preparing scallops on long skewers with bits of salty ham. Now, I have harvested sea scallops and bay scallops, known to Cape Codders as "capies." I have dined on them in just about every fashion, cooking technique, and combination, including wrapped in bacon, but none as succulent as these cooked over an open fire pit of fruitwood.

It was shaping up as a great weekend. I was tan, rested, and ready when the others started to arrive in dribs and drabs. And now I was prepared, with my day of experience, to share knowledge of the inn and the planned event. The day before, I didn't know where we were going—now I was a regular ambassador of the place and John's plan. I assumed the position of official greeter.

The most amusing arrival was Timmy Shriver and his wife, Linda. Timmy was invited not out of duty but because he was so close to John. Yet they were informed of the wedding only the evening before and left to their own devices to get to Cumberland Island. Timmy felt hoodwinked, left out, excluded, insulted, and perplexed. What was going on here? The fact that his arrival was a full day after mine, that I had come with John on a private jet, really annoyed him. Not that I would rub it in. He also learned that he and Linda would be sharing the bathroom of the master suite with me, and I could lock them out from my side—okay, that came from me.

All of this, of course, was John (and me) having some fun at his expense, which Timmy would appreciate in due time.

As the afternoon moved along and more and more guests arrived—obviously needing my knowledge and counsel—Anthony and I took it upon ourselves to move around to the different cottages. More ambassador work, under the auspices of looking for a CD player. Anthony had asked me to supply some music. I had brought soul and some ballads, including "On Raglan Road" by Sinéad O'Connor, a favorite of both Carolyn's and mine. Each cottage was unique, not just in style and structure but in clusters of guests, now fully interrogated by Anthony and me. Carolyn's friends, the fashionistas, were licking their wounds from the night before. John Perry Barlow, the onetime Grateful Dead lyricist, was already working on his own private level of beauty and refinement.

We headed back to the inn for cocktail hour and those scallops;

Kathleen—monitor for TJ in her pocket—joined me. Now we were waiting for the bride-to-be. The dinner would be the formal beginning of the
weekend's events, and there was some anxiety on Carolyn's part, naturally. So we waited. And waited. More scallops and drinks. Finally she arrived, and we headed up to the huge veranda we'd sat on the night before;
now it was arranged with large tables that sat ten, glowing with candlelight in the soft Georgia night. The tables were jammed with flowers and
party favors from the talented hand of Gordon.

I was seated next to Carolyn at her table of friends—Barlow sat on
her other side. This was a mistake, as Barlow was really on the far side of
stable by this point. The idea in mixing us up like this was for everyone to
get to know each other a little. But this rotation of personalities, which included Carolyn's sisters, was making her nervous—I could feel it. Also the
little nothing that Narciso had designed for her to wear to this evening's
event was too revealing for anyone but her physician. "I'm a bit self-
conscious about this dress," Carolyn admitted to me. So I gave her my
blazer, which was a pity, because she was absolutely radiant, and in the
tropical heat she hardly needed it. But she gladly wrapped it around her
bare shoulders.

"What do you think Mummy"—Jackie—"would think?" Carolyn kept
whispering to me. "Would she approve of this? Do you think it's okay?"
Carolyn had become obsessed with Jackie.

The rehearsal dinner, of course, is generally the responsibility of the
groom's parents, and even (or especially) with John's parents gone, it was
clear this was preying on Carolyn's mind. I assured her that Mrs. Onassis—
as I always called her—would have loved the setting, this wonderful leap
they'd taken, to get married in this exotic place. Jackie was nothing if not
her own woman, and she would have wanted John to have his own wedding in his own way. Though at the moment I didn't, of course, say all that.

I couldn't anyway, because Barlow had just pushed things too far.
We'd been talking about honor. Somebody had asked what the definition
of honor is—I don't remember why. Then Barlow, looking at Carolyn's

twin sisters, made an off-color remark about their attractiveness that re-
flected on his own honor and seemed to shock everyone.

Carolyn was mortified. The sisters simply looked stunned—was this
some sort of rude Kennedy gamesmanship? For some reason I caught the
eye of Ed Schlossberg, who was also sitting with us. Ed is a very dignified,
careful, decent man. At this moment he had the decency to pretend he
hadn't heard a word Barlow said. But something had to be done. It would
not help, of course, to tell Barlow that he had been a rude, stupid shit. I
got up, went to John's table, whispered, "We better switch seats right now.
Barlow is scaring the hell out of Carolyn." So John and I traded places.

Order was restored just by his presence; I could see her, leaning a little toward her fiancé, still wearing my blazer. Lord, she looked so tiny, so
ethereal. And radiant.

Anyway, in the weird seating arrangements, I found myself, happily,
sitting next to my wife, a good distance from the epicenter for the after-
dinner toasts. Senator Kennedy began them. Through his years as a cam-
paigner, debater, and legislator, he really has developed a great ability to
strike the right notes at important events. I marvel at Teddy: We all know
the tragedies he's been through—and there's a lot more crap that no one,
including me, knows about, though I've seen a few things—but the thing
about him is, not only did he assume leadership of the family when he
was very young, too young, but Teddy has always come through. There
is not a whiff of cynicism in Teddy at these moments—certainly not this
one. Standing up there, he was a patriarch in his element. He read a childhood poem by Caroline about John and his annoying manners that was
sweet but not too sentimental. He thanked Gogo and Dave for all that
they'd done setting this up and the beauty of Cumberland Island and how
much Jack and Jackie would have enjoyed it. (I checked on Carolyn; she
was smiling—a real smile—clearly relaxing into the moment.) "There
is one thing we know today about the Kennedys," Teddy said. "The
Kennedys can keep a secret." It was not too much—just the right touch.
Others attempted to give speeches, in the typical way of making fun of

the about-to-be-married. Timmy Shriver said it came as a shock to him that John had a reputation as a ladies' man at twenty-three, the same kid he went to Guatemala with at fifteen "and watched throw up seven times a day."

When John spoke, he said he owed us a debt of gratitude for keeping the secret, for coming from different parts of the globe, and he said that he imposed restrictions on this event that might have seemed extreme. John also noted how he was about to "learn of the pleasures of the in-law relationship." I laughed, because he seemed to mean it. The guy was thirty-five years old and had no clue about some things—Kathleen gave me a look, then, as if I might get up to suggest he submit to a reality check. For once I kept my mouth shut. This was, of course, his moment.

As the dinner wore down, now stretching into Saturday, John took me aside and asked why I didn't make a toast. That was a nice thought—that I should have, that he wanted me to.

"What was I going to add to Teddy, to Timmy?"

"Oh, for chrissake, Billy." Our closeness, not the official family thing—that's what was important to him. I appreciated that.

And that was always the thing with John and me. I used to go to the annual Profiles in Courage dinners with him in Boston, at the JFK Library. One year, during the after-dinner speeches, he was getting antsy, because John was always getting antsy. He said, "Let's go outside for some fresh air." This was black-tie, a thousand bucks a plate. We got up and walked out.

"I've got so much energy I have to do something," he said. "I'm going to do a handstand." He took his jacket off. "Here," he said. "Hold it."

"No."

"Why not?"

"I'm not holding your coat. Put it on that rail over there."

"Why won't you hold my coat?"

I said, "My mother told me, never be a Kennedy coat holder. Never be a door opener."

John looked at me in his sly way and, after a nod to my mother's memory, said, "That was pretty good advice."

So he put his coat on the railing and walked around for a couple of minutes on his hands, with Boston big-shot benefactors still inside listening to speeches. And then we went back in.

Anyway, here was the real reason he took me aside the night before his wedding. "Can I sleep in your suite tonight"—his last night as a bachelor—"in that little sitting area?"

I gave him a wild look. *You think you have to ask me that?*

Off they went, Carolyn and John—separately. John was never, as a matter of fact, much of a partier.

On the other hand, those of us who were well rested were taken to the beach by a pickup truck, to a pavilion that was loaded with enough after-dinner liquors and cigars for the Russian army. A large bonfire was lighted, and we basked in the orange glow on the last evening of summer and the last evening of the single life of our two friends. Carolyn appeared dressed in green army pants with a black shirt and her fashion-world girlfriends in tow; she looked a little spooked. We didn't leave the campfire until the morning light chased us into a moment of false sobriety, straight to our beds. On the way to mine, there was John, sleeping like a baby.

WEDDING DAY: Mostly, guests headed off to the beach, clutching their security cards. But I stayed close to the inn and watched the setup of the reception tent. Kathleen wasn't too happy that I'd crept in at daybreak. Hey, John was getting married. Of course, he had escaped the debauchery. But not me.

I had lunch, got a massage, tried to stay cool in the tropical heat and duck the recounting of jokes and stories from the night before.

That afternoon, just before we gathered to head off to the chapel, John called all his boys together: He considered us his groomsmen, but because the chapel was tiny and the guest list limited, there was no official duty. He presented each of us with a pair of blue silk boxers in a wooden box; to assure that we'd wear them with him in mind, he'd had his initials and each of ours monogrammed on the leg openings. This struck me as a cooler idea than getting a Swiss Army knife emblazoned with his name.

"When they fit you, Billy," John said, deadpan, "I will buy you dinner at any restaurant in New York." Everyone found this very funny. What juveniles. John never missed an opportunity to take off his shirt and was always on me about my weight. "You gotta get in shape, Billy."

After returning my gift to my room and checking on TJ, we assembled at the front of the inn for our carriage—that is, pickup truck—to the chapel. The heat was unreal, and those of us in starched shirts appeared to be swimming. Senator Kennedy was no exception. We were both soaked through our shirts already. Women attempting to have sophisticated hair—forget it. The hair came down and then got pulled into ponytails. The Senator and I seemed to spy the outdoor, well-stocked bar at the same instant.

What do you think? was his unspoken question.

"I will if you will," I said. I suggested a healthy Cape Codder. Teddy nodded. I went up to the guy stocking the bar for the reception. "Can I get in here?"

"Sure. What do you want?"

"I'll take care of it. Thanks." Since I got through college tending bar, I know what I'm doing, and I made Teddy and myself big, four-finger drinks. Vodka with a splash of cranberry juice.

I handed it to him, he took a big gulp, but then he said, disgusted, "Billy Noonan, what the hell are you trying to do to me? Are you trying to give me cavities?"

Huh?

As if he'd sent a boy to do a man's job: "There is way too much sugar in cranberry juice and way too much cranberry juice in this. Get out of the way, will you?"

So he got behind the bar—Teddy's a big man, and the setup guy was backing away, giving him a wide berth. "Where's the vodka?"

He found it, filled up his glass, and as he looked at me—oh, Teddy's a real devil—and put in a tiny dash of cranberry, he said, "Just for the coloring, Billy."

Never before had someone accused me of adding too much mixer, but then again there are very few of the ability of Senator Kennedy. And this was reformed Teddy.

I immediately fired my drink down—there was no way you could handle them riding in these trucks, bouncing all over. So did Teddy.

The ride was surreal. Quarter-century-old, four-wheel-drive Chevy pickup trucks took us over the sand along the water, with Chippendale chairs from the Carnegie dining room in back for the ladies. The men sat on the pickups' flatbeds. The privileged guests like Teddy and the bride's parents and grandmother rode in the cabs. Quite a sight, I'm sure, especially spied from the buzzing helicopters, on us like mosquitoes: Someone had tipped off the press. There was nothing we could do except ignore them and hope that they wouldn't descend upon the chapel.

We headed off the beach and back into a jungle of six-foot-high palmettos and other thorny shrubs, then came across a compound of houses where one of the trucks had stopped with engine trouble; they had radioed for another truck. We pushed on and finally came to a clearing with a tiny red-and-white chapel in the middle of it. There was a beehive of activity. With all the planning and thought that went into this event, it appeared that no one had bothered to unshutter the little church.

I started laughing. John had gotten us all here. Had he forgotten to make sure the church would be ready?

Effie, who had long worked for Jackie and had stayed on with John, was busy planting palm trees at the front door and lining the door with garland. Others were sweeping out the chapel and placing little fans and King James Bibles on the benches, or moving the Chippendale dining chairs from the trucks into the church. John had assured us the night before, in his short speech at the rehearsal dinner, that he had "turned Catholicism on its head" in order to perform the Catholic ceremony in a Baptist church. In fact, the history of this church meant a great deal to John. There was a small plaque with the names and dates of its builders, who were slaves freed in 1853. The church had not been used in years—the windows had been painted over in white, which created a strange look, as if the place had been muted and forgotten. Within ten feet of the front door were not just hogs and horses—you know, your typical church-yard beasts—but armadillos scurrying about, to the delight of Bobby Kennedy. Even in the terrible heat, he went after them like an errant child, returning with one by the tail, to the hysterics of the men and the squeam-ish squeals of the women. Chiggers attacked our ankles. The effect of the Cape Codders, making a wild ride into the Third World fun, had long since worn off, and we'd run out of bottled water. The sun was going down. John was tardy. The bride was nowhere to be seen. One good thing: no helicopters. They hadn't found the church.

Ah, but the replacement pickup-truck driver now delivering the stranded guests had had the foresight to include a case of Heineken on ice for his rescued party. We dove in, and the driver became, in our lore, Gunga Din.

Teddy, soaking wet, took over, telling jokes. The early-autumn sunset gave the little white church a gold tinge, with the ice-cold Heinekens bumping the effect.

Just then John showed up, frazzled and nervous that he was late, shouting, "Billy, I was going to clobber you half an hour ago!"

It seemed that John could not find his matrimonial tie. Now, this was pretty rich, John blaming *me* for *his* not being able to find something. Of course, part of the deal with John was that everyone indulged him. Who wasn't going to loan John Kennedy black shoes or a blazer? At my wedding he had decided it would be funny to hide my wedding suit and send me into a panic on my matrimonial morning, and now he was sure I'd done the same thing to him. Apparently he had the entire Greyfield Inn staff looking for his tie, and also Effie, which explained why he was late setting up the church. Effie finally found the tie after retracing John's steps. He had forgotten that he'd slept the night before in my sitting area and left it in the closet there.

Now—not in trouble because his bride was running even later, of course—he was relieved to tell us a story from a local islander he encountered on the way to the church. Apparently everyone on the island who knew about the wedding was sympathetic to John's need for secrecy and, in the spirit of southern hospitality, obliged him the courtesy. Except, that is, for one local guy—everyone seemed to know who it had to be—who found the lure of a quick buck too much and tipped off the tabloid media. That's what got those helicopters buzzing above us. According to John's source, for a few bucks more, this guy provided a "chickenshit map" to the church. An islander discovered a couple of photographers crawling out of thick underbrush, bleeding, bitten by insects (especially those godawful chiggers, which burrow under your skin), and practically begging for something to drink.

"At this point," John told us, laughing, "they didn't want any pictures, or trouble. They just wanted to get the hell out of here." What he liked best, I think, was an islander taking as much delight in thwarting the paparazzi as he did.

With the sun setting, there was concern about lighting in the church, since there was no electricity. To get so far and then have night intrude seemed terrible. There were a few flashlights from the trucks, a few candles, but they wouldn't provide much light. I suggested we pull the trucks up and use the headlights—but the whir of the engines would disturb the (increasingly dark) ambience, and to run the lights without the engines running might drain the batteries and have us hacking back through the scrub on foot.

Suddenly Carolyn and Caroline, who served as her matron of honor, showed up for the vows. Carolyn's stepfather whisked her up the steps to the altar, and the service—after all this intrigue and getting here and waiting—began immediately, lit by a flashlight and candles. It was spooky and lovely and somehow just right, as an old local black singer started in on "Amazing Grace." It happened fast: readings, blessings. Carolyn was stunning, and very stark—as if the few lights were just for her, with the rest of us in darkness and her betrothed's face leaning into her halo. It was happening! John and Carolyn exchanged vows to the nightfalling accompaniment of horses neighing. One of the world's most sought-after couples was married with forty people as witnesses, which made it even more special, forty people in this tiny old place built by slaves, in near darkness. With no buzzing helicopters—they lost us in the thick canopy of trees.

I thought of John's mother then—in certain ways so proper, so careful and set on ceremony, a woman who spoke several languages with European grace. Well, she would have loved this, even if she might have tried to talk Carolyn and John into something more formal, something larger. In the end she would have utterly embraced his idea and this spot. It was what John wanted. To hell with a big public ceremony. This could not have been better scripted.

When Father Charles declared them married, we all let out a whoop. Then we started filing out to "May the Circle Be Unbroken." The music lovers waited for the singer to finish, and the Catholics waited for the priest to leave the altar.

We immediately got back into the trucks and headed to the Greyfield Inn, as bad weather was coming. As I rode along the strand of beach in the open cab, the sky began to light up with high lightning. I was impressed with two things: The heavens were acknowledging this event, and the coming storm might break the terrible heat.

At the inn, John, Anthony, and I gathered for a few minutes under a huge tree dripping with Spanish moss—that moment of relief at every wedding before the reception begins. I think even John was surprised he could pull it off, to get us all here without the rest of the world zeroing in. He told us about getting the Catholic bishop to acknowledge the service and getting the blood test at the airport. We shared a cigarette—for once he didn't blow smoke rings; he was too jazzed for that. He just smoked and gushed. Music flowed out of the inn. "Can you believe it?" John kept saying.

Unlike at the prewedding dinner, now we sat with our friends. Robbie, Timmy, their wives, and Kathleen and I all marveled over the event, that Mr. Bachelor had gotten himself hitched, and in this wild place. Uncle Teddy stood and gave a well-deserved toast—once again with perfect timing and with exact proportions of intensity and warmth. He mentioned the silver cup that the Irish ambassador had given President-elect Kennedy before his inauguration, at the occasion of John's birth. On it a poem was inscribed:

> We wish to the new child
> A heart that can be beguiled
> By a flower that the wind lifts as it passes.
> If the storms break for him,
> May the trees shake for him
> Their blossoms down.
>
> In the night that he is troubled,
> May a friend wake for him,
> So that his time be doubled,
> And at the end of all loving and love,
> May the Man above
> Give him a crown.

Teddy remembered that at the conclusion of the ambassador's reading of the poem, JFK was quiet for a moment, then said, "I wish it could have been written about me." Teddy said that today it was written for John and Carolyn. We all raised a glass to that. Teddy was one of the few people who could refer to the President and First Lady and make it personal rather than opportunistic.

Then Caroline's daughters, Rose and Tatiana, who had served as flower girls, sang the old ditty about sitting in the tree K-I-S-S-I-N-G . . . Everyone laughed, and now John and Carolyn—she had donned his elusive blue blazer—danced to "Forever in My Life," a funky Prince song. Others got up to dance. The party was off. The only problem was that the food—artichokes for the first round—was late and surprisingly unappealing.

"Can I have a cheeseburger?" I wondered.

Everyone laughed. No one, of course, really cared about the food. The night could not be ruined, even by Teddy co-opting the DJ to let him get down to "Y.M.C.A." and "Macarena."

It wasn't until the cutting of the cake, serenaded by Senator Kennedy (the guy really got into these things), that I noticed the wedding dress and its scandalous shape. Carolyn was a truly magnificent woman—angelic-looking, with a body that . . . well, let's say that the dress hugged her posterior in a particularly careful and complete way. I took some home movies of the whole proceeding, and once I noticed the shape of that dress, my camera, which searches for a focal point, found one in the upside-down heart of her derriere. That Thanksgiving, when I shared my film noir effort with John and Carolyn, she found my cinematic obsession with her lower end hysterical. I knew she would get a kick out of it.

Because of TJ, Carolyn had arranged the earliest departure for us, along with Maurice Tempelsman. This made for an early night—the truth is, Kathleen and I were wrung out, by the heat, by the emotion. Early the next morning, the revelers were still in bed when Maurice, Kathleen, TJ, and I climbed into the van to reverse Thursday's trip. As we got back to the mainland, the presidential yacht *Honey Fitz* that I remembered as a kid in Hyannisport was docked at the St. Mary's pier next to the *Caroline K.* What was this—what were they doing there?

This seemed too weird. Later, at the airport, there was some TV coverage—vague shots of the island was all they got, coupled with shots of the two boats. Was John taking off on his honeymoon on one of them? On both of them?

Of course not.

After John and Carolyn returned from their honeymoon in Turkey, we gathered at the President's house—John's house—in Hyannisport for Thanksgiving. Once I showed my little home movie, I asked about the *Honey Fitz.*

"Oh, yeah, that." John started laughing. "It was a complete coincidence." Apparently whoever now owns the boat charters it out, and some philandering fool who'd taken his mistress south for a few days ended up on the evening news.

"This big cheese hired it for one week," John told us, "and that was the week he chose."

"What big cheese?"

"You know, some big shot."

"Who?"

"I have no idea." But photographers in the helicopters, assuming John had hired the boats (apparently it was just another weird coincidence that the *Caroline K* was there, too), buzzed the yachts all week, trying to get some pictures. The only pictures they got were of the big cheese and his girlfriend, and his wife was now filing for divorce.

"Serves him right," John said.

Nothing amused John more than turning the tables, coupled with the irony of supposed presidential indiscretions, long ago, on that yacht.

15

The Newlyweds

AFTER THE WEDDING in September, John and Carolyn had really settled into the house at Hyannisport; she and John frequented it that winter.

"My accountant told me it made more sense to charter a plane and fly here every weekend than sell," John told me. "Besides, when I start a family, I don't want to deny my kids access to this house."

We would often drive down to meet them and have a party. It went on like this for a while, and we were never closer as couples.

Those weekends John liked to make huge dinners, and we would get into huge arguments. It was a little more spirited if there were other people there, just to see if they'd weigh in, too. In March of '97, John and Carolyn came up with his friend Gary Ginsberg and his wife, whom I'd never met. They had a baby. John had given me a key to the house—he told me to use it whenever I wanted, to treat it as my own. In fact he called me before that weekend, asking if it was okay if *he* came and if he could bring somebody.

"Come on, John, reorganize that." Had he forgotten whose house it was?

I got groceries and came back and made up this big pasta sauce and salad. Ginsberg and I were like two different guys in the same camp. John was always doing that, bringing different people together to create an unusual chemistry. With occasional exceptions, it worked.

This was when Clinton was in trouble over Monica Lewinsky. We started talking about Clinton at dinner, the wine flowing. John sat where his mother used to, at the foot of the table, and I always sat on his right. Technically, it was the seat of honor. Where I had the honor of hammering him.

"How can you pardon this thing? Or condone this kind of behavior?"

"His personal life is nobody's business. And it goes on all the time."

"Yeah, but not in the goddamn Oval Office."

John said, "Hey Billy, I've been under that desk, and there's barely enough room down there for a three-year-old, never mind a fat-ass like Monica Lewinsky."

Who else could say that? We all cackled as I attempted to regain a foothold in the discussion.

What about Whitewater, and Hillary losing files in the White House, and the selling of the Lincoln Bedroom? "Listen," I said to him, "this guy can't hold on to a chief of staff. No one wants to work for the guy. For God's sake, the guy can't even get a Democrat to legally advise him." David Gergen, a Republican, had been his counsel to the president. "The guy's such an embarrassment."

"But Ronald Reagan had four chiefs of staff."

"That's not important."

"Yes it is."

"Why is it so important?"

"You brought it up."

"Yeah, well . . . let's move on."

"No. What are you trying to say?"

Now I was cornered—John always knew stuff like Ronald Reagan having four chiefs of staff. So I just fired away. "All of a sudden these files show up in the White House. You think the White House is that disorganized they can't find the Whitewater files? How the hell is he protecting us?"

John smirked. Here was Gary just watching us. The women were used to this. Carolyn said to Kathleen, "The dining room is on fire—let's go to the living room." Let the boys be boys. So the women got up.

And now John had me: "You know, Billy, that's the White House counsel—they're not even in the White House. You don't know what you're talking about. They're over in the Executive Office Building. Those offices aren't in the West Wing."

"John, you're delusional. The only reason you like Clinton is because he adores your family."

"What are you talking about? I've never been invited to the White House."

"Bullshit."

"Well, actually, we just got our first invitation."

"It must be for the Lincoln Bedroom. You giving him fifty grand to sleep there?"

"Billy . . ."

"Movie guys sleeping there for whatever money they throw at him—why don't they just put out a sign that says 'Hotel White House' in front?"

"Why shouldn't he do it? He needs these people. That's where the money is. That's what he needs to stay in there. As long as he's president, he can do those things."

"John, that's bullshit and you know it!" I yelled. "He's selling out, he's exploiting everything."

Okay, I admit it: Some of that was for Ginsberg's sake. We'd gone outside earlier—just the boys—for a walk. It was midwinter, dreary. But Gary was excited. "Is that the field where you play football and where the helicopter landed?" John smirked and nodded. "Is that the flagpole? There's the porch. Can I go get on the porch?"

Gary ran off. I said to John, "He's a little too into it, don't you think?"

"Yeah, but so what? Not a lot of people get to see it like this."

Gary came back. "Do you remember any of it, John?"—meaning, of course, when his father was alive.

John shook his head.

"I do," I said.

"You do?" John said, surprised. "How?"

I told him about my experiences with Mary Ruane, my nanny, as a five-year-old, how she'd take me to see the President's helicopter land on the compound and how special it was.

I figured that enough time had passed for me to tell him about that, that if he was willing to tolerate Gary's enthusiasm, and bring presidential memorabilia into the house, it was time to start sharing my memories. But he wasn't ready for it. He dropped his head—that's what John would do if he didn't want to deal with something, if something was too much for him. He just dropped his head, didn't say anything, and walked away. I shouldn't have ever told him that—I'd known him practically all his life, we'd been friends for almost twenty-five years, and *I* remembered his father. He didn't. Or he wasn't sure if he did. He told me once that he couldn't be sure if he actually remembered things or if he'd seen the images of his life so many times that he merely thought he remembered.

Later John and I went up on the widow's walk to have a butt. The night had gotten colder, really nasty. I said to him, "You know your father would never have done that"—rent out the White House for a night. And he said, "Yeah, I do know that. And you know, Billy, the letting of the Lincoln Bedroom, to tell you the truth, that really does piss me off. That Clinton is doing this stuff." We smoked, checked Nantucket Sound, gray and rolling like a washing machine.

The next morning I went out and got the *New York Times*, and there it was, right on the front page: "Clinton Selling Seats on Air Force One for Big Check Donors." I came home, made some breakfast, and waited. When John came down, I held it up for him. "Oh, no, is this gonna start again at breakfast? I'm going for a run." He went out the door. I said, "Go ahead, John. I'll have it all read by the time you get back, and I'll inform you about how this guy is now using the United States Air Force. I'll summarize it for you."

"Oh, am I going to listen to this all day long?"

"No. I'm actually going to go out and play golf this afternoon, so you won't have to hear about it for a couple hours."

"Thank the Lawd," he said, mimicking my accent. He looked at Kathleen, whom many have called "St. Kathleen." "How do you put up with this guy?" She gave it right back to him. "Because I love him." Which of course was much better than, "For the same reason you do."

A couple hours later, I was at the Hyannisport Golf Club; a group of Irish friends were over for St. Patrick's Day. It was a perfect Irish day for golf—cold, raw, misty. I asked one of them, Laurence Crowley, if he wanted to rethink the prospect of walking the course on a day such as this. He responded, "If the Irish didn't play golf in this kind of weather, there would be no golf played in Ireland at all." Along the back nine—by this time we're freezing and miserable, which is also typical of Irish golf—something loud and vibrating was buzzing over our heads, circling us and doing dips and swaggers.

"What the hell sort of contraption is that?" Crowley wondered.

A Buckeye, I explained. Essentially a lawn mower that flies. The group was surprised that I seemed familiar with it and wondered if they were popular down here on the Cape. Not really, I explained. You have to be a little nuts to fly in one. But I think I know who it is, I told them: the guy I'm staying with here in Hyannisport.

Later I surprised them with an invitation to the President's house for chowder and drinks. As we warmed up at John's house, he enthusiastically explained to my highly amused Irish friends how much fun he had flying his Buckeye.

ON THANKSGIVING—with John's birthday falling that weekend—he assembled a festive bunch at the President's house. Provi was there with her son, Gustavo, and his daughter, Ariel. Carolyn's friend Narciso, the designer, came up as well.

Caroline had flown in to spend Thanksgiving Day at Teddy's. I didn't give it a lot of thought at the time, but it was pretty obvious that things were frosty between John's sister and his wife; having Caroline in her corner might really have helped Carolyn as she negotiated the trials of being of Kennedy.

For now, though, things were warm and great fun. We spent the day in the usual manner, chucking a football around, going for walks, feasting, watching some football.

John told us about how he'd gone to Cuba that fall to interview Castro for *George*. He waited for days. The suspense built. He'd get a message— "He will see you for dinner tonight, and we will contact you"—then hours would pass, nothing. Finally a phone call at eight: "El Presidente cannot meet you this evening. Perhaps tomorrow." Click.

The next day John would call to inquire. "You will be contacted later today." Click. John went out for a sightseeing tour with the photographer Herb Ritts, who had accompanied him, but when they came back to the hotel, there was no message. This went on for days. At last, John called Carolyn to tell her he was coming home the next morning without the interview.

"You get on that fucking phone to whomever you need to, whether it's a U.S. diplomat or Castro's guys, and you tell them that you are not going to sit around taking this shit," Carolyn told him. "You came to see him, you are a Kennedy, you are a journalist with staff here, and if his office promised an interview, goddamnit it, you're not leaving until you get one."

Far from being put off by her attitude, John was amused by it—and jacked. He called up Castro's advance man and gave it to him verbatim. Click. Then he got a call minutes later. "El Presidente would like for you and your guests to come to the residence for dinner this evening."

He told us about how Castro had dragged the dinner on and on, speaking for what seemed to be hours at a time, so much so that he was not eating his food. The staff hovered, waiting for him to finish, but wouldn't dare touch his plate until he was done. He would make a long-winded point with a shrimp on the end of a fork, jabbing the fork for emphasis rather than eating the shrimp. When he finished his point, he would bring the shrimp to his lips and stop, beginning another point, and the staff had to keep backing off, waiting for him to gulp down his last prawn. "God, it seemed like hours," John told us. But, thanks to Carolyn, he got his interview.

Friday night was the biggest party; some of John's cousins came over for a while. Things were still a little chilly because of the editorial he'd written about them in *George*. Luckily, I had remembered the Bacardi and limes, and Provi had the blender going; it might have been cold outside, but it was warm by the fire, and those slush puppies were going down like a mouse without fur.

Carolyn carried on the Latin theme by telling us about Narciso's big show. His career had been kick-started by designing her wedding dress, and he won the MTV Designer of the Year Award. His mother was so proud at the ceremony that she was in tears, screaming to everyone in her Spanish accent, "I knew it, I knew it! From the time he was a little boy he was a yeen-yus, do you hear me, a yeen-yus!"

The rest of the night, that was his name: "Yeen-yus." Narciso's response was to draw a composite sketch of this disparate group, brought together by our connection to John and Carolyn. There was Provi with her fancy outfit on, spoon in hand; big burly Billy Noonan, wearing an Irish sweater, had TJ in his arms; Kathleen held little Kiely, our daughter, two months old. He caught Carolyn in profile, scratching at John's chiseled face, plus Gustavo, Ariel—and he included himself with pad and pencil. Then he colored it.

The striking thing was that he portrayed Carolyn as a scratching cat. I asked him about that.

"Oh, boy," he said, "you should see her with her hair up—she's just like a hissing cat with its back arched."

"Have you ever seen it?"

"No, and I don't think I want to." He'd never had it directed at *him*, anyway. Narciso described the cutthroat fashion world Carolyn had worked in, and how she survived by being willing and able to get into a catfight. "Carolyn, tell Billy about the time that I was getting a hard time in the dressing room."

Carolyn waved her hands as if she were erasing a big blackboard, getting everyone to settle down. "Okay," she said, "so I walk into the dressing room after getting a slice of pizza, and I hear this girl screaming at Narciso. I don't say a word, but this bitch gets it that something is going on behind her. She stops talking and looks around as if Calvin Klein himself had just walked in on her little tirade." They stared at each other for a moment, Carolyn and this girl. Then Carolyn glanced down at the slice of pizza in her hand, then back at the girl's face, as if to say, *If you don't want to wear this pizza* . . . The girl hurried out of the room and never confronted Narciso again. And now Narciso gazed at Carolyn fondly; he was her little pet to be taken care of.

It was a great weekend. There were, however, certain signs on the horizon. At one point John asked me, in an ominously serious way, to come upstairs with him. When we got to his bedroom, he fidgeted for a while, dancing around whatever he wanted to say. "Listen, Billy, I've been thinking about . . . You know, Carolyn's having a tough time, there's this thing with the RFKs. . . . I don't know. I was thinking that—now don't misunderstand me . . ."

I knew that Carolyn was annoyed by the paparazzi, but he was making me really nervous. Was someone sick? "John, focus. What are you trying to say?"

He sat down on the bed and looked me right in the eye, which he never did unless he was playing around or some big feeling was behind it—now he was stone-faced.

"I'm thinking about selling this house."

"John, we've been over this before." I thought he was referring to his finances.

"Billy, let me finish. I want you to buy it."

I shook my head and tried to get my thoughts around this. "John, there are about five things I can come up with immediately. First of all, you really *want* to keep this house. You own it outright, your accountant says to keep it, and you want to bring your children here. It was your father's only home. Plus, Carolyn loves it here."

"She does and she doesn't. We really don't get any privacy."

"You get enough. Anyway, I can't afford it. I've got a young family, the stock market jumps all around, plus I'm putting a family room on my house right now, and I'm strapped."

"How about if I finance it?"

"No. We have a good relationship, and that would only screw it up."

"How about if you rent it and just keep it up?"

"John, be real—I don't want to be your caretaker. Besides, do you think I want Ethel as a neighbor, with all those kids and dogs? I would have to cut through her yard to get to the beach. No, it's neither fish nor fowl. I have no interest. Why don't you sell it to someone in your family and visit?"

"They'll turn it into a function hall."

John hated the way Kennedys used their homes for fund-raisers. One year he allowed Teddy to put up a tent on his lawn. I got a call from a friend telling me he was going to JFK's house for dinner.

"How can that be?" I said. "John's in Africa."

I asked John about it when I saw him that August. Yep, a thousand dollars a head to eat chicken in a tent on the President's lawn—John decided he wasn't going to let that happen again.

Now John said, "It will do my heart good to have someone use the house, to have some life in the place. It seems so lonely on its own. Will you and Kathleen use it?"

"Sure, John, but I still don't want to be known as your houseboy."

"Who would think that?"

"What do you think they think now? It's hard being your friend without being accused of being a Kennedy kiss-ass."

"You and I know what we are—who cares what people think?"

"Okay. Let's leave it at that."

"One more thing—this addition to your house, are you okay?"

"Well, it's a lot of stress, with two babies, an au pair, a dog, construc—"

"No, I mean financially. Are you okay? You know to come to me first, right?"

Oh, Lawd, what a friend. "Yes, John, I'm fine," I said, patting him on the back. "Thanks, but I'm okay. Let's join the party."

WHAT I DIDN'T QUITE UNDERSTAND at that point was how John was grappling to find a place to live, and a lifestyle, that would suit Carolyn. But I was beginning to.

That December we received a box in the mail from Tiffany's. Not knowing what to expect, Kathleen waited until I got home to open it—she thought it might be her Christmas present. Instead it was five or six little blue boxes from Carolyn with a note: "I wasn't part of the family last year when TJ was born, but here's a little something for the kids." Two sterling baby cups with initials inscribed, two silver frames, and a piggy-bank for Kiely. This was way over the top, but it was Carolyn.

I called her husband. "Hey, John, we got a small cache of gifts from Tiffany's yesterday."

"You did? What was it?"

"Let's just say there are enough little boxes for TJ to be using them as building blocks."

I could hear him grunt as he moved the phone to his other ear, freeing up a hand to make his point. "Oh, my God, was it from Carolyn? She's doing this all over town, she's sending presents to everyone. I can't imagine what my bill is going to be."

I laughed. "Well, maybe she got something great for you, too."

"She has—there's a dozen sterling frames all over the apartment with no pictures in them. When I asked her what she was doing, she said, 'I'm just trying to make this loft feel homey. I'm trying to be a good domestic wife.'

"I told her, 'If you want to be a good domestic wife, forget the frames and make me a meat loaf.'"

16

Trouble in Paradise

RIGHT AFTER CHRISTMAS, John and Carolyn rented a home in Vero Beach down in Florida; John was getting his pilot's license there. They called to tell us the weather was great and to come down with the kids. We thanked them, but traveling with two kids under eighteen months is a lot of work We stayed home.

A few days later, I got a call from Carolyn, with a plea. "Billy, I need you to pick up John at the airport. We can't get a direct flight into Hyannis, and I don't want a car service picking him up—I want someone he knows to meet him."

"Wait a minute, Carolyn—what's going on?"

She sighed, annoyed. "Turn on the news!"

I guess I don't watch enough television. "Michael Kennedy was killed in a skiing accident last night," she told me, "and we're on our way up."

Oh, no. Things had not been going too well for Michael the past few years. He had run a lackluster campaign for Teddy; his drinking was getting the better of him; his marriage had fallen apart, mainly because of an alleged affair with an underage baby-sitter, for which he might have faced statutory rape charges; his cousin Michael Skakel had tried to sell a tell-all book about the affair. Meanwhile, his brother and confidant Congressman Joe Kennedy was trying to run for governor of Massachusetts. There was yet another problem: Joe's former wife had written a book about the hypocrisy of the Catholic Church in granting him an annulment, pointing out in the process what a mean guy he was.

Now Michael was dead, leaving young children behind in the wake of the scandal. It was not the best of times for the Robert Kennedys.

"Will you pick him up at Logan with the dog and drive him to the Cape?" Carolyn asked. A friend in need is a pest indeed. But what else could I do?

When I picked him up, John was visibly shaken.

"Bad news, huh?"

"Let me get my thoughts together, Billy."

We had driven in silence for about forty-five minutes when he finally started to talk.

"You know that stupid game they play," John said, shaking his head; he was referring to playing football while downhill skiing. "It's so dangerous. Max"—his cousin—"broke his leg last year—the same stupid game. They were warned about it, and now look what happened. It's just the Kennedys acting like Kennedys.

"At least now maybe all this shit will settle down. He can be the scapegoat that everyone can hang their problems on, and the press will let it all die down. Maybe."

We drove to the house where we'd had so much fun just a month before. It was dark out now. Provi, on call, was there with dinner. But there was another problem: Carolyn was due to land that night, and she was terrified of the paparazzi, who really swarmed when there was a scandal or death. And she was growing more terrified of them.

She called. "Can you get me without being seen?" I phoned a friend who could get me on the tarmac at the airport in Barnstable, and when Carolyn's plane landed, Gustavo and I scooped her up. That didn't stop the photographers; a car chased us, which is against the law. When I got to John's gate, I told the police, who'd been summoned to control the press, that this guy was following us. But the photographers raced in front of us anyway, jumped out, and tried to get her picture.

We slipped in through a privet hedge and avoided the paparazzi. Dinner was somber. I thought, *How quickly things can change.* Then I left for home, glad to leave the drama behind. There were, John told me later, some hysterics at the wake; it was a very sad end to a troubled life. All this was a harbinger of things to come—1998 started badly and would go downhill from there.

The next month I was in New York trying to save some Irish accounts my firm was fighting to hold on to; the investment firm's headquarters was two blocks away from John's North Moore Street loft. When I met him, I explained the situation.

"Do these guys know about you, your history in Ireland, and that you know me and I'm a client of yours?" he asked.

"They don't care, John. It's all about the money, and the London desk wants to control the accounts."

"If I were you, I'd fight them. How can you bring in the accounts and they take them?"

"John, it's business. And I'm trying to fight it."

"Do you want me to call someone?"

"No thanks, I can fight my own battles. Anyway, I call on you when I really need you."

We got to the loft, and Carolyn was there with her sister Lauren, whom I hadn't seen since the wedding. The loft was really unusual. Apart from the bathrooms and bedroom, it was a completely open space with no doors. It was filled with leftover items from 1040.

"Where's the Greek statue?" I asked John.

"At the Met."

"I see. The Met."

"What's wrong with that?"

"Nothing. It's just that you're the only guy I know who gifts five-thousand-year-old statues to the Met."

The brown velvet sofa and chairs around the TV were from the library—they looked Victorian and out of place in the modern loft, but they were a cool juxtaposition to the surroundings. John lit the candles on the two six-foot-tall candelabra, my wedding present. We checked out wedding proofs and watched a Knicks game.

There were other pieces I recognized from 1040: the large highboy with the presidential seal and initials, Jackie's painting station, artwork. There was also a beautiful picture frame from President Clinton with the presidential seal but no picture in it; in fact, the Tiffany frames were still scattered around unfilled, even though there were scores of black-and-whites of John as a kid in a baby buggy on the Truman Balcony. I asked why they weren't in the frames.

"We haven't got around to it yet," Carolyn said. Typical—so much of John always seemed to be in a state of flux, as if he enjoyed living that way.

John also had his father's scrimshaw collection, which John prized. (It was the first thing mentioned in his will, left to Caroline's son.) He took me up on his roof to point out the Woolworth Building and other sky-scrapers, but it was a tour I didn't want, since heights scare me. Back down on the street, we took a walk. Tribeca was still desolate then; you could fire a cannon in this part of town without arousing a soul.

"It's starting to get popular," John claimed.

"Because you're here?"

"No. De Niro lives down here, too."

The next morning I went off to battle for my investing rights; neither side came out with what they wanted. John and Carolyn met with their attorneys to see if there was any legal remedy to keep the photographers from hounding them. I picked up Carolyn at their loft to have lunch. She peered through the doorway, waiting for paparazzi to jump out at her; there was no one there. For the first time, I wondered if she was a little paranoid.

"They're here," she said defensively. "You wait and see—they're here."

We went to Bubby's around the corner; the maître d', who knew her, seated us in back, but Carolyn was still nervous.

"They're all staring at me," she complained.

"Carolyn, for God's sake, I'll protect you."

She smiled wanly. "You will, Big Bad Bill?"

"Yes. Now, what are you going to have? My treat."

"See that guy going to the bathroom? He just stopped to look in the mirror, and I saw him looking at me."

I put down my menu. "Carolyn, you're beautiful, you're the envy of every woman in New York, and you're the dream girl for all men. Why not enjoy this?" But I looked at the mirror, and of course she was right— people *were* staring at her in its reflection.

After lunch we went back to the apartment and talked for about an hour. She was all in a tizzy. Carolyn didn't like living in a loft in the middle of nowhere that John had designed as a bachelor, with no doors. "Our other house is his father's, and the Vineyard house is his mother's," she said. "I have no place of my own."

"Would you move to some bedroom community nearby?"

"No, he'd never do it—he thrives off the energy of the city."

"How about uptown?"

"He grew up there, and I'd still get chased by photographers every time I went out."

I could see where this was going. She was in a spot, psychologically, where she could see no solution. "Carolyn, there are more of them than you, and you're going to have to get used to it. They did the same thing to Jackie."

"Yeah, well, I need her now, but she's not here. The only one that can help me is Caroline, and she hasn't been helpful."

"Why do you think that is?" In fact, I knew why, and I hoped we didn't have to get into it. They were from utterly different backgrounds.

Once, I asked Carolyn if she wanted to go water-skiing with John and me. "Water-skiing?" she smirked. "Listen, Billy Noonan, when John was water-skiing off the back off the *Christina,* I was working in a discount store, wearing a brown smock. I can't water-ski."

It's an interesting point: Anthony, John, and I had all married girls that we loved because of their feistiness, their simplicity, their élan, and their "realness." Not because of their social position, who their father was, their wealth, and so on—we were beyond all that.

"I don't know," she said now about the frostiness between herself and Caroline. "Maybe because I have gotten her initials?" She smiled.

Sure, that was it.

"Billy, you don't understand. When I walk up a street, they walk in front of me backward, knocking over old ladies and mothers with children. They don't care. Look what happened to Princess Diana." A point I couldn't argue.

When Diana was killed, I called John. We were in Boston that Labor Day because Kathleen was expecting Kiely; she had TJ by cesarean and was going to have Kiely naturally, so things were a little tense (they finally induced her, a week late). I spoke with John. "What a pity," I said. "She was some beauty." He agreed.

"Yeah, well, I'm not sure what I'm going to do about Carolyn," he told me. "She's really spooked now."

And now I was hearing it again. When I saw John and Carolyn at the Cape, there were minor incidents, but nothing big. Yet she was frightened, and she had reason to be frightened. The bigger problem, however, was her inability to see any way to deal with the paparazzi; she'd begun to box herself in, with no way out.

"How can I bring JFK III into this world?" she went on now. "They'll never leave me alone. They treat John like a national treasure, so what are they going to do to his *son*?"

Well, put that way, it was a very good question.

"Billy, he trusts you and Robbie [Littell] the most—in fact, you're the only two who could have talked him out of marrying me, he trusts you that much. What can we do? Will you talk with him?"

I suggested that they fix up the Hyannisport house, sell some land on the Vineyard to reduce taxes, and raise some cash to find another getaway on some island somewhere.

"He won't go for that, and I'm not living up on the Cape year-round. It's too desolate."

Again, the problem with no solution.

"If I don't do something soon, I'm going to end up in a trailer park, screaming, 'I used to be married to John F. Kennedy, Jr.!'" It was too funny for words, but also a terrible little corner she was painting herself into. "Nothing, I mean nothing, could have prepared me for what I'm going through."

I was hoping that the judge they'd seen this morning would give them some relief. At this point she had John on edge with the press, and he had always handled the attention pretty smoothly. He'd come out of the water in Hyannisport not long ago to find a bunch of photographers snapping away at her alone, sunbathing on the beach, and screamed, "You can fuck with me, but stay away from my wife!" He even threw a bucket of water on some amateur-video guy who was on a private pier, after the guy called a neighbor "a bitch" when she told him to get off the pier and leave John alone. John later apologized and paid for the guy's camera; he loved telling me the story, because he knew exactly what I thought of these leeches.

But that missed the point, one that Carolyn simply couldn't grasp. The world is full of leeches, and she had to learn to deal with them.

I REALIZED THAT REAL TROUBLE was coming when I began to see how Carolyn was isolating herself and becoming too close to staff, rather than a circle of friends. John had always maintained a kitchen cabinet of friends, and he was very good at enjoying people from different spheres of his life. That kept him from becoming too insulated. Some friends, or would-be friends, would get a little too impressed with John's celebrity, but they'd eventually be spun out. John didn't like to talk about disloyalty—his standard line was, "I'd rather be screwed by a friend than an enemy." If you teased him about gossip or tabloid trash, though, you could get a verbal thrashing.

Once there was a rumor that John was going to be on a soap opera and was quitting his job at the DA's office. It had legs in New York and then hit *USA Today*; John was called on the carpet by his boss. He did not like having to explain that there was no truth to the story; yet he *was* planning on a move once his term was up, which complicated the issue. A friend of John's from Brown made light of the whole thing, and John hammered him for bringing it up, believing it, and, even worse, thinking there was something funny about the stuff he had to endure: "I had to meet with the DA, my mother is going ballistic, it's all bullshit, and you think it's funny? Well, think again, because it's not." He was hot.

The point is, though, that John maintained a solid network of friends he trusted implicitly, and outside that tight circle he enjoyed more peripheral friends he'd let in only so far, but enjoyed nonetheless. He wasn't going to live in a bubble.

Carolyn was of a different mind. She trusted few; she was from a broken family with identical twin sisters who would gang up on her when they were kids. Natural stuff. Her mother had remarried a man with children of his own; stepsiblings can be tough. Carolyn clawed her way up in the fashion industry; the friends she did maintain were edgy girls and gay guys. I knew that John would eventually put his foot down.

But now I was watching Carolyn, in becoming isolated herself, trying to isolate him, too, whittling down his friendships. She'd speculate about how some of his friends didn't trust other friends. It was classic, playing both ends against the middle so that she'd have more control.

Carolyn was using drugs, too, and it was taking a toll, making her nervous and sometimes paranoid, though, as someone once said, just because you're paranoid doesn't mean you don't have real enemies. Her behavior, and the way she was alienating people, was slopping over into John's world. John used to say that he was raised to be polite and never boast, that since he had so much more than most people, he should be modest and thankful and gracious. But now he was tolerating Carolyn's attitude about oglers. "What are you looking at?" she'd sometimes rail in public. "Do you think he's some sort of animal in a petting zoo?"

Or she'd tell friends off, and John was sort of digging it. But it was getting toxic. She'd begun complaining constantly, seeing the worst in situations and people. Cynicism can be fatal. It was all surprising and sad. As an international journalist friend of mine, trying to get some copy from me, commented, "Let's see if I have this right: The world's most eligible bachelor marries a druggy who won't leave the apartment, is that it?"

Well, it was headed that way.

Alienating those who might have helped her and courting the wrong people as intimates certainly didn't help. Effie quit and returned to Portugal because, I understand, Carolyn crossed the line between boss and employee; she couldn't help herself, she needed confessors. She was constantly on the phone with John's assistant, calling her "Lamby" and John "Mousy." She *did* make it sound like a petting zoo.

At the same time, Caroline could have been a great ally, but Carolyn couldn't connect with her. Instead she constantly told John that Caroline and Ed treated him like shit and pointed out how John was being left out of the loop, that they thought he was a fuckup. John deflected most of it and then started to listen to her. It is never, after all, the sibling that ruins family relationships; it's always the nagging spouse. John had a blunt take: "When it's just Caroline and me, we're fine—add a spouse, and look out."

Next she went after the Kennedys. Teddy was ignoring John, she claimed, avoiding a *George* event when he was just a block away; aunts and uncles were being lost to Carolyn's world of discontent. Everyone was going overboard. She needed a cause célèbre, an angle, a way to survive. She found one in Anthony. And that would be my undoing with John for a while.

ON OUR ANNUAL VISIT to the Vineyard, the third week in July that year, I flew Kathleen and the two babies over in a chartered plane. I had started going to New Bedford, because getting to the Cape on Fridays had become a time-consuming and frustrating event. It seemed as if everyone was going to the Cape now and even more to the islands. But leaving on a Thursday night, flying in, getting to Red Gate was a cinch.

We stayed at the barn, which Jackie had built just for her kids and their friends. Effie was over from Portugal to help train a new house-keeper for the two of them. He told me that he would make dinner and to come by the main house in half an hour. When I walked over, Effie said, "Carolyn wants you to call her. I think it is important."

"Why didn't you buzz me at the barn?"

"Ed made us take out the intercom system, to save money or some-thing, and I could not leave the stove."

The tone was so different; Effie would not have said something like that before, especially if Mrs. Onassis were alive. I called Carolyn at home in New York. "Billy," she said, "John is on his way up tonight, he wants to surprise you."

"Okay, then why ruin the surprise? Is something up?"

"Anthony—it's bad news. The cancer is back, and this is the beginning of the end."

We ate, and I drank wine while I waited for the bearer of bad news. Finally, in he came. Kathleen left us together in the living room, where a fire burned.

"Anthony's sick again," John announced. "It keeps coming back, eat-ing away at him. It won't leave him alone. This is bad news."

"What's the opinion?"

He stared at me for a moment. "Did you know any of this, Billy?"

"Why?"

"Because I can tell from your reaction. Who told you—was it Carolyn?"

Up to that point, I would have covered for her, but no more. "Yeah. She called to tell me, and that you were coming."

"So if you knew, why didn't you stop me?"

"Because you just started to tell me, and I would have, once you fin-ished. I wanted you to have an ear."

"She's so fucking sneaky! She is into everything, meddling and manipulating!" he yelled. Then he calmed down. "All right, it's not that bad, it's just—it's Anthony, and I wanted to get your initial reaction to this."

"Well, if it's any consolation, my reaction would be the same. I survived this thing. Watching him die makes me worry. John, I've got two little kids, I worry about it every day, but you have to live your life until one day they give you bad news or just take it away. How you live is how you die."

He said nothing, then got up and went to the fireplace. "I don't know, I just worry about Carole. . . .

"Carolyn has really been great to her," he went on, still standing at the fireplace, his hands on the mantel, staring at the flames. "In some weird way, they're bonding over this, and it's great to see. She does these little sweet things like buy her friendship rings, really nice ones, from Tiffany's." He started pacing, with his head down—his defense mechanism—still focused on the fire, not making eye contact with me. "I keep losing everyone. I really need to start thinking about having a family. This is going to suck—a baby makes everything better, right?"

"Well, things have to be in order. Everyone has to be ready. A baby is a big thing."

We talked about how Kathleen and I had started our family; he asked me to remind him how long we were married before we started having kids.

"I already have a name if it's a boy," John said, smiling. "Flynn, Flynn Kennedy—now that's a name. What do you think?"

"Flynn is my mother's maiden name. I'm down with it. By the way, what do you want my kids to call you? John, Mr. Kennedy, Uncle John—what?"

"How about Godfather?"

He was still upset that I had been chosen over him as godfather for Timmy's second son. "I did my family for TJ and Kathleen's family for Kiely, since that's their family name—you're next."

"Are you going to keep having kids? Because I'd love to have our kids grow up together."

"Well, two in one year is a lot, so we'll probably take a deep breath before we start again."

"Yeah, I want to start now, but Carolyn wants to wait and see what happens with Anthony. She wants to be around for Carole."

"Wow, that much, huh?"

"Yeah, I think it will be the three of us for a while anyway."

The next day Carolyn and her friend Jessica arrived. John was distracted and seemed low. Another guy named John—John York, a pilot friend who was supposed to come—couldn't make it. At midday John simply disappeared. Kathleen was on baby patrol, so I was left twiddling my thumbs, and that set me off.

I went to the beach to surf-cast for stripers. Finally John reappeared—he had flown to the Cape to check on the house. I was furious, so I let him have it. "What the fuck am I doing here? Why would you just leave? I'm so pissed off that I yelled at Kathleen, because you left me here and went to the Cape."

I was just warming up. "Do you know how difficult it is to get here, taking a day off, driving to New Bedford, bringing the dog, two kids? Then you show up with awful news and just escape to the Cape? What's up with that?"

"You should not have yelled at Kathleen."

"John, I yelled at her because of you, not her—don't try to shift the responsibility. Why didn't you tell me you were going to the Cape?"

"Well, I wanted to be alone, and I didn't think you'd want to fly with me."

I waited for his lower lip to start quivering—oh, he knew he was wrong, but I could barely control myself, because his skipping out like that seemed part and parcel of what he was becoming, which was selfish and insensitive and scattered and . . .

"If you wanted to be alone," I told him, "why didn't you call me and cancel?"

"Because I want you to enjoy this place. That's why I keep it, so my friends, like you, can come enjoy it."

"John, I'm no Fresh Air kid. I grew up on the Cape, and these two islands are like right field and left field for me, my playgrounds. I know these waters and islands like no other place in the world. And that doesn't answer why you left without telling me."

"Because most people won't fly with me."

"To the Cape? I would have flown to the Cape with you—I can't believe you." It was ugly.

He apologized, then said, "You're my best friend, Billy. You and Kathleen and the kids are like family to me."

I wanted to say no thanks, that I saw how he and his family were getting along, but it would have felt like whipping a puppy—he was so lost he didn't even see how selfish he'd become, how closed up into the box of his own world.

But now I was silent. He did have a lot on his mind, and I didn't think he would act so selfishly again. I was wrong.

I went back to the barn and straightened out the situation with Kathleen. Carolyn came over and sat on my bed to talk to me after I'd showered. "Billy, what did you say to John? He's white."

"I told him he acted like an asshole, and he agreed."

"Billy, you have to understand that he has a lot on his mind with Anthony and—"

"Listen, Carolyn, I've been with the Anthony thing since it started. There's no excuse for the way he acted. I was done with it, but now you're pissing me off again. Why don't you stay out of it?"

"Because John is so upset."

"He should be upset. He acted like an asshole, and it's my job to tell him that, and you should stay out of it. Let it go. Let's just have dinner and move on."

No way.

We made it through dinner, and John and I went canoeing on Squibnocket Pond under the moonlight; he showed me some work he had done at the hunting shack, the only building that came with the three-hundred-plus acres of property (plus a privy). He'd put in a water jug and decorated it with the nautical booty that had washed up on his beach. But we were going through the motions; things had gotten too bizarre and unpleasant. Kathleen and I left early in the morning.

I would not see them again until the following May at the Profiles in Courage Awards dinner. John called once in the intervening months to yell at me and to ask why I didn't call anymore.

"Let's keep it simple," I told him. "Let's talk about your investments and keep it light."

I knew that the claws were in my back. And I did not care. I stood my ground.

17

All Is Forgiven

IT WAS A STRANGE INTERLUDE before the Profiles in Courage Awards dinner in May, the longest John and I had gone without getting together in twenty-five years of friendship. We did talk business over the winter, and about a funny trip to Dublin with Timmy. I was there on business and Timmy went over to announce that the Special Olympics World Games would be coming to Ireland in 2003. We knuckleheaded around Dublin for a few days, having meetings during the day and going to discos and after-hours joints; it was a different orbit for Timmy—he was relaxed and enjoying himself like he was back at Yale on the rugby team. I also talked with Anthony over the winter. He assured me that my friendship with John and Carolyn would "work its way out. We all make bad decisions and choices. I'm not sure who was at fault, but let it go."

I could, and I was sure John could, but I knew there were people who would have gladly seen me out of the way—a few who were trying to step into John's world, to benefit from a closer relationship, always to better themselves. This played into Carolyn's hands as she looked for allies against enemies. I was, for now, a convenient enemy, but taking a strong stance makes it difficult to retreat and surrender; I felt that it was better to stay away and keep quiet. I wanted to be friends with people because of their character and strength and intellect, but also because of their weaknesses, their humanity—*them,* in other words. I wouldn't get involved in the intrigue again.

I was sure John would call me for the Profiles dinner; I had been to every dinner as his guest since the library started having events in 1985. If he did not call, our friendship, based in large part on a straightforwardness with each other that had helped both of us immensely, was probably over.

Yet I would have been okay with that. We'd had a good run, and his life was taking him in different directions. When we had talked, over the winter, he didn't mention starting a family; his conversation did include chatter about colorists, designers, image consultants—things that had nothing to do with where I was, which centered on the stock market, golf, the kids, the Cape. Who needed a personal stylist or a professional party planner? I thought the credo was, at the banquet of life, eat what you want and leave the rest. His life was changing, and it wasn't evolution; I knew he was not happy with his lot.

Before the dinner I was unsure about exposing myself to this drama again. It had been a long break, but I figured at least I could get a feel for what was going on, whether things were getting better or still crazy. Kathleen felt the same way; we were curious about John and Carolyn as a couple—where were they now?

We met them at the Boston Harbor Hotel; there had been some confusion about rooms, and apparently Teddy had walked in on Carolyn, which was an inauspicious start. We took a limo to the event—it was a quiet ride. How could she face us? Carolyn had been so close to us and now seemed so distant. Either John had told her to keep quiet, or she was seeing a psychiatrist, or she was medicated. Or a combination of all three.

"Awkward" was the word for the night. It was awkward because Carolyn had turned on us, awkward because of Anthony's illness, awkward because of the Carolyn-Caroline tension, awkward because some Kennedys, Teddy in particular, were upset with John for bringing the notorious Larry Flynt to that White House Correspondents' Association dinner just a few weeks earlier.

But after the dinner we went back to their hotel room with them, and the mood changed. John, obviously relieved that the event was behind him, became his animated self; Carolyn was still quiet, but centered. She said that Thanksgiving had not been fun without us, and she picked up her old interest in Kathleen and the kids. That was always her best quality— the way she could zero right in on *you* and need to know everything. John and I went out and walked the piers along the Boston harbor front.

"Sometimes I feel that I should just move to the Vineyard and become a gentleman farmer," John said. "I could work my magic from there, coming to Harvard and New York for meetings."

This was a momentary fantasy—he'd never be a gentleman farmer. But John clearly needed to move on in some new direction; the question was, doing what? He sounded exhausted: *George* was losing steam, and he needed to find money to keep it going. Battling Carolyn's lifestyle had taken its toll. The library events had lost their appeal to him; he was looking for alternatives to his responsibilities to the Boston-based Kennedy institutions.

He felt that Caroline was more suited to overseeing the library, and now that Ed had redesigned it, the library's purpose had shifted to fundraising and special events. The Special Olympics, the mainstay of the Kennedy Foundation, was under excellent guidance with Timmy in charge. John's interests lay in the Institute of Politics at the Kennedy School of Government. Founded by Robert Kennedy, its goal was to keep the spirit of President Kennedy's leadership alive and to foster ongoing political debate at Harvard. Jackie had designed the forum, later memorialized in John's name, to be similar to the Roman forums, where leaders and luminaries could be asked questions and, in some cases, interrogated by students. Point and counterpoint, debate—that was quintessential John.

Carolyn was better, he told me quietly as we walked into a May night growing cool. She was in intense psychoanalysis: five days a week, plus medication for depression. The recreational drugs had stopped, and there were no more blowups; they were working things out. But there was something somber in his tone, a portent of some change he didn't get into. He also didn't bring up what had happened the summer before, to acknowledge his responsibility, but he didn't have to—tonight's invitation established that.

He also told me that Anthony was failing, and staying, now, on the Vineyard.

"Why don't you come over, Billy?"

No—the days of going to Red Gate were finished for me, and I could not think of Anthony sick. I did not want to see him that way.

"Nothing is going to change until this situation does," John told me. So there it was: He was in limbo, looking ahead, but exactly what that meant, we didn't get into that night.

I was out driving around the Cape early the next weekend, Memorial Day; it's what I do when I'm up before the rest of the house. John had asked me to go over and take a look at the renovation of the Cape house. A couple years before, when John decided to keep it, he asked me to rec-ommend a contractor.

"I don't want any of these Cape Cod rip-off artists trying to make a few extra bucks off me and then parading around the fact that they reno-vated my house," he had said. "I want someone who'll keep quiet and do a good job—then I'll recommend him to people, and he'll probably take in a load of new business."

The renovator that John found was there at the house working when I arrived. He was from County Tipperary, the same village as Kathleen's family, just the sort of talented, below-the-radar guy John loved to work with. He showed me around, explaining everything he'd done and why. The floors, which had been painted for years in an old Cape Cod design, had been sanded and stained; upholstery fabric was replaced; wallpaper that had been literally hanging off the walls was replaced; and other rooms had been painted. He also regaled me with stories about how "Mrs. Kennedy"—Carolyn—had changed her mind about a number of things and was worried that she had changed the character of the house. She wanted to maintain Jackie's simple elegance, and we had a good laugh about her indecisiveness.

On my way home, I called over to the Vineyard; Carolyn answered. I told her I had just left the house and wanted to bring John up to speed— she asked what I thought about the wallpaper in Mummy's room. I explained that I was more of a floor-and-paint guy than a wallpaper-and-fabric guy. She laughed and said she'd picked it out because it was a pattern of small pink shamrocks—she ordered it thinking of me. I told her that I approved and that Jackie would have as well. She asked if I thought it would be ready by the end of July, as they were coming in August, as usual. And . . . was I going to bring Kathleen and the kids?

I was, frankly, a little weirded out by all this attention after a ten-month drought, but it was one of those things to overlook and accept for what it was: an offer of renewed friendship from both of them.

John, however, did not return my phone call, though he had a good excuse: He had crashed his Buckeye on the Vineyard and was at the hospital with a broken ankle.

A few days later, he called—John was calling all the time now. He was still laid up on the Vineyard but wanted to talk about Anthony, the house, about our upcoming weekend celebrating our wedding anniversary. I told him we had made plans to go to Nantucket with Brian and Miriam O'Neill and another couple. If he was game, there was room. He jumped right in, no excuses, no checking with Carolyn. He was in.

I had a strange premonition that July Fourth that something was deeply wrong. It was a moonless night. "Someone just walked over my grave," I said to Kathleen. "I wonder if it was Anthony."

I called him. It was quiet there, quite serene and low-key.

I was very interested in seeing John and finding out what was going on. He had been making vague references on the phone about shutting things down and starting things up. During the week before our anniversary dinner, he told me that he had something pressing to talk about, but with curious ears in the office, John was cautious. "We'll talk about it this weekend." Years earlier he had referred to a straw poll for the Senate seat that would be vacated by Daniel Patrick Moynihan. It had been floated by a guy named Mark Greene from the Green Party in New York; the poll had concluded that John would come in first, followed by Hillary and then the floater. I asked him now what was up with that poll, to rib him about how the press was pushing for Hillary Clinton to replace Moynihan.

"Wait until she gets here," John said. "She's gonna get her head handed to her." He was in.

On Thursday, July 15, Kathleen, the kids, and I left for the Cape. The next day was our fifth wedding anniversary. We had accomplished a lot in five years and were eager to celebrate. Our plan was to meet the boat in Hyannisport, assemble the four couples, and head to Nantucket for dinner. Simple enough.

18

Gone Missing

WALKING INTO THAT KITCHEN that morning was one of the hardest things I have ever done. All my memories as a kid of walking by, looking in, wondering what went on there, then hanging out with John as a teenager, parking my car out front, hanging with the Secret Service agents, driving Jackie's BMW. So many breakfasts, lunches, dinners, the holidays there with the newlyweds, TJ's initials in the cement in the gate of the fence—memories, small and large, came washing over me.

And Provi would be there, worried sick.

When I crossed the threshold, she was sitting at the small kitchen table. "Where's Yahn?" she asked me desperately. "Is he with you, Billy Noonan?"

Her head sank onto the table when I told her that he was not. Then she kept saying, "My God, what am I going to do? Where's Gustavo?" Her son was supposed to have come to the Cape from New York to attend Rory Kennedy's wedding, and no one had heard from him so far.

Dan Samson and I moved into the living room; we needed to talk. He was so jet-lagged from his flight from Seattle that he had trouble remembering exactly who had called the night before. Eventually it emerged that Carole Radziwill had called when John and Carolyn didn't arrive on the Vineyard, hoping they'd gone right to the Cape. Dan had called Timmy to ask him the protocol on informing the compound; then he was up most of the night on the phone with the coast guard and Teddy.

I called Timmy in Washington, and we had a moment of gallows humor as we laughed about John running out of fuel and standing on the wing, Carolyn yelling at him about her dress and not having anything to wear to the wedding. Some of the Kennedy cousins came by and sat for a while, watching the news. It felt like an out-of-body experience, sitting in John's living room while the rest of the nation watched the news unfold on television.

The phones rang nonstop. I checked my phone at home in Boston: 71 messages. I went through them all, hoping for John's voice. Instead, it was crying friends, reporters, and condolences.

Exhausted, I went to John's room for a shower and lay down on his bed, hoping he would wake me with a punch and a "Get the hell out of my bed." His bedroom was the President's, part of a suite; the President and First Lady had their own rooms. For years before John took it over, this room had been locked and left as it was in 1963. Now I looked up at the dings in the ceiling, remembering the day when John explained that they were the result of his father practicing his golf swing away from the public eye; Eisenhower had been accused of too much golf and not enough work, and JFK didn't want the same said of him.

I went back downstairs. Debris started washing up on John's beach— a bag with Lauren's name, Carolyn's medication, bits of plane. Max Kennedy started to cry, and I asked him not to do that, as it confirmed the unimaginable. They were having a mass next door in the tent for the wedding that was now postponed. I could not go, as I couldn't bear to see the pain in anyone else's eyes. I could only hope.

Of all the people I knew, if there was anyone, anyone at all that could survive, it was John Kennedy. He might have been the most unreliable, the messiest, the most unpredictable, the most forgetful, irresponsible guy in the world, but he took a few things seriously. One was safety, another was other people's feelings. He would have survived this, he would have gotten them out of that plane, risking his own life in the rescue.

I was sure they were hanging on to something out there—a buoy, a piece of the fuselage, a seat cushion, a piece of wood, something.

Timmy called again. He told me to put up a perimeter around the house; no one was allowed access—no one. It was Caroline's request; if there were any questions, call him. Some of the guests next door were trying to come over. One guy in particular, who considered himself a friend of John's, demanded that he be allowed in. I told him no. He would not back off and asked a cop to cajole Provi, who asked me what to do about him. I went out, told the police he was not to come in and that if he persisted, they should arrest him. Back in the living room, I told William Smith what was going on, calling the punk a pilot fish. Even now they were trying to glom on to John. Check that—*especially* now. William laughed and said that was exactly what he was, a pilot fish.

Timmy called again. "Can you believe this?" We sobbed together. "I can't believe this," was all we kept saying. I asked him if he would come here, to Hyannisport; he said he was working the phone from where he was. They were still trying to get Caroline and her family back to the East Coast from a white-water rafting trip. I tried to hold on to hope, but I was only fooling myself, and at this point I knew it.

Where was Gustavo? Dan and I thought that since Dan did not fly with John, maybe John had extended an invitation to Gustavo to fly him to the wedding. We went next door to talk to Bobby Kennedy about it— Bobby and Gustavo were like brothers—and his feeling was that if Gustavo were on the plane, this would probably kill Provi, so we decided to wait awhile. Thank God, when we got back to the house, Gustavo had arrived.

"I couldn't call," he explained, "because the phones were busy. And I couldn't get a flight, because it's the weekend and because every reporter and camera crew are headed here. I had to take a bus."

Dan and I walked around Hyannisport in a daze. The police knew me, so there was no question about access to the house. Dan was angry and willing to take on some reporter or gawker—anyone. The gate to John's house was now unattended; the press had piled up at the top of the street that leads to the compound, the hundred-yard thoroughfare I watched the President drive by a long time ago.

That afternoon Kathleen came to the house with a change of clothes. "Why don't you come home, Billy, and get some rest?"

Rest? How could I rest? My best friend was missing.

That night I drove to the Shrivers' for distraction and a couple of drinks. Driving back, I encountered a press scrum at the top of the street, blocking it. I asked them to move, they would not, I beeped, they still wouldn't move. I couldn't get back to the house. I beeped again, and some reporter yelled, "Shut up!"

I got out of the car and asked him to repeat what he'd just said; he backpedaled silently. The other reporters and camerapeople were quiet. Then I turned the car around and headed around the block, approaching the President's house a different way.

I spied an African-American woman quietly wrapping a yellow ribbon around the telephone pole in front of John's house. I could have kissed her, but she moved away as quietly as she'd appeared. John would have loved that. Gustavo and Santina used to tell me how he would coax them into taking him up to the Apollo Theater in Harlem on Saturday nights, where he would dance around oblivious to the stares and comments. I remember John once saying about someone in his family, "He's white, but he's all right"—like it was a line from a Motown hit. And John relished his father's legacy within the black community.

Rosemarie, John's assistant at *George*, had set up at his apartment on North Moore to make sure nothing even more bizarre happened. Barbara Walters was calling Rosemarie looking for someone to comment. "Who would be credible at a time like this?" asked Rosie. The press called my in-laws looking for me. I stayed where I was; I was safe here. Who was the first guy on TV? Same as the first guy blabbing after the wedding: Barlow.

What an opportunist. He was making plans to get to New York for the services, he said. I thought, *I hope he has a television in his suite.*

The next day, Dan and I walked around Hyannisport some more, taking swims rather than showering, the sweat pouring out of us. We couldn't eat. We drank some, and we were so distracted we could not finish sentences. I went up to the widow's walk, our old tree fort, and looked out over the sound, at the sleepless sea, sparkling and twinkling in the night. *Where is he? Why won't you give him up?*

"In the night that he is troubled, / May a friend wake for him, / So that his time be doubled." Those lines were from the silver cup given to JFK by the Irish ambassador; Teddy had cited it at the wedding reception, and the words kept repeating, over and over, in my mind.

I could not imagine life without him. I always thought he would be there for me, visiting my hospital room, asking if I needed money, throwing my kids up in the air, and that he was on his way to becoming something great. All I wanted was for him to fulfill the promise the President had made to my father, to be John's envoy in Dublin when he became president. That was all. If that would happen, I could die happy. Now it was all twisted around, already gone. I thought of the expression, "What's wrong? You look like you just lost your best friend." Lord.

I tried to watch TV news, but it only scared me; I couldn't fathom how the rest of the country was processing this. Thoreau had once said that a man could stand on the beach at Cape Cod and "put all of America behind him." I could not read the papers, though I did see the front page of Sunday's, with a picture of President Kennedy in the top left corner and, in the top right corner, one of John. The alpha and the omega. There would be no widow, no mother. And no child I could go to, take to a football game, watch graduate and marry, as so many had done with John. There would be no more.

On Sunday afternoon, reports came in that the fragments of plane found indicated that the plane was clearly broken apart at a force that would have killed all those on board. Still I clung to hope. Dan picked apples from the apple trees on John's lawn, and I took, from the Shrivers' house, a framed print of JFK swimming with the straps of a life preserver in his teeth, after the crash of *PT-109*. We carried them around like talismans.

That night a film crew set up little tents outside the bend in the compound stockade. We went in to see them on television telling lies and making up Kennedy stories that never happened. We went outside and threw apples over the fence at them, yelling, "Shut up, you liars! You're making that up!"

On Monday Dan and I visited the command center at Otis Air Force Base and had a sobering conversation with a commander.

"What if he's still out there hanging on to a buoy?" I asked, still clinging on myself.

"Impossible," was the answer. "In seventy-five-degree water, the human body can survive for only so long, and gripping strength decreases after two hours. Mr. Noonan, you should know that this is not a search-and-rescue mission any longer. It is now a recovery mission."

It was crystal clear, delivered as a terse military directive. There was no hope. He was gone.

Mark and Jeannie Shriver, Provi and Gustavo, and Dan and I went out to dinner. We told stories—not just of John but stories about Hyannisport and different situations. We laughed like nothing was on our minds. But when we returned to John's house, Dan and I couldn't take it; we went to the Shrivers' to try to get some sleep.

In the morning I decided that it was time to return to my family and office, and when I went back to John's to collect my things, I saw the flag snapping at half staff at Ambassador Kennedy's house. It was official. I looked around to drink it all in one last time, vowing never to return. There was nothing I wanted from that house, not at that moment. I went to his bedroom, the President's bedroom, and looked around at his personal things. Suddenly I remembered the Yeats poem: "What made us dream that he could comb grey hair?" I took John's comb. His comb *will* comb gray hairs—mine.

I returned to Boston to my family. My kids played while I sat catatonic in my chair, waving away phone calls and visitors.

The next morning, as I was driving to work in Boston, a local DJ announced that the bodies had been found. He dedicated "The End of the Innocence," by Don Henley, to John and Carolyn. The end of our innocence.

I turned around, went home, and turned on the television. Then I sat down and cried.

19

The Funeral

I GOT A CALL from William Smith. He informed me that I would be one of John's pallbearers, but an honorary one, as the bodies were to be cremated and distributed at sea. He said we should all go out to the Vineyard and celebrate John's life. But that was not a place I would return to, so I didn't think it was a great idea. Apparently others felt the same way— I didn't hear about it again.

Kathleen and I headed down to New York that Thursday. We made a quick visit to John's office to pick up a packet of information for the funeral. I looked into the office—it was all in boxes, bare. A life already packed up. We checked in to a hotel and made a quick decision not to attend the mass at St. Patrick's Cathedral. Sasha had arranged for a group of old friends to get together at an apartment. It was tough, but we smiled through the tears. I saw Jenny Christian, John's girlfriend two decades before. "The last time I saw you in New York," I told her, laughing, "we made headlines." It was the night of John's eighteenth-birthday party and the fight with the paparazzi.

"I remember you being a hero that night," Jenny said. *At last,* I thought, *someone understands.*

The next morning we assembled at St. Thomas More, waiting in the rectory before John's funeral service for instructions. Senator Kennedy's family arrived; little Teddy lost his composure, hugging me and sobbing, "Billy Noonan, you were such a good friend to him." It was a hot day; Manhattan in July is tough enough for me. This day steam was rising from me. I was hoping to find Kathleen a seat next to me but momentarily lost track of her and ended up next to Effie, who had agreed to wear shoes one last time for John. I laughed to myself about the butler's relationship with footwear in the movie *The Birdcage*. Behind me sat Kennedys and Lawfords; one of them put a comforting hand on my shoulder every once in a while during the service, but I couldn't turn and look at anyone, not at this moment. Wyclef Jean sang "Many Rivers to Cross," a Jimmy Cliff song John and I had listened to literally hundreds of times after seeing the movie *The Harder They Come*. During Communion, we sang the Bob Dylan song "Forever Young." This was all way too much for me.

Teddy, once again, performed beautifully and yet poignantly, a eulogy for John and Carolyn. It was not the first I had witnessed, but clearly the saddest for me. He touched upon John's legacy, his wit, his mischievous manner, his confidence, and his loyalty. He told us that just as the days of Camelot, he and Carolyn had shared one thousand days. To me he captured my friend beautifully. He mentioned the Yeats poem about the combing of gray hair that I remembered days before in the President's bedroom, and the poem the Irish ambassador read to President Kennedy, the one Teddy recited at the wedding that rang clearly in my head as I held out hope, on the widow's walk, for his safe return. He bade John and Carolyn good-bye, as we all did.

When the service concluded, as the pallbearers bottlenecked at the door, I found myself next to Muhammad Ali. "You know," I said to him, "one night John and I were discussing who our biggest heroes are, and he said, 'I'd have to say mine is Muhammad Ali.'" I left it at that, without explaining why. The reasons say a lot about John: the way Ali overcame poverty through sports, how he won over the Cubans at the Olympics, how he captured the heavyweight crown four times, and, especially, how he faced racism, refused to fight in Vietnam, and stuck to the ideals of his religion. Maybe it is hard to think of Ali as an underdog, given his "I am the greatest!" bravado, but that was John's view.

Muhammad Ali, when I told him how John Kennedy felt about him, heaved with emotion.

Outside, I cried with Rosemarie. "I will miss him for the rest of my life," I told her. I embraced Timmy as Senator John Kerry came by and the cameras rolled. Then I grabbed Kathleen and headed for the reception at the Sacred Heart School. I ate, and I drank until I was numb, and then I got into a limousine with some of John's friends. I took them to McSorley's Old Ale House, a quintessential Irish pub that serves its own beer two glasses at a time and goes by the motto "We were here before your grandfather was born." The walls are covered in framed photos going back to the mid-nineteenth century: portraits of presidents, Teddy Roosevelt as governor of New York, and many other luminaries. A large bust of JFK was on a shelf above the cash register. Someone had put a naval officer's hat on it cocked to the side, lending the formal expression a cavalier slant. I gave McSorley's a copy of the funeral program so that something of John would remain among the great city's elite. We stayed until dusk; I sang "Thousands Are Sailing" by the Pogues, about twilight in New York: there is a line in the song about how "we raised a glass to JFK / And a dozen more besides." Santina, I remember, started to cry and could not stop. What we all felt.

We went to a reception that night that a friend had organized on the Upper West Side. Sentimental crap was pouring out as people stood on a circular staircase and read Shakespeare and poems about loss. I saw Anthony from across the room, sitting, back braced, his hands on his cane, his chin on his hands—I could not bear to go to him. I asked Kathleen to sit with him and to tell him that I loved him. I went upstairs with Robbie Littell and a few others and hung on until sleep crept in. Laurence Leamer, in his book *Sons of Camelot*, remembered something I said that night: that in Ireland, when a young life is gone, a tree is stumped to remind them of a life lost and promise unfulfilled. I do know that ritual but have no recollection of saying it. Amazing what people remember, and don't, at a time like that.

In the morning we had breakfast in Timmy and Linda's suite with Dan and Jody Samson. They were going to Greenwich, Connecticut, to pay their respects to the Bessettes. But not me—I could not endure any more.

"Greenwich is on the way home, Billy," Timmy half pleaded.

No—I simply could not. There were no more tears left, and I needed to go home. It was TJ's third birthday, and I needed to celebrate his life. We threw a small party, people assembled quietly, and I thought, *Isn't this how John celebrated his third birthday, fresh from a funeral?*

Epilogue

THE DAYS AND WEEKS that followed John's untimely death would bring more sorrow. I responded the way I usually do when death strikes close to me—I get angry because I'm tired of loss. Sometimes I react badly.

Anthony called, a week after John's death, to say hello and to ask me how I was doing. The prince—it was him I should be concerned about, but here he was, worried about me. Since Anthony was the executor of the estate, I asked him what to do about John's securities; he told me to abide by how I was directed. He asked me what I was going to do next. I said that I was going to go to Ireland; I'd read poetry and look at the ocean and grieve.

A week later I got the call: Anthony was gone. Then there was another call from another usher; I would be a pallbearer again. I drove with Kathleen to New London, where I chartered a plane to get us across Long Island Sound. We were both scared flying in a small craft over water; I wanted to scream, but I had to stay strong for her. Anthony's friend Beth Alexander and her boyfriend, Tony, picked us up and gave us rest. We stayed with them; people were stopping by for dinner and news. We set a place for Anthony.

The day of the funeral, I brought Kathleen to the Most Holy Trinity Church in East Hampton, where we had gathered five years earlier for Anthony's greatest day (Kathleen had been in another wedding that same day, the summer of weddings). I tried to tell her about the beautiful flowers and the fun we shared; it seemed pointless. We escorted Anthony in and later went to the reception; Beth and I watched from a distance as his ashes were tossed into the sea.

Kathleen did not want to get on a plane for the return trip. "I'd rather walk," she said. I had to charter a nine-seater for her to agree to fly back over the Sound to pick up our car, and she ended up crying the whole way home.

A week later I was on an Aer Lingus jet to Shannon, heading to Ireland to grieve, as I'd told Anthony—now for him, too. From the summer of weddings to this, the summer of tragic deaths. Sitting in first class meant getting served champagne; I slugged three down and put my head back, tears streaming down my face. The stewardess asked if everything was all right. I smiled, she backed away. I closed my eyes and dreamed of happier days.

They do come back to me, still, in my dreams, full of light and music and fun. Back from the crevices of my subconscious. My father comes to me also. I can hear his voice, it is recognizable to me, and there he is, talking to me as only he could or did: "Don't bet against Notre Dame—never mind the odds, it's bad luck." No one tells me things like that anymore. And I do not have friends like the ones I lost that summer, the last summer of the second millennium. But I still have Timmy, who, I pray, will enjoy this retelling of our journey.

I have tried, since John's death, to replicate the evenings I spent at his table—first with his mother, then with our friends and wives. Evenings full of discussion and grand arguments. Nobody seems to enjoy a good fight—one that's not personal, but violently important—anymore. Oh, do I miss that. I miss those meals, and I miss the theater of ideas that John was the center of. Mostly I miss him.

John made himself known to me once since his death. It was at the christening of my daughter Bridget in June 2002. John would have been her godfather, along with Timmy. As we blessed the baby, lit the candles, and began to recite the Lord's Prayer, a loud thunderclap startled us. It had a been a beautiful day, not a cloud in the sky. The thunder was so loud that the priest stopped, visibly shaken, then started the prayer again. Rain lashed down for ten seconds. Then, just as suddenly, sun poured through the stained-glass windows of the church. It was John, angry and sad that he was not there, missing his responsibility—he was letting himself be known. Timmy confirmed it: "I believe in everything, especially when it comes to John."

In 2003, Timmy and I hosted the world in Dublin. It was really the Special Olympics World Games. "Best games ever," said the *Spirit,* the official Special Olympics magazine bulletin. It was also the fortieth anniversary of the President's visit to Ireland. We believed that John's great spirit and heart were there with us, too, John who had once told me that he could never travel to Ireland with me, that it would be "too emotional." Now we were there, I felt, as his envoy. (Timmy wore one of John's ties, as a sort of talisman.) My friends and I in Dublin; it was the greatest thing we have ever accomplished together. So far.